WILEY CIAexcel® EXAM REVIEW

FOCUS NOTES 2021

WILEY CIAexcel® EXAM REVIEW

FOCUS NOTES 2021

PART 2

Practice of Internal Auditing

S. RAO VALLABHANENI

Wiley Efficient Learning™

This book is printed on acid-free paper.

Published by John Wiley & Sons, Inc., Hoboken, New Jersey.
Published simultaneously in Canada.

For general information about our other products and services, please contact our Customer Care Department within the United States at (800) 762-2974, outside the United States at (317) 572-3993 or fax (317) 572-4002.

Wiley publishes in a variety of print and electronic formats and by print-on-demand. Some material included with standard print versions of this book may not be included in e-books or in print-on-demand. If this book refers to media such as a CD or DVD that is not included in the version you purchased, you may download this material at http://booksupport.wiley.com. For more information about Wiley products, visit www.wiley.com.

Library of Congress Cataloging-in-Publication Data:

ISBN 978-1-119-75337-7 (Paperback); ISBN 978-1-119-75329-2 (ebk); ISBN 978-1-119-75343-8 (ebk);
ISBN 978-1-119-75338-4 (Part 1); ISBN 978-1-119-75346-9 (Part 3)

Printed in the United States of America

Contents

Preface

The Certified Internal Auditor (CIA) Examination is a program of the Institute of Internal Auditors (IIA), Inc. The CIA examination certifies a person as a professional internal auditor and is intended to measure the knowledge, skills, and competency required in the field of internal auditing. The Certified Internal Auditor designation is the hallmark of an expert in internal auditing. Wiley's CIA Exam Review Products are developed to help prepare a CIA Exam candidate for the CIA Exam by reflecting the exam syllabus and to reflect the new International Professional Practices Framework of 2017 (new IPPF of 2017) issued in January 2017, consisting of professional standards.

The CIA Exam syllabus tests a CIA Exam candidate's knowledge at two cognitive levels—proficient level and basic level—as indicated in the IIA's content specifications outlines (www.theiia.org). These cognitive levels suggest allocating more time and effort to prepare for the proficient level topics and comparatively less time and effort to prepare for the basic level topics. The scope of the CIA Exam consists of three parts:

Part 1: Essentials of Internal Auditing

Part 2: Practice of Internal Auditing

Part 3: Business Knowledge for Internal Auditing

For each part of the exam, Wiley has developed a comprehensive suite of review products to study and prepare for the CIA Exam. This suite includes (1) Review Book (Study Guide), (2) Focus Notes, and (3) Web-Based Online Test Bank Software.

This book covers the Focus Notes for Part 2 of the CIA Exam.

The focus notes (index cards or flashcards) provide a quick review of the same subject matter presented in the review book but in a condensed manner to reinforce key concepts. Wiley's theme in the Focus Notes is Remember, Reinforce, and Recall the key concepts.

Wiley's goal is to provide all the required study materials for CIA Exam study and preparation in one place with one source for either a self-study or a group-study effort. Visit www.wileyCIA.com for product details and order placement.

CIA Exam Content Syllabus and Specifications

Part 2 of the CIA Exam syllabus is called **Practice of Internal Auditing** and includes four domains containing several topics. These four domains cover managing the internal audit activity; planning the engagement; performing the engagement; and communicating engagement results and monitoring progress.

Part 2 tests a CIA Exam candidate's knowledge, skills, and abilities (KSAs) related to the *International Standards for the Professional Practice of Internal Auditing*, particularly the Performance *Standards* (i.e., series 2000, 2200, 2300, 2400, 2500, and 2600). In other words, the Part 2 syllabus is greatly aligned with the IIA's Performance *Standards*.

Each domain is assigned with a relative weight of its importance to each part, expressed as a percentage of study time and effort required (i.e., higher weights require larger amounts of study time and effort). Each topic within a domain will be tested at the cognitive level of Proficient (P) or Basic (B). Here, *proficient* means the CIA Exam candidates are required to demonstrate a proficiency in their KSAs and *basic* means the candidates are required to demonstrate a basic comprehension of concepts. Here, *proficient* means greater amounts of study time and effort are required. Note that the combination of "higher weight" and "proficient level" requires a greater amount of study time and effort to earn success in the exam than the combination of "lower weight" and "basic level."

The exam duration for Part 2 is 2.0 hours (120 minutes) with 100 multiple-choice questions. The following is a breakdown of domains and topics in Part 2.

Domain I: Managing the Internal Audit Activity (20%)

1. Internal Audit Operations

A Describe policies and procedures for the planning, organizing, directing, and monitoring of internal audit operations. (B)

B Interpret administrative activities (e.g., budgeting, resourcing, recruiting, and staffing) of the internal audit activity. (B)

2. Establishing a Risk-Based Internal Audit Plan

A Identify sources of potential engagements (e.g., audit universe, audit cycle requirements, management requests, regulatory mandates, relevant market and industry trends, and emerging issues). (B)

B Identify a risk management framework to assess risks and prioritize audit engagements based on the results of a risk assessment. (B)

C Interpret the types of assurance engagements (e.g., risk and control assessments, audits of third parties and contract compliance, security and privacy, performance and quality audits, key performance indicators, operational audits, financial audits, and regulatory compliance audits). (P)

D Interpret the types of consulting engagements (e.g., control training, system design, system development, due diligence, privacy, benchmarking, internal control assessment, and process mapping) designed to provide advice and insight. (P)

E Describe coordination of internal audit efforts with the external auditor, regulatory oversight bodies, and other internal assurance functions, and potential reliance on other assurance providers. (B)

3. Communicating and Reporting to Senior Management and the Board

A Recognize that the chief audit executive (CAE) communicates the annual audit pan to senior management and the board and seeks the board's approval. (B)

B Identify significant risk exposures and control and governance issues for the CAE to report to the board. (B)

C Recognize that the CAE reports on the overall effectiveness of the organization's internal control and risk management processes to senior management and the board. (B)

D Recognize internal audit key performance indicators (KPIs) that the CAE communicates to senior management and the board periodically. (B)

Domain II: Planning the Engagement (20%)

1. Engagement Planning

A Determine engagement objectives, evaluation criteria and the scope of the engagement. (P)

B Plan the engagement to assure identification of key risks and controls. (P)

C Complete a detailed risk assessment of each audit area, including evaluating and prioritizing risk and control factors. (P)

D Determine engagement procedures and prepare the engagement work program. (P)

E Determine the level of staff and resources needed for the engagement. (P)

Domain III: Performing the Engagement (40%)

1. Information Gathering

A Gather and examine relevant information (e.g., review previous audit reports and data, conduct walk-throughs and interviews, and perform observations) as part of a preliminary survey of the engagement area. (P)

B Develop checklists and risk-and-control questionnaires as part of a preliminary survey of the engagement area. (P)

C Apply appropriate sampling (e.g., nonstatistical, judgmental, and discovery) and statistical analysis techniques. (P)

2. Analysis and Evaluation

A Use computerized audit tools and techniques (e.g., data mining and extraction, continuous monitoring, automated workpapers, and embedded audit modules). (P)

B Evaluate the relevance, sufficiency, and reliability of potential sources of evidence. (P)

C Apply appropriate analytical approaches and process mapping techniques (e.g., process identification, workflow analysis, process map generation and analysis, spaghetti maps, and RACI diagrams). (P)

D Determine and apply analytical review techniques (e.g., ratio estimation, variance analysis, budget vs. actual, trend analysis, other reasonableness tests, and benchmarking). (B)

E Prepare workpapers and documentation of relevant information to support conclusions and engagement results. (P)

F Summarize and develop engagement conclusions, including assessment of risks and controls. (P)

3. Engagement Supervision

A Identify key activities in supervising engagements (e.g., coordinate work assignments, review workpapers, and evaluate auditors' performance). (B)

Domain IV: Communicating Engagement Results and Monitoring Progress (20%)

1. Communicating Engagement Results and the Acceptance of Risk

A Arrange preliminary communication with engagement clients. (P)

B Demonstrate communication quality (e.g., accurate, objective, clear, concise, constructive, complete, and timely) and communication elements (e.g., objectives, scope, conclusions, recommendations, and action plans). (P)

C Prepare interim reporting on the engagement progress. (P)

D Formulate recommendations to enhance and protect organizational value. (P)

E Describe the audit engagement communication and reporting process, including holding the exit conference, developing the audit report (e.g., draft, review, approve, and distribute), and obtaining management's response. (B)

F Describe the chief audit executive's responsibility for assessing residual risk. (B)

G Describe the process for communicating risk acceptance (i.e., when management has accepted a level of risk that may be unacceptable to the organization). (B)

2. Monitoring Progress

A Assess engagement outcomes, including the management action plan. (P)

B Manage monitoring and follow-up of the disposition of audit engagement results communicated to senior management and the board. (P)

CIA Exam-Taking Tips

The types of questions a candidate can expect to see in the CIA Exam are fact-based, concept-based, application-based, objective-based, and scenario-based multiple-choice (M/C) questions with four choices of A, B, C, and D or a, b, c, and d. There is a systematic method in reading, interpreting, and answering the M/C questions that can make a difference between a pass or fail in the exam. Moreover, answering the M/C questions requires a good amount of practice and effort.

The following tips and techniques will be helpful in answering the CIA Exam questions:

- Stay with your first impression of the correct choice.
- Know the subject area or topic. Don't read too much into the question.
- Remember that questions are independent of specific country, products, practices, vendors, hardware, software, or industry.
- Read the last sentence of the question first followed by all choices and then the body (stem) of the question paragraph containing the last sentence. This is a reversal of the normal reading to highlight the key points quickly.

- Read the question twice, read the keywords twice, and watch for tip-off words where the latter denotes absolute conditions. Examples of keywords are *most, least, major, minor, all, not,* and *except*. Examples of tip-off words are *always, never,* and *every*.
- Do not project the question into your own organizational environment, practices, policies, procedures, standards, and guidelines. The examination is focusing on the IIA's Professional Standards and Publications and on the CIA's exam syllabus (i.e., content specifications). Also, questions require a universal answer and knowledge of best practices.
- Try to eliminate wrong choices as quickly as possible. When you get down to two semifinal choices, take a big-picture approach. For example, if choices A and D are the semifinalists, and choice D could be a part of choice A, then select choice A; or if choice D could be a more complete answer, then select choice D.
- Don't spend too much time on one question. If you are not sure of an answer, move on, and go back to it if time permits. The last resort is to guess the answer. There is no penalty for guessing the wrong answer.

Remember that success in any professional certification examination depends on several factors required of any student such as time management skills, preparation time and effort levels, education and experience levels, memory recall of the subject matter in a timely manner, calm and collected state-of-mind before or during the exam, and decision-making skills. Good luck on the exam!

Professional Standards

Professional standards for Part 2 of the CIA Exam require the knowledge of **performance standards only**. These standards include 2000, 2010, 2020, 2030, 2040, 2050, 2060, 2070, 2200, 2201, 2210, 2220, 2230, 2240, 2300, 2310, 2320, 2330, 2340, 2400, 2410, 2420, 2421, 2430, 2431, 2440, 2450, 2500, and 2600.

PERFORMANCE STANDARDS

2000—Managing the Internal Audit Activity

The chief audit executive must effectively manage the internal audit activity to ensure it adds value to the organization.

Interpretation:
The internal audit activity is effectively managed when:

- It achieves the purpose and responsibility included in the internal audit charter.
- It conforms with the *Standards*.
- Its individual members conform with the Code of Ethics and the *Standards*.
- It considers trends and emerging issues that could impact the organization.

The internal audit activity adds value to the organization and its stakeholders when it considers strategies, objectives, and risks; strives to offer ways to enhance governance, risk management, and control processes; and objectively provides relevant assurance.

2010—Planning

The chief audit executive must establish a risk-based plan to determine the priorities of the internal audit activity, consistent with the organization's goals.

Interpretation:
To develop the risk-based plan, the chief audit executive consults with senior management and the board and obtains an understanding of the organization's strategies, key business objectives, associated risks, and risk management processes. The chief audit executive must review and adjust the plan, as necessary, in response to changes in the organization's business, risks, operations, programs, systems, and controls.

2010.A1—The internal audit activity's plan of engagements must be based on a documented risk assessment, undertaken at least annually. The input of senior management and the board must be considered in this process.

2010.A2—The chief audit executive must identify and consider the expectations of senior management, the board, and other stakeholders for internal audit opinions and other conclusions.

2010.C1—The chief audit executive should consider accepting proposed consulting engagements based on the engagement's potential to improve management of risks, add value, and improve the organization's operations. Accepted engagements must be included in the plan.

2020—Communication and Approval

The chief audit executive must communicate the internal audit activity's plans and resource requirements, including significant interim changes, to senior management and the board for review and approval. The chief audit executive must also communicate the impact of resource limitations.

2030—Resource Management

The chief audit executive must ensure that internal audit resources are appropriate, sufficient, and effectively deployed to achieve the approved plan.

Interpretation:
Appropriate refers to the mix of knowledge, skills, and other competencies needed to perform the plan. *Sufficient* refers to the quantity of resources needed to accomplish the plan. Resources are effectively deployed when they are used in a way that optimizes the achievement of the approved plan.

2040—Policies and Procedures

The chief audit executive must establish policies and procedures to guide the internal audit activity.

Interpretation:

The form and content of policies and procedures are dependent upon the size and structure of the internal audit activity and the complexity of its work.

2050—Coordination and Reliance

The chief audit executive should share information, coordinate activities, and consider relying upon the work of other internal and external assurance and consulting service providers to ensure proper coverage and minimize duplication of efforts.

Interpretation:
In coordinating activities, the chief audit executive may rely on the work of other assurance and consulting service providers. A consistent process for the basis of reliance should be established, and the chief audit executive should consider the competency, objectivity, and due professional care of the assurance and consulting service providers. The chief audit executive should also have a clear understanding of the scope, objectives, and results of the work performed by other providers of assurance and consulting services. Where reliance is placed on the work of others, the chief audit executive is still accountable and responsible for ensuring adequate support for conclusions and opinions reached by the internal audit activity.

2060—Reporting to Senior Management and the Board

The chief audit executive must report periodically to senior management and the board on the internal audit activity's purpose, authority, responsibility, and performance relative to its plan and on its conformance with the Code of Ethics and the *Standards*. Reporting must also include significant risk and control issues, including fraud risks, governance issues, and other matters that require the attention of senior management and/or the board.

Interpretation:
The frequency and content of reporting are determined collaboratively by the chief audit executive, senior management, and the board. The frequency and content of reporting depends on the importance of the information to be communicated and the urgency of the related actions to be taken by senior management and/or the board.

The chief audit executive's reporting and communication to senior management and the board must include information about:

- The audit charter.
- Independence of the internal audit activity.
- The audit plan and progress against the plan.

2060—Reporting to Senior Management and the Board (continued)

- Resource requirements.
- Results of audit activities.
- Conformance with the Code of Ethics and the *Standards*, and action plans to address any significant conformance issues.
- Management's response to risk that, in the chief audit executive's judgment, may be unacceptable to the organization.

These and other chief audit executive communication requirements are referenced throughout the *Standards*.

2070—External Service Provider and Organizational Responsibility for Internal Auditing

When an external service provider serves as the internal audit activity, the provider must make the organization aware that the organization has the responsibility for maintaining an effective internal audit activity.

Interpretation:
This responsibility is demonstrated through the quality assurance and improvement program which assesses conformance with the Code of Ethics and the *Standards*.

2200—Engagement Planning

Internal auditors must develop and document a plan for each engagement, including the engagement's objectives, scope, timing, and resource allocations. The plan must consider the organization's strategies, objectives, and risks relevant to the engagement.

2201—Planning Considerations

In planning the engagement, internal auditors must consider:

- The strategies and objectives of the activity being reviewed and the means by which the activity controls its performance.
- The significant risks to the activity's objectives, resources, and operations and the means by which the potential impact of risk is kept to an acceptable level.
- The adequacy and effectiveness of the activity's governance, risk management, and control processes compared to a relevant framework or model.
- The opportunities for making significant improvements to the activity's governance, risk management, and control processes.

2201.A1—When planning an engagement for parties outside the organization, internal auditors must establish a written understanding with them about objectives, scope, respective responsibilities, and other expectations, including restrictions on distribution of the results of the engagement and access to engagement records.

2201.C1—Internal auditors must establish an understanding with consulting engagement clients about objectives, scope, respective responsibilities, and other client expectations. For significant engagements, this understanding must be documented.

2210—Engagement Objectives

Objectives must be established for each engagement.

2210.A1—Internal auditors must conduct a preliminary assessment of the risks relevant to the activity under review. Engagement objectives must reflect the results of this assessment.

2210.A2—Internal auditors must consider the probability of significant errors, fraud, noncompliance, and other exposures when developing the engagement objectives.

2210.A3—Adequate criteria are needed to evaluate governance, risk management, and controls. Internal auditors must ascertain the extent to which management and/or the board has established adequate criteria to determine whether objectives and goals have been accomplished. If adequate, internal auditors must use such criteria in their evaluation. If inadequate, internal auditors must identify appropriate evaluation criteria through discussion with management and/or the board.

2210—Engagement Objectives (continued)

Interpretation:

Types of criteria may include:

- Internal (e.g., policies and procedures of the organization).
- External (e.g., laws and regulations imposed by statutory bodies).
- Leading practices (e.g., industry and professional guidance).

2210.C1—Consulting engagement objectives must address governance, risk management, and control processes to the extent agreed upon with the client.

2210.C2—Consulting engagement objectives must be consistent with the organization's values, strategies, and objectives.

2220—Engagement Scope

The established scope must be sufficient to achieve the objectives of the engagement.

2220.A1—The scope of the engagement must include consideration of relevant systems, records, personnel, and physical properties, including those under the control of third parties.

2220.A2—If significant consulting opportunities arise during an assurance engagement, a specific written understanding as to the objectives, scope, respective responsibilities, and other expectations should be reached and the results of the consulting engagement communicated in accordance with consulting standards.

2220.C1—In performing consulting engagements, internal auditors must ensure that the scope of the engagement is sufficient to address the agreed-upon objectives. If internal auditors develop reservations about the scope during the engagement, these reservations must be discussed with the client to determine whether to continue with the engagement.

2220.C2—During consulting engagements, internal auditors must address controls consistent with the engagement's objectives and be alert to significant control issues.

2230—Engagement Resource Allocation

Internal auditors must determine appropriate and sufficient resources to achieve engagement objectives based on an evaluation of the nature and complexity of each engagement, time constraints, and available resources.

Interpretation:
Appropriate refers to the mix of knowledge, skills, and other competencies needed to perform the engagement. *Sufficient* refers to the quantity of resources needed to accomplish the engagement with due professional care.

2240—Engagement Work Program

Internal auditors must develop and document work programs that achieve the engagement objectives.

2240.A1—Work programs must include the procedures for identifying, analyzing, evaluating, and documenting information during the engagement. The work program must be approved prior to its implementation, and any adjustments approved promptly.

2240.C1—Work programs for consulting engagements may vary in form and content depending upon the nature of the engagement.

2300—Performing the Engagement

Internal auditors must identify, analyze, evaluate, and document sufficient information to achieve the engagement's objectives.

2310—Identifying Information

Internal auditors must identify sufficient, reliable, relevant, and useful information to achieve the engagement's objectives.

Interpretation:
Sufficient information is factual, adequate, and convincing so that a prudent, informed person would reach the same conclusions as the auditor. Reliable information is the best attainable information through the use of appropriate engagement techniques. Relevant information supports engagement observations and recommendations and is consistent with the objectives for the engagement. Useful information helps the organization meet its goals.

2320—Analysis and Evaluation

Internal auditors must base conclusions and engagement results on appropriate analyses and evaluations.

2330—Documenting Information

Internal auditors must document sufficient, reliable, relevant, and useful information to support the engagement results and conclusions.

2330.A1—The chief audit executive must control access to engagement records. The chief audit executive must obtain the approval of senior management and/or legal counsel prior to releasing such records to external parties, as appropriate.

2330.A2—The chief audit executive must develop retention requirements for engagement records, regardless of the medium in which each record is stored. These retention requirements must be consistent with the organization's guidelines and any pertinent regulatory or other requirements.

2330.C1—The chief audit executive must develop policies governing the custody and retention of consulting engagement records, as well as their release to internal and external parties. These policies must be consistent with the organization's guidelines and any pertinent regulatory or other requirements.

2340—Engagement Supervision

Engagements must be properly supervised to ensure objectives are achieved, quality is assured, and staff is developed.

Interpretation:
The extent of supervision required will depend on the proficiency and experience of internal auditors and the complexity of the engagement. The chief audit executive has overall responsibility for supervising the engagement, whether performed by or for the internal audit activity, but may designate appropriately experienced members of the internal audit activity to perform the review. Appropriate evidence of supervision is documented and retained.

2400—Communicating Results

Internal auditors must communicate the results of engagements.

2410—Criteria for Communicating

Communications must include the engagement's objectives, scope, and results.

2410.A1—Final communication of engagement results must include applicable conclusions, as well as applicable recommendations and/or action plans. Where appropriate, the internal auditors' opinion should be provided. An opinion must take into account the expectations of senior management, the board, and other stakeholders and must be supported by sufficient, reliable, relevant, and useful information.

Interpretation:
Opinions at the engagement level may be ratings, conclusions, or other descriptions of the results. Such an engagement may be in relation to controls around a specific process, risk, or business unit. The formulation of such opinions requires consideration of the engagement results and their significance.

2410.A2—Internal auditors are encouraged to acknowledge satisfactory performance in engagement communications.

2410.A3—When releasing engagement results to parties outside the organization, the communication must include limitations on distribution and use of the results.

2410.C1—Communication of the progress and results of consulting engagements will vary in form and content depending upon the nature of the engagement and the needs of the client.

2420—Quality of Communications

Communications must be accurate, objective, clear, concise, constructive, complete, and timely.

Interpretation:

Accurate communications are free from errors and distortions and are faithful to the underlying facts. Objective communications are fair, impartial, and unbiased and are the result of a fair-minded and balanced assessment of all relevant facts and circumstances. Clear communications are easily understood and logical, avoiding unnecessary technical language and providing all significant and relevant information. Concise communications are to the point and avoid unnecessary elaboration, superfluous detail, redundancy, and wordiness. Constructive communications are helpful to the engagement client and the organization and lead to improvements where needed. Complete communications lack nothing that is essential to the target audience and include all significant and relevant information and observations to support recommendations and conclusions. Timely communications are opportune and expedient, depending on the significance of the issue, allowing management to take appropriate corrective action.

2421—Errors and Omissions

If a final communication contains a significant error or omission, the chief audit executive must communicate corrected information to all parties who received the original communication.

2430—Use of "Conducted in Conformance with the International *Standards* for the Professional Practice of Internal Auditing"

Indicating that engagements are "conducted in conformance with the *International Standards for the Professional Practice of Internal Auditing*" is appropriate only if supported by the results of the quality assurance and improvement program.

2431—Engagement Disclosure of Nonconformance

When nonconformance with the Code of Ethics or the *Standards* impacts a specific engagement, communication of the results must disclose the:

- Principle(s) or rule(s) of conduct of the Code of Ethics or the *Standard*(s) with which full conformance was not achieved
- Reason(s) for nonconformance
- Impact of nonconformance on the engagement and the communicated engagement results

2440—Disseminating Results

The chief audit executive must communicate results to the appropriate parties.

> **Interpretation:**
> The chief audit executive is responsible for reviewing and approving the final engagement communication before issuance and for deciding to whom and how it will be disseminated. When the chief audit executive delegates these duties, he or she retains overall responsibility.

2440—Disseminating Results (continued)

2440.A1—The chief audit executive is responsible for communicating the final results to parties who can ensure that the results are given due consideration.

2440.A2—If not otherwise mandated by legal, statutory, or regulatory requirements, prior to releasing results to parties outside the organization the chief audit executive must:

- Assess the potential risk to the organization.
- Consult with senior management and/or legal counsel as appropriate.
- Control dissemination by restricting the use of the results.

2440.C1—The chief audit executive is responsible for communicating the final results of consulting engagements to clients.

2440.C2—During consulting engagements, governance, risk management, and control issues may be identified. Whenever these issues are significant to the organization, they must be communicated to senior management and the board.

2450—Overall Opinions

When an overall opinion is issued, it must take into account the strategies, objectives, and risks of the organization and the expectations of senior management, the board, and other stakeholders. The overall opinion must be supported by sufficient, reliable, relevant, and useful information.

Interpretation:
The communication will include:

- The scope, including the time period to which the opinion pertains.
- Scope limitations.
- Consideration of all related projects, including the reliance on other assurance providers.
- A summary of the information that supports the opinion.
- The risk or control framework or other criteria used as a basis for the overall opinion.
- The overall opinion, judgment, or conclusion reached.

The reasons for an unfavorable overall opinion must be stated.

2500—Monitoring Progress

The chief audit executive must establish and maintain a system to monitor the disposition of results communicated to management.

2500.A1—The chief audit executive must establish a follow-up process to monitor and ensure that management actions have been effectively implemented or that senior management has accepted the risk of not taking action.

2500.C1—The internal audit activity must monitor the disposition of results of consulting engagements to the extent agreed upon with the client.

2600—Communicating the Acceptance of Risks

When the chief audit executive concludes that management has accepted a level of risk that may be unacceptable to the organization, the chief audit executive must discuss the matter with senior management. If the chief audit executive determines that the matter has not been resolved, the chief audit executive must communicate the matter to the board.

Interpretation:

The identification of risk accepted by management may be observed through an assurance or consulting engagement, monitoring progress on actions taken by management as a result of prior engagements, or other means. It is not the responsibility of the chief audit executive to resolve the risk.

Domain 1: Managing the Internal Audit Activity (20%)

This domain addresses several major theoretical topics. It describes the scope of internal audit operations and its administrative activities. It establishes a risk-based internal audit plan using a risk management framework to assess risks and to prioritize audit engagements. It defines the scope of assurance engagements and consulting engagements. It describes how to coordinate among internal auditors, internal nonauditors, and outside auditors. It requires the chief audit executive (CAE) to communicate the audit plan and governance, risk management, and control issues to the board and senior management. It recommends that the CAE report the audit metrics and key performance indicators (KPIs) to the board and senior management.

Internal Audit Management Functions

Internal audit operations are no different from other business operations, such as manufacturing, service, marketing, finance, and human resources operations. Each of these operations needs the same basic management functions, such as planning, organizing, directing, and controlling (monitoring) activities, which are performed in the order shown next.

Management Functions = Planning ⟶ Organizing ⟶ Directing ⟶ Controlling

Internal audit planning requires developing and periodically revising (updating) its comprehensive audit plan and ensuring that audit coverage for all identified auditable areas within the audit universe is appropriate for the size and complexity of the organization's activities. This should be accomplished either through a multiyear plan approach with the plan revised annually or through an approach that utilizes a framework to evaluate risks annually, focusing on the most significant risks. There should be a mechanism in place to identify when a significant risk area will not be audited in the specified time frame and a requirement to notify the audit committee and seek its approval for any exception to the framework.

Internal Audit Management Functions (continued)

It is a common practice to audit business functions on a cycle-based plan every three-year or four-year audit cycle. But high-risk areas should be audited at least every year or even more often. Regardless, the internal audit plan should consider the risk assessment, and internal audit's approach to audit coverage should be appropriate based on the risk assessment. An effective audit plan covers individual business areas or functions and risk disciplines as well as cross-functions or cross-departments.

Because the internal planning process operates in a dynamic environment, it should allow for changes when necessary. The process should include a procedure for modifying the internal audit plan to incorporate significant changes that are identified either through continuous monitoring process or during a routine/repeat audit work.

The internal audit plan also identifies the types of audits to perform in terms of assurance audits and consulting audits consisting of operational audits, performance audits, value-for-money audits, information technology audits, compliance audits, big data audits, and agile audits (i.e., targeted audits).

Internal audit organizing means deciding how to structure the audit function and how to staff the audit function with management levels and job positions. Depending on the size of the audit function, it can be organized into assurance audit division or group, consulting audit divisions or groups, and compliance audit divisions or groups. The CAE can decide whether the audit function should be organized with a tall structure (too many job levels) or a flat structure (too few job levels). Job descriptions are required for each job to describe duties, responsibilities, and qualifications. Examples of job positions can be staff auditor, senior auditor, in-charge auditor, lead auditor, audit supervisor, audit manager, and audit director. An audit manual is also developed describing audit policies, procedures, and continuing education guidelines to run the audit department.

Internal audit directing involves leading the entire audit department, similar to leading any other department. It involves motivating all employees to work toward a common goal of delivering the audit work products and services like a world-class internal audit function. In this regard, the CAE wears several hats, such as supervisor, manager, leader, change agent, coach, mentor, delegator, motivator, inspirer, agile performer, and above all futurist.

Internal audit monitoring involves formal continuous monitoring practices as part of the audit function's risk assessment processes to support adjustments to the audit plan or audit universe (risk universe) as changes occur. An effective continuous monitoring process should include written standards to ensure consistent application of monitoring processes throughout the audit function. These standards can consist of who would conduct the monitoring activities and whether they are full-time or part-time auditors, insiders or outsiders, or auditors or nonauditors.

Continuous monitoring results should be documented through a combination of metrics, management reporting, periodic audit summaries, and updated risk assessments to substantiate that the process is operating as designed. Critical issues identified through the monitoring process should be communicated to the audit committees. Computer-assisted auditing techniques (CAATs) are useful tools to highlight issues that warrant further consideration within a continuous monitoring process.

Internal Audit Management Theories

Three theoretical research topics include managers' styles, managerial roles, and audit management skills as they apply to the internal audit management function in managing internal audit operations on a daily basis.

Managers' Styles

The quality of a decision is a direct reflection of how the decision maker processes information. Managers approach decision making and problem solving in very different ways, depending on the availability of such information. Their approaches, perceptions, and recommendations vary because their minds work differently. Researchers have identified four management styles such as the directive style, the analytic style, the behavioral style, and the intuitive style. One is not superior to the others.

The **directive style** focuses on "more telling and less doing," instead of "less telling and more doing." This style comes across as a "command and control" style, representing an autocratic management style. Most employees get turned off with this style.

The **analytic style** managers tend to be logical, precise, and objective. They prefer routine assignments that require attention to detail and systematic implementation. The manager uses deductive reasoning. The analytic style is good to use in model-building exercises and forecasting involving projections.

Managers' Styles (continued)

The **behavioral style** takes into account an employee's emotions and feelings that people go through. This style considers what people are saying, what they mean, and why they are saying if, requiring a participative management approach. Most employees favor this style.

The **intuitive style** manager is creative, is comfortable in handling a dynamic and nonroutine environment, follows his hunches, and is mostly subjective. He likes to address broad issues and use inductive reasoning. This manager sees things in complex patterns rather than as logically ordered bits and pieces. The intuitive style is good to use in brainstorming sessions and where traditional assumptions need to be challenged.

In practice, many managers use a combination of directive, analytic, behavioral, and intuitive styles.

Managerial Roles

Henry Mintzberg studied what managers do by focusing on the key roles they play. He then isolated 10 roles he believed are common to all managers. These 10 roles have been grouped into three major categories: (1) interpersonal (i.e., figurehead, leader, and liaison); (2) informational (i.e., nerve center, disseminator, and spokesperson); and (3) decisional roles (i.e., entrepreneur, disturbance handler, resource allocator, and negotiator).

Audit Management Skills

Audit management skills (management skills or managing skills) can be broadly classified as conceptual, human, and technical skills to manage people. These skills are not exhibited equally across management levels. They vary with the nature of the job, the level of decision making, and the type of interaction with people.

Audit Process

Conducting an audit is a process with a series of activities to be reviewed and a series of procedures to be followed. A structured methodology, consisting of audit phases or stages, can be used during the audit process to ensure quality and to ensure that all required activities are accomplished—starting from the beginning of an audit to the completion of the audit. Each phase has defined tasks to be completed. Five such phases include:

1. Preliminary survey
2. Audit program
3. Fieldwork
4. Reporting
5. Monitoring and follow-up

The audit report is the end product of the audit process.

Administrative Activities in Internal Audit

Budgeting, resourcing, recruiting, staffing, training and development, and continuing education programs are some examples of administrative activities that can occur in an internal audit department. The risk-based internal audit plans drive these administrative activities. Significant changes to audit budgets and timelines for the completion of audits should be reported to the audit committee with documented reasons and rationale. The audit committee's approvals are required for significant changes. An important administrative audit activity is developing and updating an audit manual useful for the entire audit department. The manual should contain comprehensive policies, procedures, and guidelines in running and operating the audit department on a daily basis. Existence of an audit manual can facilitate effective, efficient, and consistent audit practices.

Sourcing the Internal Audit Function

The board of directors, audit committee, senior management (chief executive officer [CEO] and other C-level executives), and the CAE might have discussions whether to keep the internal audit function in-house (in-source) or outsource it either fully or partly to external service providers. If they decide to outsource the audit function either partly or fully, then the audit committee and CAE of the outsourcing organization should ensure that the next items are in place:

- A written charter, an engagement letter, or similar service agreement with the outsourced vendor.
- Confidentiality requirements in protecting the company's sensitive information and personal information by the outsourced vendor.

Sourcing the Internal Audit Function (continued)

- Selection, renewal, and retention of outsourced vendor must be based on competencies (i.e., qualifications and experiences) and competitive bidding procedures to ensure that a high-quality vendor is selected to deliver a high-quality audit work.
- The audit committee receives information on audit engagements from the outsourced vendor similar to an in-house audit function.
- Contingency procedures are in place for managing temporary or permanent disruptions in the outsourced vendor services to ensure that the outsourced internal audit function can meet its intended audit objectives.
- The outsourced vendor should maintain similar work standards expected of an in-house internal audit function.
- The outsourced vendor should provide the board of directors, audit committee, and senior management with an accurate report on the control environment and recommendations to improve controls.
- The outsourced vendor is subjected to a due diligence review before entering into a third-party relationship and is subjected to an oversight and control review after entering into the third-party relationship.

Sourcing the Internal Audit Function (continued)

- The scope of the due diligence review can include a review of elements such as:
  - An organization's strategic plans
  - Proper due diligence in selecting a third party
  - Written contracts or agreements that outline the rights and responsibilities of all parties
  - Ongoing monitoring of the third party's activities and performance levels
  - Clear roles and responsibilities for overseeing and managing the relationship and risk management process
  - Documentation and reporting that facilitate oversight, accountability, monitoring, and risk management
  - Contingency plans for terminating the third-party relationship in an effective manner
- The written contract and agreement for the outsourced vendor should contain:
  - Procedures for changing the terms of the agreement and how audit scope can be expanded or reduced

Sourcing the Internal Audit Function (continued)

- Stipulating that the internal audit reports and the workpapers become the property of the outsourcing organization (i.e., the company that is contracting to outsiders); if not, the outsourcing organization will have access to the workpapers
- Statement regarding record retention requirements, data destruction plans, and security breach notifications
- A process for resolving problems (e.g., arbitration, mediation, and ombudsman) and clarifying who bears the cost of consequential damages arising from errors omissions, and negligence
- Statement that the third party will not perform management functions, make management decisions, or act as an employee or management
- Statement requiring access to the outsourced vendor's audit reports, audit programs, audit workpapers, and audit-related memorandums and correspondence

- Statement requiring access to software escrow (source code escrow) for using the outsourced vendor's proprietary software. The quality of audit work performed by the third party should be consistent with the outsourcing organization's standards of work expected to be performed by an in-house internal audit function.

TQM in Internal Audit Operations

Many internal audit departments have installed total quality management (TQM) approaches to improve internal audit operations. One such approach is recommended by the U.S. Government Accountability Office, which outlines eight steps to apply and implement TQM approaches in audit operations.

1. **Initial quality assessment.** This step includes:
   - Identifying the audit department's customers
   - Establishing the needs of customers
   - Setting priorities so as to best meet customer needs
   - Assessing the quality of the audit products (audit reports) as perceived by audit customers in regard to timeliness, usefulness, responsiveness, and cost
   - Interviewing customers so as to reveal pertinent information about the audits, audit staff performance, and the audit department as a whole
2. **Chief audit executive awareness.** Awareness training should stress the importance of TQM as a philosophy or an approach, not a program.
3. **Formation of a quality council.** Audit managers, audit supervisors, and audit staff members should be part of the quality council, and they should acquire the knowledge of TQM principles, practices, and tools. This council should report to the CAE. It should coordinate training and participate in prototypes.

TQM in Internal Audit Operations (continued)

4. **Fostering teamwork in audits.** The audit department should establish a participative environment that fosters teamwork and quality work. Audit plans, audit work programs, fieldwork, workpapers, and audit reports all require quality orientation and thinking.

5. **Development of prototypes.** To convince some auditors who are doubtful about the TQM philosophy, the quality council should demonstrate the practical value of new ways of organizing the audit work with highly visible prototype and productivity initiatives. When tested and proven successful, these prototypes can convince the cautious of the audit staff.

6. **Celebration of success.** The audit department should publicize the achievements of the prototype to encourage the cautious and hesitant audit staff.

7. **Organizational implementation.** All units and all locations of the audit department should successfully implement audit quality methods, and appropriate recognition should be given for those units that are most successful. This provides motivation and promotes healthy competition.

8. **Annual audit quality review.** There should be an annual audit quality review for audit departments that are spread throughout the organization. The annual review, together with a rating system, will demonstrate the success of the implementation of quality in the audit department.

RISK-BASED INTERNAL AUDIT PLAN

This section defines risk-based auditing, presents a process for assessing internal audit risk, discusses a risk assessment model, presents audit risk factors, and discusses several approaches for risk assessment.

Risk-Based Auditing Defined

Risk-based internal auditing is a methodology that links internal auditing risk to an organization's overall risk management framework. The audit risk assessment is a process by which an auditor identifies and evaluates the quantity of risk-types and the quality of risk-controls. The organization's board, audit committee, and the CAE use the results of the risk assessments to focus on the business areas of greatest risk and to establish priorities for audit work. An audit function should not ignore areas that are rated low risk. An effective risk-based audit plan ensures adequate audit coverage for all auditable activities. The frequency and depth of each area's audit should vary according to the audit risk assessment. Risk-based auditing allows internal audit management to provide assurance to the board that risk management processes are managing risks effectively in relation to organization's risk appetite. Risk appetite represents aggregated risks. An organization's risk appetite should be commensurate with its business size, business complexity, and management risk tolerance levels. The larger the size of the business, the greater the complexity, the higher management's tolerance for risk, the bigger the risk appetite, and vice versa.

Risk appetite = Business size + Business complexity + Management's risk tolerance levels

Internal Audit Risk Assessment

A comprehensive risk assessment should effectively analyze the key risks and critical risk functions for an organization and prioritize auditable entities within the audit universe (risk universe). During the risk assessment, internal auditors can refer to other types of risk assessments performed by the organization's senior management, risk management function, and risk committee. However, internal auditors need to apply independent professional judgment in integrating the various risk assessments conducted by nonaudit functions such as management, risk management function, and risk committee due to their lack of independence and objectivity.

Total audit risk = Internal audit's risk + Senior management's risk + Risk manager's risk
+ Risk committee's risk

Major **risk factors** commonly used in the audit risk assessment are listed next.

- Nature and scope of the business units, product lines, service lines, and business functions
- Nature of transactions, such as volume, size, and geographic locations (e.g., domestic and foreign)
- Nature of the operating environment (e.g., technology levels—high, medium, or low); laws and regulations (new or current); complexity of transactions (high, medium, and low); organizational changes (people, systems, and processes); and decision-making levels (e.g., centralization and decentralization)

Internal Audit Risk Assessment (continued)

- Nature and severity of internal and external threats facing the organization (high, medium, or low)
- Nature and scope of third-party services and providers utilized (breach of contracts, remedies, and damages)
- Human resources (experience, turnover, and competency levels of employees and management)
- Nature and strength of internal controls (weak, medium, or strong)
- Degree and level of governance and oversight activities by the board and senior management (weak, medium, or strong)
- Timing, scope, and results of internal audit's quality assurance assessments (acceptable or unacceptable)
- Quantified risk levels (high, medium, and low)

  Risk = Impact × Likelihood

Internal auditors and risk managers should develop written guidelines on the use of risk assessment tools and risk factors and review the guidelines with the board, senior management, risk committee, and audit committee. These guidelines need to be updated as a reference book for all parties involved in the risk assessment. Items the written guidelines should include are listed next.

Internal Audit Risk Assessment (continued)

- Length of the audit cycles (high risk means every 12 months, medium risk means every 18 months, and low risk means every 24 months)
- Risk-scoring methodology (define the basis for risk grades, risk weights, and risk scores)
- Risk assessments overrides (notification and approval on an exception basis is required and must be tracked)
- Timing of audit risk assessment for each business function or activity (a separate risk assessment is required for each audit engagement)
- Systemic control issues (size and severity of control deficiencies and their impacts)
- Minimum documentation requirements (written assessment analysis and scoring of assessment decisions is required)

Risk assessments typically analyze the risks inherent in a given business function or activity, the mitigating controls, and the resulting residual risk exposure to the organization. The board, senior management, and internal audit management should ensure that the risk measurement approaches or risk-scoring systems are simple, understandable, consider all relevant risk factors, and avoid subjectivity.

Internal Audit Risk Assessment (continued)

Outputs of the risk assessment exercise include overall audit plan containing audit universe, audit coverage, audit plan changes, audit plan staffing, audit cycles, and audit work programs. A relationship between risk levels, audit priorities, and audit cycles is shown next.

High-Risk Areas ⟶ High-Priority Audit Cycle

Medium-Risk Areas ⟶ Medium-Priority Audit Cycle

Low-Risk Areas ⟶ Low-Priority Audit Cycle

Risk Assessment Model

Audit resources are limited and expensive; hence they should be properly allocated and scheduled for maximum utilization. Risk models or risk analysis is often used in conjunction with development of long-range audit schedules. Performing risk analysis and risk assessment is a major step in audit planning work. A **risk** is defined as the probability that an unfavorable event occurs that could lead to a financial or other form of loss. The potential occurrence of such an event is called **exposure**. Risks are caused by exposures. Controls can reduce or eliminate risks and exposures.

STEPS INVOLVED IN A RISK ASSESSMENT MODEL

- Identifying risk factors
- Judging the relative importance of the risk factors
- Measuring the extent to which each risk factor is present in an audit unit
- Quantifying and evaluating the risk level
- Allocating the audit resources according to the risk level

Risks are inherent when business activities and transactions are processed either manually or in an automated manner. Intentional or unintentional errors, omissions, and irregularities (e.g., theft, fraud) do occur when people handle transactions during analyzing, recording, approving, classifying, computing, processing, summarizing, posting, and reporting activities. These risks represent potentially damaging events that can produce losses.

Audit Risk Factors

High-risk areas should receive high priority, and low-risk areas should be given low priority. A systematic risk assessment approach is better than a haphazard, trial-and-error, approach. An IIA survey identified 19 potentially important audit-risk factors. Each factor might be related to the risk or to the allocation of internal audit resources when the objective is to minimize losses to the firm.

1. **Quality of internal control system (most important factor).** The design and past performance of an internal control system is important in judging the probability of errors in the system. Audit units with a weak system of internal controls pose a higher risk of loss. Consequently, units with weak internal control should receive a larger share of audit resources.

2. **Competence of management.** Although difficult to measure objectively, the competence of a unit's management influences the confidence that the internal auditor has in the operations of the unit. The less competent the management, the higher the risk of losses to the firm.

3. **Integrity of management.** Although it is even more difficult to assess or measure, the integrity of management bears an obvious relationship to the probability of losses to the firm through overrides of the control system.

4. **Size of unit.** The size of a unit normally affects the magnitude of its potential losses. Thus, the larger an audit unit (in terms of total assets, revenue, cash flow, etc.), the larger the demand for audit resources.

Audit Risk Factors (continued)

5. **Recent change in accounting system.** A recent change in systems may invalidate past performance as a measure of control strength and usually increases the probability of errors during the system's break-in period.

6. **Complexity of operations.** As the operating complexity of an audit unit increases, the information and control system will also become more complex. This complexity can increase both the probability of error and the effort required to monitor the system.

7. **Liquidity of assets.** Highly liquid assets normally receive more audit attention than their asset size alone would indicate. Liquid assets are active, mobile resources that are an attractive target for defalcations. Thus, the more liquid the resources of an audit unit, the greater the level of internal auditing.

8. **Recent change in key personnel.** Control systems depend on competent judgments by key personnel. A lack of continuity in personnel may mean the control system is less effective than in previous periods.

9. **Economic condition of unit.** Because of pressure on management to produce improved economic results, the risk of control breakdowns is often greater in units with poor economic performance. In addition, poor economic performance may be a signal of such breakdowns. Thus, units with poor economic conditions are likely to pose more risk for the firm.

Audit Risk Factors (continued)

10. **Rapid growth.** Rapid growth stretches the personnel and the management control system of an operation. While growth provides significant opportunities for profit, it also provides the opportunity for control problems to emerge.
11. **Extent of computer automation.** Automation cannot be undertaken just for the sake of automation. Bleeding-edge (new) technologies can be costly and risky when compared to proven technologies. A company management should follow its industry's standards regarding automation so that it is not below the industry level.
12. **Time since last audit.** Because the internal audit detects and deters inappropriate activity, the effects of internal auditing will likely be greatest just before and just after an audit. As the time since the last audit increases, the risk of loss of internal control increases.
13. **Pressure on management to meet objectives.** For the same reasons discussed in item 9, increased performance pressure increases the pressure to circumvent controls.
14. **Extent of government regulation.** This factor reflects the fact that the firm may be subject to some unpredictable forces, which may serve to increase risk.

Audit Risk Factors (continued)

15. **Level of employee morale.** This factor may be important because low morale may indicate significant differences between the objectives of the top management and those of individuals at lower levels. Such differences can lead to increased risk.
16. **Audit plans of independent auditors.** Although internal and external auditors have differing concerns and objectives in auditing, their activities do overlap. The plans of external auditors can influence individuals in units, which might be subject to external and internal auditing.
17. **Political exposure.** Risk comes in many forms. The cost of events can be direct (i.e., lost profits and fraud losses) or indirect (i.e., reputation).
18. **Need to maintain appearance of independence by internal auditor.** This factor was included to see if the internal auditor's resource allocation would be significantly affected by the need to maintain the appearance (in addition to the substance) of independence within the firm. Given its low rating, this factor apparently is not a significant influence.
19. **Distance of unit from home office (least important factor).** This factor was included to determine if the out-of-sight, out-of-mind approach applied to internal audit risk. It may also reflect the foreign versus domestic aspects of relative risk.

Approaches to Risk Assessment

The purposes of risk analysis and assessment are to identify risks and exposures, calculate the damage or loss, and make cost-effective control recommendations. Several risk assessment techniques and approaches are available to quantify risks. Some of them, used in combination, are listed next.

- Judgment and intuition
- Scoring approach
- Delphi technique
- Quantitative methods

Judgment and intuition always play an important role in risk assessment. The auditor calls on personal and professional experience and education. This is often called a gut-feel approach. Under this approach, risks may be labeled as high, medium, or low.

The **scoring approach** assigns a weight factor and a risk level to each characteristic. The product of these two numbers is the weighted risk score of the characteristic, and the sum over the risk scores of an area yields the area risk score. These areas can be ranked according to the weighted risk score.

The weight factors can be derived using the **Delphi technique**. The audit department can use the Delphi technique to get the weights from the audit staff using their expertise in operational, financial, compliance,

Approaches to Risk Assessment (continued)

program, and computer system audits. The rationale for using the Delphi technique is that it is sometimes difficult to get a consensus on the cost or loss value and the probabilities of occurrence.

An example of a **quantitative method,** as recommended by Federal Information Processing Standards (FIPS) Publications (PUB) 65, involves calculating an annual loss exposure value based on estimated costs and potential losses. The annual loss exposure values are considered in the cost-effective selection of controls and safeguards. The essential elements of risk analysis are an assessment of the damage, which can be caused by an unfavorable event, and an estimate of how often such an event may happen in a period of time. Quantitative means of expressing both potential impact and estimated frequency of occurrence are necessary in performing a quantitative risk analysis. The annual loss exposure is calculated as

$$ALE = I \times F$$

where **ALE** is annual loss exposure, **I** is estimated impact in dollars, and **F** is the estimated frequency of occurrence per year.

ASSURANCE ENGAGEMENTS

Assurance engagements are objective examinations of evidence for the purpose of providing an independent assessment on governance, risk management, and control processes for the organization. Assurance services provide an assessment of the reliability and/or relevance of data and operations in specific areas of business functions. With these engagements, internal auditors provide reasonable assurance that organizational goals are being accomplished. Assurance audits are bounded work with a predefined audit scope that is fixed (e.g., accounts payable audit and accounts receivable audit).

Note that an internal auditor's role in conducting assurance engagements and performing consulting engagements is different due to the different objectives and outcomes of these objectives. Under these conflicting situations, the best audit practice is not to assign the same auditor to perform the assurance engagement and consulting engagement on the same audit area of interest. Specifically, assurance engagements can include these 15 topics:

1. Risk and control assessments
2. Third-party audits
3. Related-party audits
4. Construction audits

ASSURANCE ENGAGEMENTS (CONTINUED)

5. Security audits
6. Privacy audits
7. Performance audits
8. KPI reviews
9. Balanced scorecard reviews
10. Contract audits
11. Financial audits
12. Operational audits
13. IT audits
14. Compliance audits
15. Quality audits

Risk and Control Assessments

Assessing risks and controls is a major responsibility of the board, senior management, and internal auditors alike, as part of an organization's governance, risks management, and control processes or activities. This section is divided into two subsections—audit objective and audit program, and tools to conduct risks and control assessments. Here, a business goal is to ensure that risks are controlled.

Audit Objective and Audit Program

An audit objective of risk and control assessment is to determine whether an organization's risk assessment system allows the board and senior management to plan for and respond to existing risks and emerging risks. An audit program is suggested next.

- Determine whether the board and senior management involve outside risk consultants and internal control experts in the risk assessment and risk evaluation process and that these personnel are competent and knowledgeable.
- Determine whether the board and senior management discuss and evaluate risks and consider control issues during the pre-planning stages of introducing new products and new services. Does this evaluation consider technological, environmental, social, and governance issues with appropriate attention paid to all of these issues?

Audit Objective and Audit Program (continued)

- Determine the adequacy of de-risking approaches taken such as surety bonds, blanket bonds, and risk insurance policies in relation to risk profiles. Ascertain how residual risk will be handled.
- Determine whether a chief risk officer and staff computes value-at-risk (VAR) amounts for each type or category of risks for each business division and for the entire business organization.

VaR is an estimate of the maximum amount of loss that can occur in a given time period (e.g., one year) and at a given confidence level (e.g., 95%). The VAR needs to be established for each risk type or risk category that is documented in risk descriptions and risk discussions. The amount of VAR is the amount of risk capital (i.e., capital at risk) needed to withstand a particular loss. The Monte Carlo method can be used to compute the VAR amount. Risk appetite is directly related to VAR, meaning that the higher the risk appetite level, the larger the amount of VAR, implying more value is at risk. An example of VAR is that we are 95% confident that our organization will have to incur $500,000 loss in the next year due to cyberattacks, resulting from cyberrisks of data breaches. **Back-testing** can help in comparing and reconciling the estimated VAR to the actual VAR to make future estimates better.

Tools to Conduct Risk and Control Assessments

At least five tools exist to conduct risk and control assessments:

1. Risk matrix
2. Risk maps
3. Risk and control maps
4. Risk and control matrix
5. Risk and control testing

There is a built-in link between risks and controls in that controls reduce risks. Each tool is described next.

Risk Matrix

A **risk matrix** is a tool for ranking and displaying risks with their maximum and minimum values for consequences (impacts) and likelihoods (probabilities). A risk matrix expresses the same thing as the level of risk.

Risk matrix = Consequences (impacts) + Likelihoods (probabilities)

Risk Maps

A risk map or risk mapping involves profiling risk events to their sources (i.e., threats and vulnerabilities), determining their impact levels (i.e., low, medium, or high), and evaluating the presence of or lack of effective controls to mitigate risks. Risks are mapped to a business area that will be affected. A risk map describes the primary control procedures in place and indicates the areas that need control-related investment. Risk mapping is a part of developing risk profiles. Risk maps establish the relationship between vulnerabilities, threats, risks, and controls, as shown next.

Vulnerabilities → Threats → Risks → Controls

Risk and Control Maps

Strong and effective controls can reduce vulnerabilities, which in turn reduce threats. Risks come from threats and controls reduce risks. This means risks are under control. Internal auditors must assess whether the level of a control is appropriate for the risk it mitigates. A risk and control map can help auditors to document the relationship between risks and controls. Possible outcomes from the risk and control mapping are listed next.

Some high risks are undercontrolled (open to fraud, threats, and vulnerabilities).

Some low risks are overcontrolled (waste of resources, delays in operations).

Risk and Control Maps (continued)

Some risks are not controlled at all (open to fraud, threats, and exposures).

Some controls are not needed (waste of resources, delays in operations).

Some controls do not address any risks (waste of resources, open to threats).

Some weak controls are overdesigned (waste of resources, delays in operations).

Some strong controls are underdesigned (open to fraud, threats, and vulnerabilities).

Some simple controls are overcomplicated (waste of resources, delays in operations).

Some complex controls are oversimplified (open to fraud, threats, and vulnerabilities).

Risk and Control Matrix

A **risk and control matrix** documents the links between risks, controls, testing approaches, summaries of interviews, auditor observations, audit test results, audit evidence, and auditor conclusions that can be documented in audit workpapers. This matrix identifies the risks that may impact an auditable area's objectives, resources, systems, processes, and operations. Moreover, this matrix provides important feedback on the key risks that were identified, including mitigating controls.

Risk and Control Testing

Engagement objectives help internal auditors determine which audit procedures to perform. They also help auditors to prioritize risk and control testing of systems and processes during an audit engagement. This testing provides assurances regarding deign accuracy, operating effectiveness and efficiency, compliance to requirements, control accuracy, and reporting.

Third-Party Audits

Third Parties Defined

A third-party relationship can occur between two or more organizations either through a formal written contract or through an informal memorandum of understanding or agreement to buy/sell goods or provide/receive services. Examples of third-party relationships include:

- Outsourced vendors with products and services
- Use of independent consultants
- Computer network vendors
- Services provided by affiliates, subsidiaries, and joint ventures
- Services with other business partners (e.g., insurance companies, banks, and healthcare providers) with ongoing relationships

At least two entities are involved: One is the company engaging a third party to provide products and services (i.e., engaging company) and the other is the third party itself, where the latter can be one entity or several entities. Third parties are different from related parties because third parties consist of outsiders, such as suppliers, vendors, and contractors, whereas related parties consist of insiders, such as employees and their families.

Risks in Third-Party Relationships

Several new risks can arise or existing risks can increase when employing third parties because the third party is not under the direct control of the engaging company or hiring company. Increased risk most often comes from greater complexity of the nature and scope of the business, ineffective risk management by the engaging company, and inferior performance by the third party.

Governance Risk

Oversight risk may arise when the engaging company's management has exercised ineffective due diligence and oversight of third parties that market or originate certain questionable activities on the engaging organization's behalf. Ineffective oversight of third parties can also result in poor account management, customer service, and debt/receivables collection activities.

Strategic Risk

Strategic risk can arise if the engaging company does not use third parties when it is prudent to do so. For example, an engaging company may introduce strategic risk when (1) it does not leverage third parties that possess greater expertise than the engaging company does internally, (2) the third party can more cost-effectively supplement internal expertise, or (3) the third party is more efficient at providing a service with better risk management than the engaging company can provide internally.

Strategic risk exists in an engaging company that uses third parties in an effort to remain competitive, increase earnings, or control expense without fully performing due diligence reviews or implementing the appropriate risk management infrastructure to oversee the activity. Strategic risk also arises if management does not possess adequate expertise and experience to oversee properly the third-party relationship.

An engaging company is exposed to strategic risk if it uses third parties to conduct core functions or offer core products and services that are not compatible with the engaging company's strategic goals, cannot be effectively monitored and managed by the engaging company, or do not provide an adequate return on investment (ROI).

Operational Risk

Operational risk is present in all products, services, functions, programs, delivery channels, and work processes because an engaging company may not have direct control of the activities performed by the third party. Another risk is business concentrations when the engaging company relies on a single third party for multiple activities, particularly when several of the activities are critical to the engaging company's operations. Additionally, geographic concentrations can arise when the engaging company's operations and those of its third parties, its contractors, and its subcontractors are all located in the same region or are dependent on the same critical power and telecommunications infrastructures. This means that risk concentrations are increased, requiring backup and contingency plans.

Compliance Risk

Compliance failures by the third party could result in litigation cases or loss of business to the engaging company and damage to the engaging company's reputation. Compliance risk exists in a number of ways, such as when:

- Products, services, or systems associated with third-party relationships are not properly reviewed for compliance.
- The third party's operations are not consistent with laws, regulations, ethical standards, or the engaging company's policies and procedures.

Compliance Risk (continued)

- A third party implements or manages a product or service in a manner that is unfair, deceptive, or abusive to the recipient of the product or service.
- The engaging company licenses or uses technology from a third party that violates a third party's intellectual property rights.
- The third party does not adequately monitor and report transactions for suspicious activities to the engaging company.
- The engaging company's oversight function does not include appropriate audit and control features, particularly when the third party is implementing new company activities or expanding existing ones.
- Activities are further subcontracted.
- Activities are conducted in foreign countries.
- Customer and employee data is transmitted to foreign countries.
- Conflicts of interest between the engaging company and a third party are not appropriately managed.
- Transactions are not adequately monitored for compliance with all required laws and regulations.
- The engaging company or its third parties have not implemented appropriate controls to protect customer privacy data and customer and company records.

Reputation Risk

Third-party relationships that do not meet the expectations of the engaging company's customers and other stakeholders can expose the company to reputation risk. Poor service, frequent or prolonged service outages and disruptions, significant or repetitive security lapses, or violations of consumer laws can result in litigation cases, loss of business to the company, or negative perceptions in the marketplace.

Publicity about adverse events surrounding the third parties also may increase the company's reputation risk. In addition, many products and services involved in franchising arrangements expose the company to higher reputation risks. In some cases, it is not until something goes wrong with the third party's products, services, or client relationships that it becomes apparent to the engaging company that it is too late to get involved. When the engaging company is offering products and services actually originated from third parties as its own, the engaging company can be exposed to substantial financial loss and damage to its reputation if it fails to maintain adequate quality control over those products and services and adequate oversight over the third party's activities.

Third-Party Risk Management Process

An effective third-party risk management process consists of five phases at the beginning of a relationship life cycle:

1. Planning
2. Due diligence reviews and third-party selection
3. Contract negotiation
4. Ongoing monitoring
5. Termination

Planning

Developing a plan to manage the relationships is often the first step in the third-party risk management process. Planning is essential especially when contracting with third parties that involves core critical activities.

Due Diligence Review and Third-Party Selection

Conducting a due diligence review of a potential third party before signing a contract helps ensure that the engaging company selects an appropriate third party and understands and controls the risks posed by the relationship. The due diligence review should be consistent with the engaging company's risk appetite levels. Specific topics covered include:

- Strategies and goals
- Legal and regulatory compliance
- Financial condition
- Business experience and reputation
- Fee structure and incentives
- Risk management, physical security, and information security
- Resilience
- Human resource management
- Insurance coverage
- Conflicting contractual agreements with other parties

Contract Negotiation

Developing a contract that clearly defines expectations and responsibilities of the third party helps to ensure the contract's enforceability, limit the engaging company's liability, and mitigate disputes about performance. This section is further expanded under the heading "Third-Party Contract Compliance."

Ongoing Monitoring

Performing ongoing monitoring of the third-party relationships when the contract is in place is essential to the engaging company's ability to manage risk of the third-party relationship.

Termination

Developing a contingency plan is necessary to ensure that the engaging company can transition the activities to another third party, bring the activities in-house, or discontinue the activities when a contract expires, the terms of the contract have been satisfied, in response to contract default, or in response to changes to the engaging company's or third party's business strategy.

Third-Party Contract Compliance

Once the engaging company selects a third party, management should negotiate a contract that clearly specifies the rights and responsibilities of each party to the contract. Additionally, when a third-party relationship will involve critical activities, senior management should obtain board approval of the contract before its execution. The engaging company should review existing contracts periodically, particularly those involving critical activities, to ensure they continue to address pertinent risk controls and legal protections. Where problems are identified, the engaging company should seek to renegotiate at the earliest opportunity.

The third-party contracts should generally address these 17 items at a minimum:

1. Nature and scope of arrangement
2. Performance measures or benchmarks
3. Responsibilities for providing, receiving, and retaining information
4. Right to audit and require remediation
5. Responsibility for compliance with applicable laws and regulations
6. Cost and compensation
7. Ownership and license

Third-Party Contract Compliance (continued)

8. Confidentiality and integrity
9. Business resumption and contingency plans
10. Indemnification
11. Insurance
12. Dispute resolution
13. Limits on liability
14. Default and termination
15. Customer complaints
16. Subcontracting
17. Foreign-based third parties

Related-Party Audits

Related Parties Defined

Related parties include affiliates, subsidiaries, employees of a company (e.g., executives and officers), and nonemployees of a company (e.g., shareholders and corporate promoters), among others. Note that related parties are different from third parties because related parties mostly are insiders, such as employees and officers, whereas third parties mostly are outsiders, such as suppliers, vendors, and contractors.

Who are These Related Parties Anyway?

Related parties are of two types: related persons and related firms. **Related persons** include employees, directors, officers, executives, attorneys, corporate promoters, investors, owners, shareholders, and beneficiaries. **Related firms** include affiliates, subsidiaries (financial or operating subsidiaries), and holding companies. However, an independent real estate company owning and renting its land on its premises to an independent company is not an affiliate of the latter company. Similarly, an independent company renting safe deposit boxes to a bank's customers and private citizens is not an affiliate of the bank.

Covered Transactions in Related Parties

Covered transactions are those specific transactions applicable to related parties and are listed next.

- Loans and extensions of credit to affiliates and employees
- Purchase of assets from affiliates
- An investment in securities (bonds and stocks) issued by an affiliate
- The acceptance of securities issued by an affiliate as collateral for a loan or extension of credit to any person
- The issuance of a guarantee, acceptance, or letter of credit on behalf of an affiliate

For example, a bank's policy may state that (1) no member bank shall pay to related persons a greater rate of interest on their deposits than that paid to other depositors on similar deposits with such member bank; (2) no member bank can extend credit in any manner to any of its own officers and executives; and (3) no executive or officer of any member bank may become indebted to that member bank except by means of extension of credit with the bank that is authorized to make it.

Risks in Related-Party Transactions

- Misreported sales between affiliates
- Unspecified intercompany transactions
- Failure to disclose and account for a compensation arrangement with a former CEO
- Personal loans to current CEO or other executives

Audit Program for Related-Party Transactions

An audit program for a bank's related-party transactions should focus on major issues and risks that can arise in the future, as described next.

- Review the names, locations, nature of business, and manner of all affiliates of a bank and its related firms, including their relationship with the bank and their fee schedules for services performed.
- Determine the amount of loans made to, investment in, and credit extensions offered to the related persons and firms.

Audit Program for Related-Party Transactions (continued)

- Determine whether any collateral is pledged to secure credit extensions to the related persons and firms. Ascertain whether the collateral is computed at its fair market value. A low-quality asset should not be acceptable as collateral for a loan, extension of credit to, or a letter of credit issued on behalf of an affiliate.
- Determine whether a bank's debt was not used to serve as collateral for loan advances made to related persons or firms.
- Review any litigation cases and other financial commitments made to related persons or firms.
- Assess the scope and adequacy of the internal audit and external audit of related-party transactions and management's response to those audit findings and recommendations.
- Assess the amount of risk accepted and the amount of the residual risk not accepted by management.

Review of Transfers and Receivables to or from Shareholders

Transactions involving the major shareholders (e.g., close family and relations), either directly or indirectly, are potentially the most difficult type of transactions to review and monitor. In some jurisdictions, shareholders above a limit as low as five shareholdings are obliged to report transactions. Disclosure requirements include the nature of the relationship where control exists and the nature and amount of transactions with related parties, grouped as appropriate. Given the inherent opaqueness of many transactions, the obligation may need to be placed on the beneficiary to inform the board about the transaction, which in turn should make a disclosure to the market. This should not absolve the company from maintaining its own monitoring, which is an important task for the board.

Related-Party Disclosure Requirements

The Securities and Exchange Commission (SEC) has issued statements on the role of management's discussion and analysis related to the effects of transactions with related parties and certain other parties. The SEC statements make it clear that transactions involving related parties should not be presumed to be carried out on an arm's-length basis, as the requisite conditions of a competitive market may not exist. Disclosures of the following may be necessary, where related-party transactions are material:

- The business purpose of the related-party arrangement
- Identification of the related parties transacting business with the registrant
- How transaction prices were determined by the parties
- If disclosures represent that transactions have been evaluated for fairness, a description of how the evaluation was made
- Any ongoing contractual or other commitment as a result of the arrangement

In management buyouts of a company, which fall outside of the definition of related parties, is a company established and operated by former management of the registrant? This means previous senior managers and officers of a company become new owners of the same company. Disclosure rules apply to management buyouts of a company because the registrant may have a relationship that enables the parties to negotiate terms of material transactions that may not be available for other, more clearly independent parties on an arm's-length basis.

Construction Audits

Many opportunities exist in contract auditing in terms of cost recovery due to fraud, deception, kickbacks, overcharges, and conflicts of interest. Similar to IT system development audits, internal auditors should participate early in construction audits due to their large investments. Early participation is required in planning, developing a request for proposal document, bidding procedures, cost estimates, contractual terms, contractors' accounting (billing) systems, cost control, and project control procedures. A provision should be provided in the contract for overall project reviews, billing reviews, and progress reviews and to facilitate cost recovery audits. The right-to-audit clause is needed.

Types of Construction Contracts

Construction audits generally fall into one of the three categories: fixed-price contracts (lump sum or hard bid), cost-plus contracts, and unit-price contracts. Regardless of the type of contract, all contracts must use a formal request-for-proposal document and competitive bids and negotiations prior to the start of the actual contract work in order to avoid potential losses and risks.

Under **fixed-price contracts**, contractors agree to work for a fixed amount. The auditor should review escalation clauses, progress payments, incentive provisions, adjustments for excess labor and materials costs, and change orders. Risks in the fixed-price contracts include:

- Inadequate insurance and bond coverage
- Charges for equipment and materials that are not received

Types of Construction Contracts (continued)

- Overhead cost items included as additional charges
- Inadequate inspection relative to specifications
- Extra costs, changes, and revisions that are already part of the original contract

Under **cost-plus contracts**, the contractor is reimbursed for costs plus a fixed fee (which is encouraged) or costs plus a fee based on percentage of costs (which is discouraged). Some cost-plus contracts provide for maximum costs and sharing of any savings generated. Risks in the cost-plus contracts include:

- Overhead cost items are also billed directly
- Duplication of costs between headquarters and field offices
- Poor-quality work practices
- Poor physical protection of materials and equipment
- Excessive costs incurred due to idle rented equipment

Types of Construction Contracts (continued)

- Excessive staffing of project
- Uncontrolled overtime cost

Unit-price contracts are useful when large amounts of similar work are required from the contractor (e.g., clearing land by the acre and surveillance of a building). A price is agreed on for each unit of work. Risks in the unit-price contracts include:

- Excessive progress payments
- Improper or inaccurate reporting of units completed
- Unauthorized escalation adjustments
- Inaccurate field records

Other types or categories in the construction contracts are margin-at-risk contracts (i.e., contribution margin is not enough to cover profits where contribution margin is revenues minus variable costs), time-and-material contracts, and guaranteed maximum price contracts.

Types of Construction Audits

Regardless of the type and category of contract used, all construction contracts share some common phases and associated tasks. In the past, construction project managers, contractors, and owners focused on interim construction audits and postconstruction audits (postmortem or postcompletion audits) as a way to manage and control construction projects. Most of the time, these audits are too late for management to benefit from because they are done on a reactive and after-the-fact basis. Innovative thinking leads to focus on preconstruction audits on a proactive basis to prevent major problems, avoid cost overruns, and anticipate and control project delays. Here, the preconstruction audit can be considered as phase 1, interim construction audit as phase 2, and postconstruction audit as phase 3. These three phases and their associated tasks are shown in the next table.

Pre-audit	Interim audit	Post-audit
Proactive thinking	Reactive thinking	Reactive thinking
Modern approach	Traditional approach	Traditional approach
Represents best practices	Represents legacy practices	Represents legacy practices
Identifies contract leakages earlier	Reacts to contract leakages later	Handles contract leakages much later

Types of Construction Audits (continued)

Contract leakages occur due to overpayments, erroneous payments, and double payments to contractors with misunderstanding between contracting parties about what was agreed to and how, and misapplication of confusing contractual terms and conditions, which can be prevented. However, contract leakages do not result from fraud or collusion. Instead, they arise from careless management approval of noncompliant and nonreimbursable payments to contractors without checking the terms and conditions of their contracts prior to approval due to simple negligence. Contract leakages are handled much differently in these three phases. For example, during preconstruction audits, contract leakages are identified much earlier in the project even before they occur. During the interim construction audits, midcourse corrective actions are taken to control the contract leakages on a reactive basis. Traditionally, postconstruction audits handled the contract leakages with payment reconciliations and remediations on an after-the-fact basis to recover excess or erroneous payments made to contractors (i.e., cost recovery efforts).

Audit Program for Construction Projects

A suggested audit work program for internal auditors to use during construction audit engagements is presented next.

- Review a contract's terms and conditions and make sure they do not contradict one another and are not ambiguous. Recommend changes to contradictory language.
- Ensure that the contract contains a clause about fines and penalties for breach of contractual terms and conditions and other violations. Make sure that possible remedial actions are clearly stated.
- Ensure that the original contract is kept separate from the change work orders and that the original contract is not updated directly whenever a change order is issued. The goal is to keep the original scope of the project separate from the frequent changes to allow tracking of accountability and responsibility.
- Review the composition of payroll burden rates and benefits cost multipliers, usually made on the basis of hourly wage rates for construction workers. Understand the assumptions made, hourly base wage rates used, inflation factors applied, and markup percentage used to derive an hourly wage rate. Recompute and revalidate the hourly wage rates, payroll burden rates, and benefit cost multipliers to determine their accuracy. Cost recovery amounts at the end of a project are based on these hourly wage rates.
- Ensure that the project manager is continuously monitoring the status and costs of the project with proper project management controls.

Security Audits

Basically, security audits can be divided into physical security reviews and system security reviews where the latter is focused more than the former due to their relative risk and importance levels. Eleven specific topics in security audits are listed next.

1. Mobile technology audit
2. Ransomware audit
3. Bitcoin audit
4. Data security audit
5. Identity theft audit
6. Social media audit
7. Cloud security audit
8. User authentication and authorization reviews
9. Information systems security control reviews
10. Web and mobile analytics
11. Software piracy audit

Mobile Technology Audit

The scope of mobile technology audit includes mobile device attacks, mobile device use policies, web and mobile attacks, security controls over websites and mobile devices, and mobile applications (apps) review. A mobile device can be a smartphone, digital tablet, electronic reader, or personal digital assistant (PDA).

Mobile Device Attacks

Attacks against mobile devices generally occur through four different channels of activities: software downloads, visiting a malicious website, direct attack through the communication network, and physical attacks.

1. **Software downloads.** Malicious applications may be disguised as a game, device patch, or utility program, which is available for download by unsuspecting users and provides the means for unauthorized users to gain unauthorized use of mobile devices and access to private information or system resources on mobile devices.

2. **Visiting a malicious website.** Malicious websites may automatically download malware to a mobile device when a user visits that site. In some cases, the user must take action (such as clicking on a hyperlink) to download the application while in other cases the application may download automatically.

Mobile Device Attacks (continued)

3. **Direct attack through the communication network.** Rather than targeting the mobile device itself, some attacks try to intercept communications to and from the device in order to gain unauthorized use of mobile devices and access to sensitive information.
4. **Physical attacks.** Unauthorized individuals may gain possession of lost or stolen devices and use those devices to access sensitive information stored on them.

Mobile Device Use Policies

Management needs to create acceptable-use policies for all portable media devices and educate/train employees about those policies. Management needs to conduct cost-benefit analysis and perform risk – return analysis with either distribute locked-down, corporate-controlled devices or ask employees to bring or choose their own devices. An organization's mobile device use policy can have positive or negative consequences with the four choices listed next. For example, these choices can lead to risks such as data leakage, data loss, data stealing, and data destruction. Consider banning from the workplace personal portable media devices that management cannot control and monitor.

1. **Bring your own device (BYOD)** is a policy that permits employees to bring personally owned devices to their workplace and use them to access restricted company's data, information, and applications. This policy is risky.
2. **Bring your own applications (BYOA)** is a policy similar to BYOD that involves employees using third-party applications in the workplace or on a work device. This policy is risky.
3. **Choose your own device (CYOD**) is a program that differs from BYOD by allowing end users to select from a predetermined and approved list of personal device types for work rather than any device. This policy is not risky.
4. **Wear your own device (WYOD)** is a program similar to BYOD that allows end users to use personal wearable devices (watches and virtual reality goggles) to perform a company's tasks and functions. This policy is risky.

Mobile Device Use Policies (continued)

Exhibit 1.1 summarizes attacks or exploits against mobile devices and suggests controls to reduce risks.

Attack or exploit	Description of the attack and controls
Zero-day exploit	A zero-day attack takes advantage of a security vulnerability before an update for the vulnerability is available. By writing exploits for unknown vulnerabilities, attackers create a potential threat because mobile devices generally do not have software patches to prevent the exploit from succeeding. A security control is to install all software patches and updates without fail.
Theft or loss of device	Because of their small size and use outside the office, mobile devices can be easier to misplace or steal than a laptop or notebook computer. If mobile devices are lost, it may be relatively easy to gain access to the information they store. Security controls are to exercise the kill option on the device, use a remote data-wiping tool, and turn on the device location tracking software (global positioning software [GPS]).
Browser exploits	Browser exploits are designed to take advantage of vulnerabilities in software used to access websites. Visiting certain web pages and/or clicking on certain hyperlinks can trigger browser exploits that install malware or perform other adverse actions on a mobile device. A security control is to avoid clicking on unknown hyperlinks.
Tampering	Modifying data, software, firmware, or hardware without authorization; modifying data in transit; inserting tampered hardware or software into supply chain; repackaging legitimate app with malware; modifying network or device configuration (e.g., jailbreaking or rooting a phone). A security control is to use an anti-tampering tool to make tamper-proof or tamper-resistant.

Mobile Device Use Policies (continued)

Attack or exploit	Description of the attack and controls
Denial of service	Deny or degrade service to users. Jamming or wireless communications, overloading networks with bogus traffic, ransomware, theft of mobile device or mobile services. A security control is to use anti-jamming tool.
Information disclosure	Unauthorized access to information or service. Interception of data in transit; leakage or exfiltration of user, app, or enterprise data; tracking of user physical location (geolocation); eavesdropping on voice or data communications; and surreptitiously activating the phone's microphone or camera to spy on the user. A control is to use encryption with passwords and passphrases.
Spoofing	Impersonating something or someone. Email or short message service (SMS) message pretending to be from a boss or colleague (social engineering); fraudulent Wi-Fi access point or cellular base station mimicking a legitimate one. A control is to use anti-spoofing software, such as digital signatures.
Malware	Malware is often disguised as a game, patch, utility software, or other useful third-party software application (app). It includes spyware, Trojan horses, keystroke logging, unauthorized location tracking, and viruses. It is self-spreading and repackaging. A control is to use antivirus and antimalware software.

Mobile Device Use Policies (continued)

Attack or exploit	Description of the attack and controls
Network exploits	Network exploits take advantage of software flaws in the system that operates on local Bluetooth, Wi-Fi, or cellular networks. They can propagate malware and hijack the users' credentials to impersonate users online. A bluesnarfing attack enables attackers to gain access to contact data by exploiting a software flaw in a Bluetooth-enabled device. A control is to turn off the Bluetooth and Wi-Fi services when the device is not needed.
Phishing and spamming	**Phishing** is a scam that frequently uses email or pop-up messages to deceive people into disclosing sensitive information. Internet scammers use email bait to "phish" for passwords and financial information from mobile and Internet users. A control is to use anti-phishing software. **Spamming** is sending unsolicited commercial email advertising for products, services, and websites. Spam can appear in text messages and email, can be used for phishing attempts, and can be used as a delivery mechanism for malware. A control is to use anti-spamming software.
Jamming	**Jamming** is an attack in which a mobile device is used to emit electromagnetic energy on a wireless network's frequency to make it unusable by the network. Jamming is used in the denial-of-service attack. A control is to use anti-jamming and anti-skimming tools.

Exhibit 1.1: Summary of attacks or exploits against mobile devices and suggested controls to reduce risks

Mobile Device Use Policies (continued)

BYOD mobile devices that employees are allowed to bring to their workplace are called **rogue devices** due to the risk these devices can pose to a company. These mobile devices become rogue devices when they are unofficially connected to unauthorized, unsecured, and controlled nonbusiness external websites such as social media, sports, gaming, and film networks. Hackers can insert rogue software (i.e., malware and bots) into these BYOD devices and can reach a company's official network to cause a data breach or other damage. This means hackers use these mobile devices as an entry point to access a company's official network.

Web and Mobile Attacks

Several attacks can occur using electronic mail (email) and mobile devices such as smartphone, digital tablets, and PDAs in order to perpetrate fraud. The integration of email, voice, text messages, and web browser functionality increases the likelihood that users will fall victim to various social engineering frauds, such as phishing, spear phishing, vishing, smishing, and click fraud.

Phishing is the fraudulent practice of sending mass emails to innocent people (untargeted victims) claiming to be from legitimate sources, such as companies and individuals, to induce victims to reveal personal and sensitive information, such as passwords and credit/debit card details online. Phishing is a criminal act using the social engineering approach of masquerading as a trustworthy individual or entity. Vishing and smishing acts are variants of phishing and of social engineering approaches.

Spear phishing is a targeted form of email deception through social engineering, resulting in exploitation or compromise of an individual's mobile device and a company's networks. This deception is an entry point into the company's networks and computer systems. Attackers glean personal information about an individual, which allows them to masquerade as a trusted source in an electronic communication. This may lead the individual to click on links, accept software updates, or open attachments via email, social media messages, or electronic popup messages. Security controls include installing anti-phishing software, user education and training to become phishing-aware, users acting as second lines of defense, and users becoming more vigilant at work.

Vishing is the act of using the telephone voice calls (cell/mobile, landline, or interactive voice recording system) in an attempt to scam the user into surrendering private information that will be used for identity theft, such as credit/debit card activation, income tax refund, rewards redemption, winning a lottery, receiving a job promotion, and free vacation, travel, and gifts. Advanced vishing attacks can take place over voice communications by exploiting voice over Internet protocol (VoIP) solutions and broadcasting services. VoIP easily allows caller ID to be spoofed.

Smishing is a type of phishing attack where cell/mobile phone users receive text and multimedia messages containing a website hyperlink, which if clicked would download a Trojan horse to the cell/mobile phone to spread viruses. Smishing exploits SMS and multimedia messaging service (MMS) messages.

Click fraud involves deceptions and scams that inflate online advertisement bills with improper, inaccurate, and illegal numbers of clicks made on the web. Either software bots are deployed or imposter users are hired by advertising firms to keep on clicking the ad either continuously or periodically to indicate that actual users are reading the ad. Later, the advertising firm bills its client for the number of clicks made (the billing rate is based on cost per click). A security control against click fraud is to use heat maps that track website visitors' click behavior and browsing habits. Heat maps help a web administrator visualize how web visitors are interacting with the website.

Security Controls over Websites and Mobile Devices

A list of security controls over websites and mobile devices and their associated attacks is presented next.

- Be suspicious of unsolicited phone calls, visits, or email messages and text messages from individuals asking about employees or other internal information. If an unknown individual claims to be from a legitimate organization, try to verify his or her identity directly with the organization.
- Do not provide personal information, customer information, or information about your organization, including its organizational structure, computer networks, or data centers, unless you are certain of a person's identity and authority to request this information.
- Do not reveal personal or financial information in email, and do not respond to email solicitations for this information. Do not follow the links sent in email.
- Do not send sensitive information over the Internet before checking a website's security.
- Pay attention to the universal resource locator (URL) of a website you receive. Malicious websites may look identical to a legitimate website, but the URL may use a variation in spelling or a different domain (e.g., .com vs. .net). If you are unsure of the URL, contact the original company directly. Information about known phishing attacks is available online from groups such as the Anti-Phishing Working Group.

Security Controls over Websites and Mobile Devices (continued)

- Install and maintain antivirus software, firewalls, and email filters to reduce some of this unwanted network traffic. Also, take advantage of anti-phishing features offered by your email servicer and web browser providers.
- Do not "jailbreak" or "root" the mobile device. Jailbreaking or rooting is removing the limitations imposed on a device by the manufacturer, often through the installation of custom operating system components or other third-party software. Jailbreaking makes a device more vulnerable to attacks because it removes important safeguards against malware attacks. Some users prefer to bypass the operating system's lockout features in order to install apps that could be malicious in nature. Doing jailbreaking and rooting is risky.
- Secure all sensitive data stored on a USB drive (e.g., jump drives, flash drives, and thumb drives), CDs, and DVDs using strong encryption. Consider using jump drives with onboard antivirus capability to perform automatic virus scans. Also use antimalware software on mobile devices.
- Set up a local firewall on the device to filter inbound and outbound traffic and to block malicious software.
- If a device is lost, stolen, or misplaced, activate GPS to track the location of the device and enable a remote-wiping feature to erase all data on the device.

Security Controls over Websites and Mobile Devices (continued)

- Disable Bluetooth and Wi-Fi services when not using them. When using Wi-Fi, encrypt the network or use a virtual private network (VPN) connection. When using the Bluetooth, set it to “nondiscoverable” mode to make the device invisible to unauthenticated devices.
- Create acceptable-use policies for all portable media devices and educate/train users about those policies.
- Develop an inventory of mobile devices that carry sensitive company information and audit the inventory on a regular basis.
- Configure Secure Socket Layer (SSL) security features on organizational web servers to encrypt data being transmitted.

Mobile Applications Review

Mobile apps defined

Mobile applications (apps) are small-size computer programs that operate on mobile devices using mobile operating systems for users' convenience. These apps are primarily used on mobile devices, such as smartphones, digital tablets, and PDAs, and secondarily on personal, laptop, and notebook computers. Data loss, data theft, and security glitches are examples of potential risks in apps. Mobile apps are different from applets; applets are small computer applications written in various programming languages that are automatically downloaded and executed by applet-enabled Internet browsers. Examples include Active-X applets and Java applets, both of which have security concerns in that applets are much riskier than apps.

Mobile apps' design features

Mobile apps are developed at an alarming rate per day by all types of organizations to provide convenience to their customers to do business with them, such as to place orders, pay, and track products and services; to receive marketing advertisements and promotional programs; to make appointments and schedules; and to download coupons and rewards.

Mobile apps are very popular and efficient tools for retail customers and retail store associates alike for use on their mobile devices. Apps are convenient tools for customers to use during shopping and productivity tools for retail store associates (retail employees) to assist customers. Regardless of the person, apps design must be

Mobile apps' design features (continued)

easy to use on a regular basis and must be designed keeping the context of their use in mind. Here, the **context** means that the app's format and function are carefully aligned to fully engage customers.

Specifically, **format** means layout, size, font, appearance, graphics resolution, readable and relevant information, display quality, appealing presentation, and form. Similarly, **function** means substance, features, usability, and applicability. The format and function are an example of classic discussion of substance over form or form over substance.

One way to classify mobile apps is basic apps and advanced apps. It is obvious that going from a basic app to an advanced app requires a huge investment in development, the difference being the number and type of features and functions built into the app. Note that the features of advanced apps contain the features of basic apps and more.

- **Basic app features**—Accessing a retailer's coupons, rebates, price discounts, and special deals with sales promotions; browsing a retailer's inventory system to find a product; locating retail stores; and downloading a store's navigation map
- **Advanced app features**—Scanning a product's bar code inside a store to show a product's price, description, availability, and customer reviews; searching for a product and finding matching products; connecting customer purchases to the loyalty program for rewards and points, which links customer engagement with customer retention; and mobile checkout to pay for purchases from anywhere in the store (i.e., tap-and-go)

Security risks in mobile apps

Several security risks exist in mobile apps, including:

- Improper platform usage—Misuse of a platform's features or failure to use the platform's security controls
- Insecure data storage—Unintended data leakages and insecure authentication
- Insecure communication—Poor handshaking and weak negotiations between systems and devices and cleartext communication of sensitive information, such as passwords
- Insecure authentication—Failure to identify the user at all when that should be required and weaknesses in session management; it also means granting anonymous access to some system resources or services during the authentication process
- Insecure authorization due to incorrect authorization decisions
- Poor programming quality resulting in buffer overflow attacks
- Code tampering—Provides an attacker a direct method of subverting the intended use of the software for personal or financial gain
- Unauthorized functionality—Software developers insert a hidden backdoor, place a password as a comment in the programming code, and disable the two-factor authentication mechanism during software testing
- Reverse engineering the final binary code to reveal its source code to understand the functions of back-end servers and to analyze the inner workings of intellectual property such as trademarks and patents

Security controls over mobile apps

In a rush to shorten the time-to-market metric, app software developers often focus on improving app functions and features and not so much on establishing security controls over apps. Apps can be classified as complex or simple; complex apps require maximum security controls and simple apps require minimum security controls. In other words, apps require a customized security approach, not a one-size-fits-all approach. The absence of effective and strong security controls can lead to vulnerabilities, such as data breaches, data snoops, and identity theft attacks. Apps that are more complex may rely on remote servers for storing and manipulating users' data; app developers must be familiar with securing app software, securing transmission of data between two points, and securing servers.

A list of suggested security guidelines over apps is presented next.

- Take an inventory of the data you collect and retain. Doing this requires practicing the data minimization principle, meaning collecting all the relevant data needed and ignoring all the irrelevant data not needed.
- Understand the differences between mobile platforms. Each mobile operating system uses different application programming interfaces (APIs) and provides its own minimum-security features, which may require add-on security features to make them security strong.
- Use transit-encryption feature for storing and validating user credentials (e.g., usernames, passwords, passcodes, and API keys) and recognize that the apps will be used on unsecure Wi-Fi access points in public places, such as airports, coffee shops, restaurants, and retail stores. Hackers use these access

Security controls over mobile apps (continued)

points to conduct data snooping and data interception attacks. **Data snooping** is an attack where data is read off a network while in transit without modifying or destroying the data. **Data interception** can occur when an attacker is eavesdropping on communications originating from or being sent to a mobile device. Electronic eavesdropping is possible through various techniques, such as man-in-the-middle attacks, which occur when a mobile device connects to an unsecured Wi-Fi network and an attacker intercepts and alters the communication; and Wi-Fi sniffing, which occurs when data are sent to or from a mobile device over an unsecured network connection without encryption, thus allowing an eavesdropper to "listen to" and record information that is exchanged.

- Use due diligence reviews on programming libraries and software development kits that third-party providers use to make apps and to ensure that the apps are secure.
- If an app is communicating with a cloud provider's server, make sure that there is a division of responsibility between securing the app and updating the app (i.e., separation of duties) to make it conflict-free.
- Protect users' data stored on their mobile devices, including data stored on central or local servers, with encryption. Note that servers can be subjected to injection attacks, cross-site scripting, and other threats.

Security controls over mobile apps (continued)

Injection attacks occur when untrusted data is sent to a system interpreter as part of a command or query. An attacker's hostile data can trick the interpreter into executing unintended commands or accessing data without proper authorization. **Cross-site scripting** attack occurs whenever an application includes untrusted data in a new web page without proper validation. This attack allows an attacker to execute scripts in the victim's browser that can hijack user sessions, deface websites, or redirect the user to malicious websites.

- Do not store users' passwords in plaintext, and consider using an iterated cryptographic hash function to hash passwords and then verify against those hash values. That way, if your server suffers a data breach, passwords are not left totally exposed.
- Keep improving apps functions and features, including security controls, with frequent updates and patches. Solicit feedback from users on this matter.
- Pay attention to laws and regulations dealing with financial data, health data, and children's data, as these laws are very strict, requiring full compliance. Protect users' privacy rights.

Ransomware Audit

Ransomware Defined

Ransomware is malicious software (malware) that denies access to computer files until the victim pays a ransom. Ransomware is a type of cyberattack that prevents a user from using a computer until the user pays a certain amount of money. It is essentially extortion with all the data on the user's computer at risk unless the user pays.

How Does Ransomware Work?

Scammers, data-nappers, or computer kidnappers send emails that look like courtesy messages from legitimate companies—especially shipping companies—to spread a new ransomware called CryptoLocker botnet. Other names for this type of malware include WannaCry, WannaCrypt, CryptoWall, or Cryptomining. CryptoLocker works by encrypting all the files on a user's computer (e.g., photos, documents, and tax refunds) that the user has saved to the hard drive or to any shared folders. Once the files are encrypted, the user will not be able to open the files without the decryption key, which the user can get only from the criminals behind CryptoLocker. Hackers or criminals hold user files "hostage," often encrypting them and demanding payment, typically in bitcoins, for the user to get the files back.

How Does Ransomware Work? (continued)

After CryptoLocker has encrypted the user files, it displays a message like this: "Your personal files are encrypted." The criminals demand payment through an anonymous payment type like bitcoin or Green Dot cards and promise to give the user the decryption key if the user pays the ransom amount in time (e.g., $300 to be paid within 72 hours). Unfortunately, once CryptoLocker has encrypted the user files, there is no way to recover them. Users could pay the ransom, but there is no guarantee that they will get the decryption key to open the files.

Common Ransomware Attacks

Ransomware attacks can occur on any organization's computer systems and networks and on any individual's personal computers (i.e., Windows and other platforms). At least four common attack methods exist in ransomware: exploit kits, malicious email attachments, malicious email links, and multiple attack vectors.

Exploit kits are sophisticated toolkits that exploit vulnerabilities. Most often these kits are executed when a user (victim) visits a compromised website. Malicious code hidden on the site, often in an advertisement (adware), redirects the user to the exploit kit landing page without his or her knowledge. If websites are vulnerable, a drive-by-download of a malicious payload will be executed, the system will become infected, and the files will be held for ransom.

SOURCES OF RANSOMWARE ATTACKS

Sources of ransomware attacks include portable executable file (PEFs), Word documents, .JS files, compressed file attachments, zip file attachments, and double extension files, such as a .pdf.exe. Specifically, sources include:

- Clicking on email links
- Downloading attachments and apps
- Spear phishing emails (most common)
- Visiting a compromised website
- Opening malicious online advertisements (spam emails)
- Using outdated and unpatched software (e.g., applications software, operating system software, and antivirus software)

Common Ransomware Attacks (continued)

Malicious email attachments are crafted emails likely from a believable internal source (e.g., a human resource department or an IT department) and attached to a malicious file (e.g., a portable executable file [PEF], Word document, or.JS file). The recipient opens this attachment thinking the email came from a trusted source. Once the file is opened, the ransomware payload is unknowingly downloaded, the system is infected, and the files are held for a ransom amount.

Malicious email links are URLs in the body of the email. Likewise, these emails are sent from someone or some organization that a recipient believes to be a trusted source. When clicked, these URLs download malicious files over the web, the system is infected, and the files are held for a ransom amount.

Multiple attack vectors include regular networks, cloud-based networks, and network end points.

Security Measures over Ransomware Attacks

Similar to any other computer attacks, organizations can develop security measures over ransomware attacks, including prevention, detection, and response (recovery) measures. It has been said that the recovery costs from ransomware attacks will be much higher than the ransom money paid to hackers due to damage-control costs and the losses of revenues, employee productivity, employee morale, and company reputation (i.e., increase in reputation costs).

Specific preventive measures are listed next.

- Do not click on links in an email unless you know who sent it and what it is. Instead, type the URL.
- Minimize drive-by downloads. CryptoWall ransomware is spread primarily via spam email and infects victims through drive-by downloads and malvertising (i.e., advertising with malware attached).
- Do not open double extension files, such as .pdf.exe.
- Use a cloud-based backup method with an add-on system that is secure, scalable, and effective that can move large amounts of data from data center, thus avoiding network bottlenecks. A cloud backup is like an insurance policy.
- Make sure that all applications, operating system, antivirus, and mobile device software have been patched with the latest updates.
- Set up your operating system, web browser, and security software to update automatically.

Security Measures over Ransomware Attacks (continued)

- Use an external hard drive to back up all personal computer files every day. However, disconnect the backup device from the computer when it is not actively backing up the files. In other words, never use the automatic option for backing up files when you are using the computer for work. If the CryptoLocker program strikes while your backup device is connected to your computer, the program will try to encrypt both the internal hard drive files and the external hard drive files. Consequently, the damage is multiplied.
- Use the application whitelisting feature, where only known computer programs can execute, based on security policy permissions.
- Separate networks and data categories by implementing physical security and logical security controls for different organizational units.
- Configure access controls on data files, data directories, and network share permissions with least privilege in mind. If a user needs only read access to specific files, the user should not have write access to those files, directories, or shares.
- Execute operating system software or specific application programs in a virtualized environment.
- Manage the use of privileged accounts based on the principle of least privilege. This means that no users should be assigned administrative access unless it is absolutely needed, and those with a need for administrator accounts should use them only when necessary.

Security Measures over Ransomware Attacks (continued)

Examples of other preventive measures include:

- Conducting user awareness and training programs
- Using spam filters to prevent phishing emails
- Authenticating inbound emails to prevent email spoofing attacks
- Scanning all incoming and outgoing emails to detect threats and to filter executable files from reaching end users
- Configuring firewalls to block access to known malicious Internet provider (IP) addresses
- Patching operating system software and firmware on devices using a centralized patch management system
- Installing antivirus and antimalware programs to conduct regular file scans automatically

Specific recovery measures are discussed next.

All organizations and all individuals using computer systems and networks should develop a recovery plan with the details about the backup source methods, backup storage policy, backup schedules, backup duration, and rotation and retention of backup files. Verify the integrity of the backup files and programs and test the restoration process to ensure it is working.

Security Measures over Ransomware Attacks (continued)

Specifically:

- Contain the attack, meaning disconnecting the infected devices from your network to keep ransomware from spreading.
- Isolate or power-off affected devices that have not yet been completely corrupted.
- Immediately secure backup data or systems by taking them offline and by ensuring that those backups are free of malware.
- Restore your computer only after all files have been backed up and any malware has been removed. Then reboot the computer.
- Change all online account passwords and network passwords after removing the system from the network. Furthermore, change all system passwords once the malware is removed from the system.
- Contact law enforcement authorities immediately with information such as criminals' email addresses or bitcoin wallet numbers.
- Implement security incident responses and business continuity plans. Having a data backup can eliminate the need to pay a ransom to recover data. Conduct an annual penetration test and vulnerability assessment. Store backups in the cloud or physically offline. Backups are critical in ransomware recovery and response. If computer files are infected, a backup may be the best way to recover critical data.

Risk Factors for Ransomware Victims

The cryptocurrency bitcoin is a payment mechanism that is increasing the success rate of ransomware attacks because bitcoin has no central authority. Due to lack of the central authority, law enforcement authorities cannot take any action against the attackers. Other payment mechanisms include Green Dot cards. Law enforcement authorities do not recommend paying ransom to criminals because doing so could send a signal to criminals that the user files are not backed up and protected, which could increase the ransom price and increase the criminals' bargaining power.

Ransomware victims may wish to consider the next risk factors either before or after paying the ransom amount. Law enforcement authorities do not encourage or recommend that victims pay a ransom to criminal actors. Victims will want to evaluate the technical feasibility, timeliness, and cost of restarting systems from backup. Ransomware victims may also wish to consider these factors:

- Paying a ransom does not guarantee that an organization will regain access to their data; in fact, some individuals or organizations were never provided with decryption keys after they paid a ransom.
- Some victims who paid the ransom were targeted again by cyberactors.
- After paying the original ransom amount, some victims were asked to pay more to get the promised decryption key. Paying the ransom amount could inadvertently encourage this criminal business model.

Bitcoin Audit

Bitcoins are technically called cryptocurrencies with cryptography as the supporting technology. Nontechnically they are called virtual currency, digital currency, digital gold, or digital wallets. Bitcoins are called virtual currency because there is no real currency (real money or flat money, such as U.S. dollars) involved. Credit/debit cards or wire transfer funds from banks, cash, prepaid/money/cash cards can be used to buy the digital currency through standard bitcoin exchange places or smartphone applications (apps), including major retail stores (e.g., Walmart and Amazon), local convenient stores, local currency exchanges, and local pharmacies. Bitcoins can also be used to purchase gift cards from a retail store. Here, the key point is that a virtual currency is exchanged for flat currency, funds, or other forms of virtual currency, all for a fee.

Blockchain or hash chain technology support bitcoins where the disruptive technology is facilitating transactions between mutually distrusting entities without the need for a trusted arbiter (i.e., no trusted middleperson, intermediary, or a central bank). Blockchain is a fully distributed and decentralized ledger that is synchronized through consensus between entities or parties. It facilitates fully decentralized operations, processes peer-to-peer transactions, and is tamper evident and resistant.

Risks of Using Bitcoins

Bitcoins can be used legally for making and receiving business payments. Bitcoins can also be used for illegal purposes, such as drug dealings, money laundering, hacking, fraudulent activities, and other related crimes. For example, hackers demanded their payment through bitcoins during ransomware attacks.

- Bitcoins and blockchains together deploy a disruptive technology that is not fully tested or proven, resulting in major risk to businesses and individuals.
- Public participation in bitcoin transactions is riskier than private participation.
- Privacy rights of participants can be violated due to lack of centralized recordkeeping for controlling and monitoring purposes.
- There is a lack of security best practices over digital wallets. Lack of mitigating controls is associated with the risk of irreversible transactions. This means that incorrect transactions cannot be corrected; once transactions are added to a blockchain, they cannot be changed. Buyers can get a refund for their purchases only if the seller is willing (i.e., voluntary or discretionary).
- Lack of effective identity and access management practices for validating users' electronic credentials.
- The bitcoin currency market is volatile due to the speculative nature of the bitcoin market (i.e., sudden high or low prices).

Risks of Using Bitcoins (continued)

- Data-loss risk due to potential hackers when they break into bitcoins distributed ledger.
- Bitcoin data cannot be changed when necessary because bitcoins were not designed to allow changes. Data source data immutability is not helpful when there are accusations of tampering after the fact.
- Fraudsters are ready to cheat innocent people with fake opportunities using a variety of bitcoin scams, such as:
  - "Guaranteed" high investment returns
  - No net worth or no income requirements
  - Pressure to buy right now
  - Unsolicited offers
  - Unlicensed individuals and unregistered firms offering and selling investments in bitcoins

  Above all, the entire deal sounds too good to be true (i.e., a high risk).

Data Security Audit

The scope of a data security audit includes a review of data breaches, understanding data leakages, a review of methods to protect customer information, and an audit of data storage and backup methods.

Data Breaches

Data breaches are examples of cybersecurity incidents that have occurred at several public sector organizations (e.g., the U.S. Office of Personnel Management, governmental agencies, and cities) and private sector organizations (e.g., Target, Yahoo, Sony, and Equafax) with severe financial losses and poor public relations with a high reputation risk. Hackers stole information from millions of customers, financial data and personal data, then sold that information to others, creating more identity fraud.

Organizations that are victims of data breach attacks must calculate the total costs resulting from such attacks. Victim organizations will quickly find out that the actual costs are much higher than the expected costs. These total costs can be classified in four ways: direct costs, indirect costs, opportunity costs, and one-time costs, as follows.

Direct costs include external digital forensic cost, internal hotline support cost, external technical consulting cost, and external legal consulting cost. Costs incurred for post-breach remedies include discounts given to the affected customers toward future purchase of products and services; credit monitoring services for the affected customers; and reestablishing accounts for old customers and opening accounts for new customers.

Data Breaches (continued)

Indirect costs include internal investigation cost, internal communication cost, lost sales, lost profits, and lost goodwill and reputation.

Opportunity costs include (1) increased customer defection rates and costs, resulting from increased turnover of current customers and (2) increased customer acquisition rates and costs, resulting from searching for new customers.

One-time costs include legal costs, resulting from customer lawsuits; court fines and penalties; and related court filing fees and handling costs.

WHAT CUSTOMER INFORMATION IS STOLEN IN DATA BREACHES?

Hackers are interested in stealing customers' online login data, debit/credit card number, bank account information, Social Security number, date of birth, driver's license number, financial data, personal data, medical data, tax data, phone numbers, name and address, and biometric data so they can re-create the charge cards and do other fraudulent activities.

Data Breaches (continued)

Major reasons for data breaches are poor authentication, authorization, and identity controls combined with weak session management procedures placed at the front door to security. For example, it was reported that retail customers were using plain charge cards (credit and debit cards) without using a combination of smart chip and a personal identification number (PIN) when they presented their charge cards at the retailers' point-of-sale (POS) registers. In the past, most retailers used weak and unsecure methods with a combination of (1) card and no signature, (2) card and signature, (3) card and PIN, (4) card and no PIN, and (5) card chip and no PIN. The best security control at the retail POS register is a combination of card chip and PIN, which can protect every customer, every retailer, and every card-issuing company. For online shopping, the best security control is username, password, passcode, charge card number, and personal security questions where customers provide answers to such questions, referred to as multifactor authentication.

Organizations can protect customers' data with basic user identification and authentication (e.g., username, passwords, passcodes, and personal security questions); strong encryption for data in storage, data in process, and data in transit; cloud storage; multilevel firewalls; and multifactor authentication mechanisms. Of course, user education and training always help in avoiding phishing and spamming emails, answering pretexting phone calls and robotic phone calls, and analyzing system logs. In summary, organizations need to invest resources to prevent data breaches with timely prevention, detection, and response capabilities.

Data Leakages

Whereas data breaches are primarily conducted by outsiders (hackers), data leakages are performed primarily by insiders (employees and contractors). It has been reported that more than one-third of cybercrime incidents were caused by inside knowledge workers (employees) of a company due to their familiarity and access to internal computer systems. Of these insiders, two-thirds were found to be negligent employees and one-third were found to be malicious employees. These inside threat sources include disgruntled employees and contractors, either actively employed or departing employees who are stealing sensitive company information (e.g., customer data, email lists, strategic plans, and research and development materials) and proprietary information (e.g., intellectual property data such as software code, trademarks, and patents). These insiders are abusing their positions of trust.

This type of data leakage includes data loss, data stealing, and data destruction acts, which are possible when employees are given permission to bring their own devices (BYOD) and due to the availability of online file-sharing apps. Insiders think that it is acceptable to transfer work documents that they have created to their personal computers, removable storage media, cloud-based data storage services, digital tablets, and smartphones. Some disgruntled employees and contractors destroy company data by deleting or erasing it. These insiders are ignoring or violating confidentiality agreements, conflict-of-interest statements, code-of-conduct rules, code-of-ethics documents, noncompete agreements, and intellectual property agreements that they have signed and are showing no respect for laws.

Data Leakages (continued)

Recommended security controls against insider incidents are listed next.

- Automatic daily data file backup systems
- End-point backup systems that enable restoration to the last known good state of data files, thus providing visibility into when and how data was deleted
- Filing lawsuits against inside cybercriminals
- Restricting access to file-sharing services and cloud-based data storage services
- Developing acceptable-use policies for mobile devices
- Establishing a legal hold policy where courts require companies to document their security controls and the steps taken to prevent negligent or intentional destruction of data when companies bring lawsuits against inside cybercriminals. (Courts request a proof of documented security controls that are in place to prevent data leakage, data loss, and data stealing; such controls show "due care" on the company's part.)

Customer Information Protection Review

Protecting valuable and sensitive customer information is a major goal of many organizations in light of increased occurrences of data breaches and data leakages in private and public sector organizations. Customer information is defined as information that is personal and nonpublic (private) in nature, whether it is maintained on paper, electronic, or other form. It consists of medical records, marital information, health records, wage records, prescription drug records, and name and address information. In addition to a company's employees, outsiders such as third-party service providers can have access to a company's customer information.

Internal auditors should make sure that the next security controls are in place and that those controls are actually protecting the customer information.

- Access controls to authenticate individuals and permit access only to authorized individuals. Controls to prevent employees from providing customer information to unauthorized individuals who may seek to obtain this information through fraudulent means, such as pretext calling used in perpetrating identity theft.
- Access restrictions at physical locations containing customer information, such as buildings, computer facilities, and records storage facilities to permit access only to authorized individuals.
- Encryption of electronic customer information, including while in transit or in storage on networks or systems to which unauthorized individuals may have access.

Customer Information Protection Review (continued)

- Procedures designed to ensure that customer information system modifications are consistent with the organization's security program.
- Dual control procedures, joint custody, segregation of duties, and employee background checks for employees with responsibilities for or access to customer information.
- Monitoring systems and procedures to detect actual and attempted attacks on or intrusions into customer information systems.
- Response programs that specify actions to be taken when the organization suspects or detects that unauthorized individuals have gained access to customer information systems, including appropriate reports to regulatory and law enforcement agencies
- Measures to protect against destruction, loss, or damage of customer information due to potential environmental hazards, such as fire and water damage or technological failures
- Ensure that your browser is up-to-date and security patches applied.
- Never click on hyperlinks within emails. Instead verify and type the URL independently without copying blindly.

Customer Information Protection Review (continued)

- Use updated antivirus, antiphishing, and firewall software.
- Train staff to implement the organization's information security program.
- Regularly test the key controls, systems, and procedures of the information security program. The organization's risk assessment results should determine the frequency and nature of such tests. Tests should be conducted or reviewed by independent third parties or staff independent of those who develop or maintain the security programs.
- Make sure that due diligence reviews are conducted before selecting third-party service providers. In addition, a written contract, a risk assessment exercise, and continuous monitoring are needed for the service providers.

Data Storage and Backup Audit

The scope of computer storage media audits includes review of rotation of computer files to and from offsite storage, electronic vaulting at remote locations, environmental controls at offsite as well as onsite, and adequacy of storage media capacity for future computing needs. Due to their safe and uncorrupted backups, Data backup and storage are important in case of ransomware attacks, data breaches, and data leakage attacks.

Both the original site and the backup site must utilize the same computer hardware and software (i.e., have the same configuration) in order to operate the same ways at all times. This means that when the original site is down or has crashed due to a major or minor disaster, the backup site must kick in and be ready to take over (i.e., disaster ready), as if nothing ever happened to the original site. The goal here is that no one will notice the difference between the original site and the backup site during normal operation.

The backup site could be owned by the same retailer that operates the original site, or it could be rented, leased, or hosted by commercial third parties. Additional problems can occur when the backup site is leased or hosted by the third parties, including how much testing was done to ensure preparedness and how fast they can be when disaster occurs. Commercial banks, financial institutions, and airline companies are known to have well-managed and well-tested backup sites due to the time-sensitive and heavy customer traffic nature of their business. Each minute a website is down leads to lost revenues and profits with associated reputation risk and risks of customer defection.

Original Site versus Backup Site

- Original site operates all the time, 24/7 (Plan A).
- Backup site operates only when the original site is down (Plan B).

Identity Theft Audit

Identity theft or fraud happens when someone steals personal information and uses it without that person's permission. It's a serious crime that can wreak havoc with people finances, credit history, and reputation—and can take time, money, and patience to resolve. There are three specific types of identity theft: tax-related identity theft using someone's Social Security number, child identity theft using a child's personal information, and medical identity theft using someone's personal information to get medical care or services.

Identity theft can occur in several ways:

- Data breaches by hackers in a retail environment where hackers steal customers' personal and financial information.
- Data leakages by company insiders, such as employees and contractors.

Pretext calling by a fraudster in a banking environment. Pretext callers use pieces of a customer's personal information to impersonate an account holder to gain access to that individual's account information. Armed with personal information, such as an individual's name, address, and Social Security number, a pretext caller may try to convince a bank's employee to provide confidential account information. While pretext calling may be difficult to spot, there are measures banks can take to reduce the incidence of pretext calling, such as limiting the circumstances under which customer information may be disclosed by telephone. A bank's policy could be that customer information is disclosed only through email, text message, a letter, or in-person meeting.

Identity Theft Audit (continued)

Specific control actions to prevent identity theft include:

- Placing both extended fraud alerts and credit freezes on credit reports to make it more difficult for an identity thief to open new accounts in your name.
- Repairing credit after identity theft by disputing fraudulent charges and accounts related to identity theft.
- Reissuing lost or stolen credit/debit/ATM cards because federal law limits liability, but that liability may depend on how quickly the loss or theft is reported.

If identity thieves have your personal information, they can drain your bank account, run up charges on your credit cards, open new utility accounts, or get medical treatment on your health insurance. It is important to safeguard your personal information, whether it is on paper, online, or on your computers and mobile devices.

The U.S. **Red Flags Rule** was issued in 2007 under the Fair and Accurate Credit Transactions Act, clarified with the issuance of the Red Flag Program Clarification Act of 2010. This rule, which amended the Fair Credit Reporting Act, requires many businesses and organizations to implement a written identity theft prevention program designed to detect the red flags of identity theft in their day-to-day operations, take steps to prevent the crime, and mitigate its damage. The bottom line is that a program can help businesses spot suspicious patterns and prevent the costly consequences of identity theft.

Social Media Audit

Social media platforms with extensive and sophisticated use of technologies include Facebook, Twitter, You Tube, Google +, Instagram, Pinterest, Snapchat, and several others. Social media can drive customer traffic into physical stores (offline stores) and nonphysical stores (online stores). Today's retailers are using YouTube, Google+, and Pinterest more than Facebook and Twitter.

Members of the Millennial generation (Generations Y and Z) use social media more than other generations. It is difficult for retailers to keep up with social media technology, as it changes constantly and continuously.

Today more and more customers are interacting and transacting with social media platforms (e.g., Facebook or Google) rather than directly with retailers. Retailers now have to have a greater presence on social media and offer personalized services. These customers ignore security and privacy concerns and are willing to share their information in exchange for more personalized services. Customers are using social channels to place and track their purchase orders with retailers. When most customers go to social media, retailers must follow.

Internal auditors must make sure that only authorized company employees can respond to comments posted by customers on social media platforms. Unauthorized employees responding to customer postings and comments can lead to and increase the company's negative reputation risk. The marketing staff, public relations office, or social media administrator should be given authority to respond to customer comments.

Social Media Audit (continued)

A retailer's marketing strategy today must use social channels to introduce new products, announce improvements made to existing products, and offer sales promotions.

Because it is common for customers to post negative comments about a retailer's products on social media, retailers should publish "comment and post" policies describing what types of comments are allowed or acceptable for posting. Retailers should also provide a procedure to handle negative comments and posts to escalate and resolve problems and issues. Be aware that disgruntled employees (former and current) can post negative comments in addition to customers.

A positive side to the social channel is that it should be viewed as a modern "suggestion box" system where employees and customers can suggest new products, improvements to existing products, and better ways of doing things, all online and instantly.

Cloud Security Audit

Cloud computing is a model for enabling ubiquitous, convenient, on-demand network access to a shared pool of configurable computing resources (e.g., networks, servers, storage, applications, and services) that can be rapidly provisioned and released with minimal management effort or service provider interaction. This cloud model promotes availability and is composed of five essential characteristics—on-demand self-service, broad network access, resource pooling, rapid elasticity, and measured service—three service models—cloud software as a service, cloud platform as a service, and cloud infrastructure as a service—and four deployment models—public, private, community, and hybrid cloud. Cloud technology provides three major services—computing, storage, and networking. The backup storage service is a very useful function to address ransomware attacks.

Types of Clouds

Users can subscribe to different types of clouds depending on their needs. Home users or small business owners will most likely use public cloud, where the clouds included are a mixture of public, private, or community.

Cloud Security

The information housed on the cloud is often seen as valuable to individuals with malicious intent. People store a lot of personal information and potentially secure data on their computers, and this information is now being transferred to the cloud. It is critical for users to understand the security measures that a cloud provider has in place, and it is equally important for users to take personal precautions to secure their data. Some security-related questions to ask cloud providers are listed next.

What encryption methods do the providers have in place?

What methods of protection do they have in place for the actual hardware that your data will be stored on?

Will they have backups of my data?

Do they have firewalls set up?

If case of a community cloud, what barriers are in place to keep user information separate from other companies?

The standard terms and conditions of many cloud providers may answer these questions.

The emergence of cloud computing promises to have far-reaching effects on the systems and networks of many organizations. Many of the features that make cloud computing attractive, however, can also be at odds with traditional security models and controls. The major issues include security and privacy of data. Next, we discuss security downsides (bad news) and security upsides (good news) of a cloud computing environment.

Security Downside and Solutions

Some of the more fundamental concerns in cloud computing include:

- System complexity
- Shared multitenant environment
- Internet-facing service
- Loss of control

As with any technology, cloud computing services can engage in improper or illicit activities, such as botnets and cracking mechanisms, such as Wi-Fi protected access (WPA) crackers.

The next security controls can mitigate the security downsides of cloud computing environment:

- Deploy access control and intrusion detection technologies at the cloud provider, and conduct an independent assessment to verify that they are in place. The scope of work partly includes traditional perimeter security measures in combination with the domain security controls. Traditional perimeter security includes:
  - Restricting physical access to network and devices
  - Protecting individual components from exploitation through security patch deployment

Security Downside and Solutions (continued)

- Setting as defaults most secure configurations
- Disabling all unused ports and services
- Using role-based access control
- Monitoring audit trails
- Minimizing the use of privileges
- Using antivirus software
- Encrypting communications

- Define trust boundaries between service providers and consumers to ensure that the responsibility for providing security is clear.
- Support application and data portability such that customers can take action to change cloud service providers when needed to satisfy availability, confidentiality, and integrity requirements. This action includes the ability to close an account on a particular date and time and to copy data from one service provider to another.

Security Upside

The cloud computing paradigm provides opportunities for innovations in provisioning security service that hold the prospect of improving the overall security of some organizations. The biggest beneficiaries are likely to be smaller organizations that have limited numbers of IT administrators and security personnel and lack the economies of scale available for larger organizations with sizable data centers. Potential areas of improvement where organizations may derive security benefits from transitioning to a public cloud computing environment are listed next:

- Staff specialization
- Platform strength
- Resource availability
- Backup and recovery
- Mobile endpoints
- Data concentration
- Data center oriented (e.g., redirecting electronic mail records to a cloud provider via mail exchange records to discover widespread spam, phishing, and malware campaigns and to carry out remedial actions such as quarantining suspect messages and content)
    - Cloud oriented (e.g., reverse proxy products are available that enable unfettered access to a cloud environment yet maintain the data stored in that environment in encrypted form)

Key Security Considerations in Cloud Computing

Major security considerations in cloud computing include the need to:

- Carefully define security and privacy requirements during the initial planning stage at the start of the system development life cycle.
- Determine the extent to which negotiated service agreements are required to satisfy security requirements and the alternatives of using negotiated service agreements or cloud computing deployment models which offer greater oversight and control over security and privacy.
- Assess the extent to which the server and client-side computing environment meets organizational security and privacy requirements.
- Continue to maintain security management practices, controls, and accountability over the privacy and security of data and applications.

Potential Vulnerabilities in Cloud Computing

Potential vulnerabilities associated with various cloud computing service and deployment models include:

- The inherent system complexity of a cloud computing environment and the dependency on the correctness of these components and the interactions among them.
- The dependency on the service provider to maintain logical separation in a multitenant environment. (This vulnerability is not unique to the cloud computing model.)
- The need to ensure that the organization retains an appropriate level of controls to obtain situational awareness, weigh alternatives, set priorities, and effect changes in security and privacy that are in the best interests of an organization.

Security Requirements

The goal is to ensure a safe and secure cloud solution is available to provide a prospective IT service. The solution should consider these security needs:

- Statutory compliance to laws, regulations, and organization requirements
- Data characteristics to assess which fundamental protections an application's dataset requires
- Privacy and confidentiality to protect against accidental and nefarious access to information
- Integrity to ensure data is authorized, complete, and accurate
- Data controls and access policies to determine where data can be stored and who can access physical locations
- Governance to ensure that cloud computing service providers are sufficiently transparent, have adequate security and management controls, and provide the information necessary for the organization to appropriately and independently assess and monitor the efficacy of those controls

Potential Security Benefits

Potential security benefits of using cloud computing services are listed next.

- The ability to focus resources on areas of high concern as more general security services are assumed by the cloud provider
- Potential platform strength resulting from greater uniformity and homogeneity, and resulting improved information assurance, security response, system management, reliability, and maintainability
- Improved resource availability through scalability, redundancy, and disaster recovery capabilities; improved resilience to unanticipated service demands
- Improved backup and recovery capabilities, policies, procedures, and consistency
- Ability to leverage alternative cloud services to improve the overall security posture, including that of traditional data centers
- Reduced time-to-market metric regarding access provisioning of new applicants

General and Specific Security and Privacy Issues

Data processed in a public cloud computing environment and applications running in a public cloud facility can experience different security and privacy exposures than would be the case in an onsite hosted environment. For example, cloud subscribers, who are ultimately responsible for their data processed on provider systems, will need to require assurances from providers that they are in compliance with the appropriate regulations.

Examples of *general security and privacy issues* in a public cloud environment include:

- Not meeting the subscriber's data protection requirements
- Not providing encryption of data at rest in storage
- Not knowing the strengths of the encryption algorithm
- Not knowing the attack surface of a cloud and the likely pool of attackers
- Not knowing the expertise level of cloud administrators

General and Specific Security and Privacy Issues (continued)

Examples of *specific security and privacy issues* in public cloud computing environment are listed next.

- Storing sensitive data without adequate protection due to risk of unintended data disclosure
- Lack of subscriber awareness over where data is stored and who has or can have access, leading to privacy concerns due to distributed nature of clouds
- Inability to partition access rights between subscribers, providers, and administrators, thus compromising system integrity
- Not having both logical separation and physical separation of systems required to protect a subscriber's resources due to multitenancy
- Using a subscriber's browser as a graphical interface, account setup, and resource administration, leading to security flaws
- Lack of proper protection of a subscriber's cryptographic keys to ensure a safe use of cryptography from inside a cloud

User Authentication and Authorization Reviews

This section discusses identification purpose, application authentication techniques for system users and for devices, identity management and privilege management, and integrating identification and authentication methods. In addition, it presents a brief discussion of digital signatures, digitized signatures, electronic signatures, and digital certificates.

Identification Purpose

Identification means establishing the identity of a user, process, or device prior to authentication. It is the means by which a user provides a claimed identity to the system. **Authentication** means verifying the identity of a user, process, or device, often as a prerequisite to allowing access to system resources. It is the means of establishing the validity of this claim. **Authorization** is the process of defining and maintaining the allowed actions. **Accountability** is making individuals responsible for their actions and inactions equally, and it supports the identification, authentication, and audit requirements, nonrepudiation, deterrence, fault isolation, intrusion prevention and detection, and after-action recovery and legal action. Accountability should be reflected in audit trails. Access rules support accountability.

Identification and authentication (I&A) establishes the basis for accountability, and the combination of I&A and accountability enables the enforcement of identity-based access control. The correct sequence of actions taking place in an access control mechanism is:

Identification ⟶ Authentication ⟶ Authorization ⟶ Accountability

Identification Purpose (continued)

Note that identification comes before authentication, authorization comes after authentication, and accountability comes after authorization.

The user's identity can be authenticated using these basic I&A mechanisms:

- Knowledge-based I&A techniques (e.g., what you know using password, user ID, username, or PIN).
- Token-based I&A techniques (e.g., what you have using memory, , smart, personal identification verification [PIV] cards; hardware token, noncryptographic key, and digital certificate).
- Physical location-based I&A techniques (e.g., where you are using GPS and wireless sensor network).
- Biometrics-based I&A techniques (e.g., what you are using fingerprints, iris recognition, and dynamic biometrics, such as handwriting and voice recognition, for).

Biometrics is the science and technology of measuring and statistically analyzing biological data. In IT, the term "biometrics" usually refers to technologies for measuring and analyzing human body characteristics, such as voice and facial pattern recognitions, eye retina scans, and hand measurements (e.g., fingerprints, handwriting, hand geometry, wrist veins, and thumb impressions). Unfortunately, equipment used in biometrics can lead to two types of errors: Types I and II. In practice, it is generally necessary to adjust the equipment for a compromise between false rejection of correct individuals (Type I error) and false acceptance of imposters (Type II error). The goal is to obtain low numbers for both types of errors. An equal error rate (crossover error rate) occurs when false rejection rates and false acceptance rates are equal. Biometrics provide a strong security control as a part of multifactor authentication process.

Identification Purpose (continued)

Examples of Weak and Strong Authentication Methods

Weak authentication methods include user IDs, PINs, and reusable (static and simple) passwords.

Strong authentication methods include:

- Dynamic passwords (i.e., one-time passwords using challenge-response protocols)
- Hardware tokens
- Passphrases
- Encrypted time-stamps
- Smart cards
- Location-based authentication
- Memory cards
- Multiple factors of authentication
- Biometrics
- Public key infrastructure (PKI) systems such as digital signatures and digital certificates

Identification Purpose (continued)

The principal forms of authentication include static, dynamic, and multiple factors.

- **Static authentication** reuses a specific authenticator (e.g., static password) where an attacker cannot obtain this authenticator. The strength of the authentication process is highly dependent on the difficulty of guessing or decrypting the authentication value.
- **Dynamic authentication** uses cryptography to create a one-per-session authenticator that changes with each authentication session between a claimant and verifier.
- **Multiple factor authentication** requires two or more types of authentication techniques. It can include both static and dynamic authentication mechanisms. One example is the user of a password along with a smart card token.

Authorization mechanisms fall into four major categories, such as local, network, single sign-on, reduced sign-on, single log-in and single log-out.

1. **Local authorization** is performed for each application and computer to which a user requires access. The local operating system and applications are employed to set up and maintain the authorizations for that computer or application.

Identification Purpose (continued)

2. **Network authorization** is performed at a central, authorization server, providing access to a user's account from one or more workstations on the network and giving access to a single user account or multiple accounts. Security tokens (e.g., memory cards, flash memory, USB tokens, and smart cards) are used to allow access first to a computer and then to a network.

3. **Single sign-on (SSO)** employs a central authorization server to enable a user to authenticate once and then access all the resources that the user is authorized to use. This achieves access to multiple applications, computers, workstations, and domains operating with a variety of authentication mechanisms (e.g., a Kerberos implementation used within a heterogeneous network). The central server establishes and maintains the authorizations at each application, computer, workstation, or domain that the user is allowed to access.

   Reduced sign-on (RSO) is a technology that allows a user to authenticate once and then access many, but not all, of the resources that the user is authorized to use.

4. **Single log-in** is similar to single sign-on, and it eliminates the need for authorization at each resource and for individual authentications to each resource.

   Single log-out is closing all open programs, files, functions, sessions, and screens with one system command so no computer resource is vulnerable to attackers.

Application Authentication Techniques for System Users

Organizational users include employees and outsiders such as contractors. Users must uniquely be identified and authenticated for all accesses. Unique identification of individuals in group accounts (e.g., shared privilege accounts) may need to be considered for detailed accountability of activity. Authentication of system user identities is accomplished through the use of passwords, tokens, biometrics, or, in the case of multifactor authentication, some combination thereof.

Access to systems is defined as either local or network. **Local access** is any access to an organizational information system by a user (or process acting on behalf of a user) where such access is obtained by direct connection without the use of a network. **Network access** is any access to an organizational information system by a user (or process acting on behalf of a user) where such access is obtained through a network connection. **Remote access** is a type of network access which involves communication through an external network (e.g., the Internet). Internal networks include local area networks (LANs), wide area networks (WANs), and virtual private networks (VPNs) that are under the control of the organization. The VPN is considered an internal network if the organization establishes the VPN connection between organization-controlled endpoints in a manner that does not require the organization to depend on any external networks across which the VPN transmits to protect the confidentiality and integrity of information transmitted.

Specific controls for system users are listed next.

- The system should use multifactor authentication for network access to privileged and nonprivileged accounts.

Application Authentication Techniques for System Users (continued)

- The system should use multifactor authentication for local access to privileged and nonprivileged accounts.
- The organization should (1) allow the use of group authenticators only when used in conjunction with an individual/unique authenticator; and (2) require individuals to be authenticated with an individual authenticator prior to using a group authenticator.
- The system should use multifactor authentication for network access to privileged and nonprivileged accounts where one of the factors is provided by a device separate from the information system being accessed.
- The system should use replay-resistant authentication mechanisms for network access to privileged and nonprivileged accounts. An authentication process resists replay attacks if it is impractical to achieve a successful authentication by recording and replaying a previous authentication message. Techniques used to address this include protocols that use nonces or challenges (e.g., transport layer security [TLS]) and time-synchronous or challenge-response one-time authentication.
- The organization should conduct a risk assessment to determine the risks of identifying and authenticating nonorganizational users. Factors such as scalability, practicality, and security must be considered simultaneously to balance between the ease of use and protection.

Application Authentication Techniques for Devices

An information system should uniquely identify and authenticate specific types of devices before establishing a connection. Devices include mobile devices (e.g., USB memory sticks, external hard disk drives, notebook/laptop computers, cellular/mobile telephones, digital cameras, audio recording devices, and PDAs) and mobile ID devices (used to acquire fingerprint, face, and iris images in personal identity verification program). These devices can use either shared known information (e.g., Media Access Control [MAC] or Transmission Control Protocol/Internet Protocol [TCP/IP] addresses) for identification or authentication solutions (e.g., IEEE 802.1x and Extensible Authentication Protocol, RADIUS server with EAP-Transport Layer Security authentication, or Kerberos) to identify and authenticate devices on LANs, WANs, and wireless networks. The required strength of the device authentication mechanism is determined by the security categorization of the information system.

General controls over devices are listed next.

- The information system should authenticate devices before establishing local network, remote network, and wireless network connections using bidirectional authentication between devices that is cryptographically based.
- Usage restrictions and operational guidance include proper configuration management, device identification and authentication, implementation of mandatory protective software (e.g., malicious code detection and firewall), scanning devices for malicious code, updating virus protection software, scanning for critical software updates and patches, conducting primary operating system integrity checks, and disabling unnecessary hardware (e.g., wireless and infrared).

Application Authentication Techniques for Devices (continued)

- Travel guidance for traveling employees includes providing computers with sanitized hard drives, limited applications, and additional hardening with stringent configuration settings. Security measures for employees returned from travel include examining devices for signs of physical tampering and purging or reimaging the hard disk drive.
- Regarding dynamic address allocation for devices, the organization should standardize Dynamic Host Control Protocol (DHCP) lease information and the time assigned to devices and its lease information when assigned to a device. DHCP-enabled clients typically obtain leases for IP addresses from DHCP servers.
- Using the remote authentication dial-in user service (RADIUS) protocol, a remote client can exchange authentication, access control, accounting, and device configuration information with a RADIUS server. The RADIUS server can authenticate a user or a device from its database or user I&A parameters.
- Using the Terminal Access Controller Access Control System + (TACACS+) protocol enables a network resource to offload the user administration to a central server.

Application Authentication Techniques for Devices (continued)

Specific controls over mobile devices are listed next.

- Smart card authentication (i.e., proof by possession)
- Password authentication (i.e., proof by knowledge)
- Fingerprint authentication (i.e., proof by property)

Specific controls over mobile ID devices are listed next.

- The data encryption algorithm should use advanced encryption system-256 (AES-256) for transmission and should provide for the encryption and decryption of bidirectional traffic.
- Data at rest should use encryption for all data residing on the device either as a temporary file or a part of the database.
- Data storage cards should use encryption for all of the device data, files, or databases written to the storage medium.
- Operator authentication should be achieved by a two-factor authentication, one of which should be biometric.

Application Authentication Techniques for Devices (continued)

- A password of minimum length with alphabetical, numerical, and/or special characters should be used for biometric operator authentication.
- The device should provide the capability for biometric operator reauthentication after a designated length of time expired; the device should be reauthenticated itself after a designated amount of idle time, or result in a device shut-off.
- The device should provide the capability to lock or render it inoperable, erase selected file, and/or erase all files on it based on failed security protocols.
- The device should provide the capability to establish a maximum limit of failed authentication attempts before the handheld device clears all application data or requires unlock only by a security administrator.
- After a biometric operator's authentication and authorization is established, the device's identification should be verified by matching against a list of specified devices (i.e., blacklists, or lost/stolen lists). A matched device should not be authorized to communicate with the central system.
- All devices should be updated whenever policies change or software is updated to provide greater protection.

Application Authentication Techniques for Devices (continued)

- When inserting a protected (encrypted) memory card into the mobile device's expansion slot, the device should be able to detect an encrypted card and prompt the biometric operator for the card's authentication code. Access to information would be granted only when the correct authentication code has been provided.
- The data authentication algorithm should use the Rivest, Shamir, Adelman-2048 (RSA-2048) key size. The secure hash function for the signature should use secure hash algorithm (SHA-256) key size.

WHAT ARE USER AUTHENTICATORS AND DEVICE AUTHENTICATORS?

Examples of user authenticators include passwords, tokens, biometrics, PKI certificates such as electronic signatures and digital certificates, and keycards.

Examples of device authenticators include passwords and PKI certificates such as electronic signatures and digital certificates.

Identity Management and Privilege Management

Identity management is the comprehensive management and administration of user permissions, privileges, and profiles. It provides a single point of administration for managing the lifecycle of accounts and profiles. **Identity** is the distinguishing character or personality of an individual based on a set of physical and behavioral characteristics by which that individual is uniquely recognized.

Access control ensures that only authorized access to resources occurs. It helps protect confidentiality, integrity, and availability and supports the principles of legitimate use, least privilege, and separation of duties. Access control simplifies the task of maintaining enterprise network security by reducing the number of paths that attackers might use to penetrate system or network defenses. Identity and access management ensures that adequate safeguards are in place to secure authentication, authorization, and other identity and access management functions.

In the past, users typically subscribed to each system or resource separately, as needed for their job functions, by undertaking multiple systems and user registration processes. This resulted in users having to manage multiple security credentials (i.e., certificates, usernames, and passwords). This arrangement was tedious, expensive, time-consuming, unattractive, and frustrating for users, as it scaled or performed poorly as the number of resources increased.

In light of these problems, a single solution is needed that allows user management processes to be efficiently and effectively leveraged and reused across trust domains, thereby facilitating interoperability between various

Identity Management and Privilege Management (continued)

information systems. This solution is accomplished through an access life cycle consisting of five phases: provisioning, permissioning, credentialing, analyzing, and revoking.

1. **Provisioning** (vetting) is a procedure for enabling end users to access and use system services. It involves creating for each user an account in a directory service and populating the account with the user-specific information needed by each service. It asks this question: What can you access?
2. **Permissioning** is the authorization given to users that enables them to access specific resources on the network, such as data files, applications, printers, and scanners. User permissions also designate the type of access, such as read-only (view) or update-only (read/write). It asks this question: What can you access?
3. **Credentialing** involves a certification authority issuing a certificate after validating an applicant that is requesting the access. It asks this question: How do I know it is you?
4. **Analyzing** is reviewing current, old, and expired accounts for correctness and appropriateness against their approved access rights and permissions for such accounts.
5. **Revoking** includes canceling user accounts, expired accounts, illegal accounts, and decertifying users who are no longer valid, appropriate, or correct.

Identity Management and Privilege Management (continued)

In addition, identity binding and identity proofing are required. **Identity binding** is binding of the vetted claimed identity according to the credential-issuing authority, perhaps through biometrics. **Identity proofing** is the process by which a credential-issuing authority validates sufficient information (e.g., source documents, credentials, personal ID cards, and photo IDs) and validates them to uniquely identify an individual.

Major benefits of identity and access management include providing SSO, RSO, and SLO capabilities to end users for accessing multiple online systems and services. This method eliminates the need for registering end user identity information in multiple systems and services. This method is supported by several basic security technologies, including cryptographic trust model, identity management standards and middleware, and a metadata model for securely exchanging information about users.

Although the SSO system is designed for user convenience, cost savings, and efficiency, it can be subjected to a single point of failure due to concentration of risks in one place and at one time. This means that if the SSO system is compromised, all the connected multiple systems can be compromised too.

Privilege management creates, manages, and stores the attributes and policies needed to establish criteria that can be used to decide whether an authenticated entity's request for access to some resource should be granted. Enterprise-level privilege management fits under the umbrella of enterprise-level access control. At the enterprise level, **access management** encompasses all the practices, policies, procedures, data, metadata, and technical and administrative mechanisms used to manage access to the resources of an

Identity Management and Privilege Management (continued)

organization. Access management includes access control, privilege management, and identity management, as below:

Access management = Access control + Privilege management + Identity management

Access control ensures that resources are made available only to authorized users, programs, processes, or systems by reference to rules of access that are defined by attributes and policies. In privilege management, resources can be both computer-based objects (e.g., files and web pages) and physical objects (e.g., buildings and vault safes). The entities requesting access to resources can be users (people) and processes running on a computer, application, or system. Identity management deals with identification and authentication, authorization, decision, and enforcement processes.

Integrating Identification and Authentication Methods

It has been proven that four-factor authentication methods are stronger and better than single-factor authentication methods.

- Any one of these methods can represent a **one-factor authentication method**, which is not strong and secure: Something you have: photo ID, memory card, smart card, personal identity verification PIV card with PIN for swiping into a reader with photo, decal mounted onto a motorized vehicle, transponder mounted on a motorized vehicle used for operating an automated entry point, visitor badge without name and photo, physical key, digital certificate, hardware token, and mobile ID device
- Something you know: password, passcode, passphrase, or PIN; shared or unshared combination, such as electronic safe, cipher lock, PIN pad combination, and digital certificate.
- Something you are: photo ID, PIV card with PIN or photo, fingerprint identification (one to many), fingerprint verification (one to one), hand geometry (one to many), iris scan (one to many), colleague (peers and coworkers) recognition, and user (peers or security guards) recognition. (Colleague and user recognitions are considered attended access.)
- Somewhere you are: geodetic location, such as a building, city, sate, or country using a GPS for employees traveling to and from the company's remote location or to and from vendor/customer location

Integrating Identification and Authentication Methods (continued)

Any one of the next methods can represent a **two-factor authentication** method. Note that there are many combinations due to use of several authentication devices.

- Combination of something you have and something you know (e.g., digital certificate where digital signature is used with a PIN to unlock the private key; cryptographic hardware token with one-time password device and PIN; and PIV card with PIN or password for after-hours entry without after-hour attendant).
- Combination of something you have and something you are (e.g., verified digital or optical photo ID with driver's license and personal identity card with photo or attended/unattended access; hardware token with biometrics.
- Combination of something you know and something you are (e.g., User ID, PIN, password, and biometric sample).
- Combination of something you have, something you know (i.e., PIN), and something you are (e.g., personal identity card with attended access and PIN). It is an attended access or two-person access control method using the card and the PIN and is not the strongest two-factor authentication because of the attendant present (i.e., another person is present to allow the access, could be doing a favor).

Integrating Identification and Authentication Methods (continued)

Combination of something you have (PIV card), something you have (e.g., digital certificate), and something you know (e.g., PIN). This option illustrates that multiple instances of the same factor (i.e., something you have) results in a stronger two-factor authentication. However, this implementation represents a higher level of assurance than other instances of two-factor authentication due to no attendant present. Two-factor authentication is better than one-factor authentication. **Three-factor authentication methods** combine something you have (i.e., PKI keys or a hardware token), something you know (i.e., PIN or password), and something you are (i.e., comparing the cardholder to his biometric image stored on the biometric database and/or on the access card), which is the strongest three-factor authentication. A hardware token can be used in support of this level of assurance in logical access control. Three-factor authentication is better than one-factor and two-factor methods.

Four-factor authentication methods combine something you have (i.e., card, key, or mobile ID device), something you know (i.e., PIN or password), something you are (i.e., fingerprint or signature), and something about where you are (i.e., building or company/remote location, or vendor/customer location) and represent the strongest and highest form of all authentication methods.

Digital Signatures, Digitized Signatures, Electronic Signatures, and Digital Certificates

A **digital signature** is an electronic analog of a handwritten signature in that it can be used to prove to the recipient, or a third party, that the originator in fact signed the message. Digital signatures are also generated for stored data and programs to verify data and program integrity at any later time.

Digital signatures authenticate the integrity of the signed data and the identity of the signatory. They verify to a third party that data were actually signed by the generator of the signature. Digital signatures are used in electronic mail, electronic funds transfer, electronic data interchange, software distribution, data storage, and other applications requiring data integrity assurance and data origin authentication. Digital signatures can address potential threats such as spoofing, masquerading, replay attacks, and password compromise. They cannot address denial-of-service attacks.

The security of a digital signature system is dependent on maintaining the secrecy of users' private keys. Users must, therefore, guard against the unauthorized acquisition of their private keys. A digital signature can also be used to verify that information has not been altered after it was signed; this provides message integrity. A simpler alternative to a digital signature is a hash function.

Digital signatures offer protection not available by alternative signature techniques such as **digitized signature**, which is created as a visual form of a handwritten signature to an electronic image. Although a digitized signature resembles its handwritten counterpart, it does not provide the same protection as a digital signature. Digitized signatures can be forged as well as duplicated and appended to other electronic data. They cannot be used to determine whether information has been altered after it is signed.

Digital Signatures, Digitized Signatures, Electronic Signatures, and Digital Certificates (continued)

An *electronic signature* is a cryptographic mechanism that performs a similar function to a handwritten signature. It is used to verify the origin and contents of a message.

Digital certificates are basically containers for public keys and act as a means of electronic identification. The certificate and public keys are public documents that, in principle, anyone can possess. An associated private key, possessed only by the entity to which the certificate was issued, is used as a means of binding the certificate to that entity. Users not possessing this private key cannot use the certificate as a means of authentication. Entities can prove their possession of the private key by digitally signing known data or by demonstrating knowledge of a secret exchanged using public key cryptographic methods. A digital certificate is a password-protected and encrypted file. It should not contain any owner-related information that changes frequently. In practice, anyone can generate public-private key pairs and digital certificates; consequently, it is necessary to determine whether the certificate holder is trustworthy.

ELECTRONIC SIGNATURES VERSUS HANDWRITTEN SIGNATURES

Electronic signatures are very difficult to forge, although handwritten signatures are easily forged. In general, electronic signatures have received the same legal status as that of written signatures. Cryptography can provide a means of linking a document with a particular person, as is done with a written signature. If a cryptographic key is compromised due to a social engineering attack, then the electronic originator of a message may not be the same as the owner of the key. Trickery and coercion are problems for both electronic and handwritten signatures (i.e., social engineering attacks).

Information Systems Security Control Reviews

This section presents security objectives, security controls, security policies, and security impact analysis. In addition, it includes a brief discussion about firewalls, encryption, and risks and threats in system development and in operational systems.

Security Objectives

There are five security objectives: confidentiality, integrity, availability, accountability, and assurance. However, information systems literature primarily focuses on the first three security objectives—confidentiality, integrity, and availability—which form the three legs of the Confidentiality, Integrity, and Availability (CIA) triad. Another definition of security according to ISO/IEC 13335 standard is that it encompasses all aspects related to defining, achieving, and maintaining confidentiality, integrity, availability, accountability, authenticity, and reliability.

1. **Confidentiality.** Confidentiality of data and information is the requirement that private or confidential information not be disclosed to unauthorized individuals. Confidentiality protection applies to data in storage, during processing, and while in transit. Confidentiality is the preservation of authorized restrictions on information access and disclosure, including means for protecting personal privacy and proprietary information. Thus, confidentiality is related to privacy.

Security Objectives (continued)

2. **Integrity.** Integrity of the system and data is required as protection against intentional or accidental attempts to violate either (1) data integrity—the property that data has not been altered in an unauthorized manner while in storage, during processing, or while in transit; or (2) system integrity—the quality that a system has when performing the intended function in an unimpaired manner, free from unauthorized manipulation. In other words, integrity is lack of improper modification, alteration, or destruction.

3. **Availability.** Availability of a system and data is a requirement intended to assure that systems work promptly and service is not denied to authorized users. This objective protects against (1) intentional or accidental attempts to either perform unauthorized deletion of data or otherwise cause a denial of service/ data and (2) attempts to use system or data for unauthorized purposes. Availability is continually and reliably accessible and usable in a timely manner, including the ability to share.

4. **Accountability.** Accountability is the requirement that actions of an entity may be traced uniquely to that entity. Accountability (i.e., taking responsibility for one's own actions and inactions) is dependent on confidentiality and integrity. If confidentiality or integrity is lost, accountability is threatened. Note that availability and accountability share the same concerns and controls. Accountability is often an organizational policy requirement and directly supports nonrepudiation, deterrence, fault isolation, intrusion detection

Security Objectives (continued)

and prevention, and after-action recovery and legal action (e.g., audits, investigations, and courts). Here accountability is at the individual level. Accountability is the ability to associate actors with their acts and to include nonrepudiation (i.e., ensuring that actors are unable to deny—repudiate—an action).

5. **Assurance.** Assurance is the basis for confidence that the security measures, both technical and operational, work as intended to protect the system and the data it processes. Assurance verifies that the other four security objectives—confidentiality, integrity, availability, and accountability—have been adequately met by a specific implementation. "Adequately met" means:

    a. The required functionality is present and performs correctly.

    b. There is sufficient protection against unintentional errors (by users or software).

    c. There is sufficient resistance to intentional penetration or bypass.

Assurance is the basis for confidence that the security measures, both technical and operational, work as intended to protect the system and the data it processes. Assurance is addressing the question of the amount of uncertainty one should have in software system.

Security Objectives (continued)

When designing an information system, a system architect or system designer should establish an assurance level as a target. This target is achieved by both defining and meeting the functionality requirements in each of the other four security concepts and doing so with sufficient "quality." Assurance highlights the fact that for an information system to be secure, it must not only provide the intended functionality but also ensure that undesired actions do not occur. Assurance is essential; without it the other security objectives are not met. However, assurance is a continuum; the amount of assurance needed varies between information systems.

Another viewpoint of an information system is that it must be dependable at all times; here "dependable" is a qualitative, umbrella term. Dependability is an integrating concept that encompasses six properties: confidentiality, integrity, availability, reliability, safety, and maintainability. Although properties such as reliability (i.e., continuity of correct service), safety (i.e., absence of catastrophic consequences on the user and the environment), and maintainability (i.e., the ability to undergo modifications and repairs) may not directly result in secure software, they all contribute to keeping the security up to date and showing that the software is secure.

Security Controls

Access controls fortify the CIA triad by identifying, authenticating, and authorizing users to access systems and data. Poor access controls and inadequate disaster recovery plans can prevent an organization from reasonably ensuring the CIA triad's objectives or goals.

The interdependencies between the CIA triad and security controls are described next.

Confidentiality (i.e., sensitivity, criticality, secrecy, nondisclosure, and privacy) is dependent on integrity, in that if the integrity of the system is lost, then there is no longer a reasonable expectation that the confidentiality mechanisms are still valid. So, confidentiality is tied to integrity. Implementing the safeguards (controls) suggested in the next table can help toward achieving the confidentiality objective.

Security Controls (continued)

Controls to Achieve the Confidentiality Objective

Security objective	Security controls
Confidentiality	Use encryption techniques during data/program storage and transmission. Use digital signature verification techniques. Develop data classification schemes. Require all employees sign nondisclosure statements to ensure transaction privacy. Implement accountability principle by logging and journaling system activity. Implement security policies, procedures, and standards. Implement system user identification, authentication, and authorization techniques. Implement Reference Monitor concept in the design of an operating system. Implement layers of controls to prevent impersonation and tailgating. Implement logical and physical access controls. Establish employee security awareness and training programs. Establish document and file disposition controls. Establish security labels and tags to storage media and data files to reflect their sensitivity. Install audit trails and journals to provide transaction monitoring capability. Audit the adequacy of confidentiality safeguards.

Security Controls (continued)

Integrity (i.e., accuracy, authenticity, nonrepudiation, accountability, and completeness) is dependent on confidentiality, in that if the confidentiality of certain information is lost (e.g., due to the use of the superuser password), then the integrity mechanisms are likely to be bypassed. Implementing the safeguards (controls) suggested in the next table can help toward achieving the integrity objective.

Controls to Achieve the Integrity Objective

Security objective	Security controls
Integrity	Implement system/user identification, authentication, and authorization techniques. Implement logical and physical access controls. Use encryption techniques during data/program storage and transmission. Use digital signature verification techniques. Implement intrusion detection and response programs. Install data editing and validation routines for data input, process, and output. Install antivirus software. Implement security policies, procedures, and standards. Implement layers of controls to prevent impersonation and tailgating.

Security Controls (continued)

Security objective	Security controls
	Establish data reconciliation controls. Implement Reference Monitor concept in the design of an operating system. Use disk repair utility programs for personal computers. Make system and data backups. Establish employee security awareness and training programs. Implement variance detection techniques in sensitive transaction processing. Install audit trails and journaling to provide transaction monitoring capability. Audit the adequacy of integrity safeguards.

Availability (i.e., usability and timeliness) is dependent on confidentiality and integrity, in that (1) if confidentiality is lost for certain information (e.g., superuser password), the mechanisms implementing these objectives can be bypassed easily; and (2) if system integrity is lost, then confidence in the validity of the mechanisms implementing these objectives is also lost. Implementing the safeguards (controls) suggested in the next table can help toward achieving the availability objective.

Security Controls (continued)

Controls to Achieve the Availability Objective

Security objective	Security controls
Availability	Establish software configuration controls. Implement disaster recovery and contingency plans. Purchase insurance coverage. Implement logical and physical access controls. Implement user/system authorization mechanisms. Implement intrusion detection and response programs. Implement records management programs. Install asset management system for tracking software and hardware inventory. Implement logical and physical access controls. Make system and data backups. Use loosely coupled parallel processor architecture for fail-safe operation. Implement incident logging and reporting. Install fault-tolerant hardware and software for continuous operation. Require extra power supplies and cooling fans.

Security Controls (continued)

Security objective	Security controls
	Establish employee security awareness and training programs. Conduct computer capacity planning. Implement redundancy and recovery features. Audit the adequacy of availability safeguards.

Another way of presenting the security controls is to classify them from a technical viewpoint and according to their action, such as preventive controls, detective controls, and recovery controls.

Preventive controls focus on inhibiting security breaches from occurring in the first place. They include identification, authentication, authorization, access control enforcement, cryptographic key management, nonrepudiation, system protections, transaction privacy, protected communications, and security administration.

- **Identification.** This control provides the ability to uniquely identify users, processes, and information resources. To implement other security controls (e.g., discretionary access control, mandatory access control, and accountability), it is essential that both subjects and objects be identifiable. Identification control recognizes an entity (e.g., user, program, device, or process) prior to access.

Security Controls (continued)

- **Authentication.** The authentication control provides the means of verifying the identity of a subject to ensure that a claimed identity is valid. Weak authentication mechanisms include passwords and PINs; strong authentication mechanisms include tokens, smart cards, digital certificates, and Kerberos. Authentication often acts as a prerequisite to allowing access to resources in a computer system.
- **Authorization.** The authorization control enables specification and subsequent management of the allowed actions for a given system (e.g., the information owner or the database administrator determines who can update a shared file accessed by a group of online users).
- **Access control enforcement.** Data integrity and confidentiality are enforced by access controls. When the subject requesting access has been authorized and validated to access particular computer processes, it is necessary to enforce the defined security policy (i.e., discretionary or mandatory access control). These policy-based access controls are enforced via access control mechanisms distributed throughout the system (e.g., mandatory access control-based sensitivity labels, discretionary access-based control file permission sets, access control lists [ACLs], roles, file encryption, and user profiles). The effectiveness and the strength of access control depend on the correctness of the access control decisions (e.g., how the security rules are configured) and the strength of access control enforcement (e.g., the design of software or hardware security). Checking identity and requested access against ACLs and using file encryption methods are examples of access control enforcement mechanisms.

Security Controls (continued)

The correct sequence of access to a computer or information resource is shown next.

Identification ⟶ Authentication ⟶ Authorization ⟶ Access Control Enforcement

- **Cryptographic key management.** Cryptographic keys must be securely managed when cryptographic functions are implemented in various other controls. The scope of key management includes key generation, distribution, storage, and maintenance.
- **Nonrepudiation.** System accountability depends on the ability to ensure that senders cannot deny sending data and that receivers cannot deny receiving it. The nonrepudiation control provides an unforgeable proof of sending and/or receiving data, and its scope spans prevention and detection categories. It has been placed into the prevention category because the mechanism implemented prevents the successful repudiation of an action (e.g., the digital certificate that contains the owner's private key is known only to the owner). Consequently, this control is typically applied at the point of transmission or reception.
- **System protections.** Underlying a system's various security functional capabilities is a base of confidence in the technical implementation. This represents the quality of the implementation from both the perspective of the design processes used and the manner in which the implementation was accomplished. Some examples of system protections are residual information protection (also known as object reuse), least privilege (need to know), process separation, modularity, layering, abstraction, encryption, data hiding, and minimization of what needs to be trusted.

Security Controls (continued)

- **Transaction privacy.** Both government and private sector systems are increasingly required to maintain the privacy of individuals using secure systems. Transaction privacy controls (e.g., Secure Sockets Layer and secure shell) protect against loss of privacy with respect to transactions performed by an individual.
- **Protected communications.** In a distributed system, the ability to accomplish security objectives is highly dependent on trustworthy communications. The protected communications control ensures the integrity, availability, and confidentiality of sensitive and critical information while it is in transit. Protected communications use data encryption methods (e.g., VPN and IP security [IPsec] protocol), and deployment of cryptographic technologies (e.g., DES, Tripe DES, RAS, MD4, MD5, and secure hash standard), and escrowed encryption algorithms (e.g., Clipper) to minimize network threats, which include replay, interception, packet sniffing, wiretapping, and eavesdropping. Protected communications must be safe from disclosure, substitution, modification, and replay attacks.
- **Security administration.** The security features of an IT system must be configured (e.g., enabled or disabled) to meet the needs of a specific installation and to account for changes in the operational environment. System security can be built into operating system security or the application system. Commercial off-the-shelf add-on security products are available.

Detective controls focus on detecting security breaches. Specifically, detective controls warn of violations or attempted violations of security policies and procedures. They are needed to complement or supplement the preventive controls because preventive controls are not perfect. Detective controls include audit, audit trails, checksums, intrusion detection and containment, proof of wholeness, and virus detection and eradication.

- **Audit.** The auditing of security-relevant events and the monitoring and tracking of system abnormalities are key elements in the after-the-fact detection of, and recovery from, security breaches. The after-the-fact events include audits, investigations, and court evidence.
- **Audit trails.** Audit trails show a chronological record of system activities that are sufficient to enable the reconstruction and examination of the sequence of events surrounding or leading to an operation, procedure, or event, from beginning to end. They show who has accessed a system and what operations are carried out and aid in tracing system activities.
- **Checksums.** Checksums show a value automatically computed on data to detect errors or manipulations during transmission and to ensure the accuracy of data transmission. The number of bits in a data unit is summed and transmitted along with the data. The receiving computer then checks the sum and compares, and any changes are noticed.

Security Controls (continued)

- **Intrusion detection and containment.** It is essential to detect security breaches (e.g., network break-ins and suspicious activities) so that a response can occur in a timely manner.
- **Proof-of-wholeness.** The proof-of-wholeness control (e.g., a system integrity tool) analyzes system integrity and irregularities and identifies exposures and potential threats. It determines whether integrity has been compromised and whether the information state or system state has been corrupted. However, this control does not prevent violations of security policy; it detects violations and helps determine the types of corrective action needed.
- **Virus detection and eradication.** Virus detection and eradication software installed on servers and user workstations detects, identifies, and removes software viruses to ensure system and data integrity.

Recovery controls focus on recovering from security breaches as they restore lost computing resources. Recovery controls are needed as a complement or supplement to preventive controls and detective controls, neither of which is perfect. Recovery controls include backups, checkpoints, contingency plans, and controls to restore a system to its secure state.

- **Backups.** Backup methods copy files and programs to facilitate recovery in a timely manner.
- **Checkpoints.** Checkpoints provide restore procedures before, during, or after completion of certain transactions or events to ensure acceptable level of fault-recovery.

Security Controls (continued)

- **Contingency plans.** Contingency plans provide policies and procedures designed to maintain or restore business operations and computer operations, both at the primary processing center or at an alternative processing site.
- **Restore to a secure state.** This control enables a system to return to a state that is previously known to be secure, after a security breach occurs.

Security Policies

Effective security policies and procedures are the first step or the first line of defense to ensure secure systems and networks. To make the security policy effective, it must be practical and enforceable, and compliance with the policy must be possible. The policy must not significantly impact productivity, be cost prohibitive, or lack support. This delicate balance is best accomplished by including both functional management and information security management in the policy development process.

Four basic types of security policies—program policy, issue-specific policies, system-specific policies, and acceptable use policies—are discussed next.

1. **Program policy** is used to create an organization's information security program. Contents of program policy include purpose, scope, responsibilities, and compliance (i.e., penalties and disciplinary actions). It contains scope, responsibilities, strategic direction, and resources.

2. **Issue-specific policies** address specific issues of concern to the organization. Examples of specific issues include:

   - Internet access
   - Email privacy
   - Approach to risk management and contingency planning

Security Policies (continued)

- Protection of confidential and proprietary information
- Use of unauthorized software
- Acquisition of software
- Doing computer work at home
- Bringing in disks from outside the workplace
- Access to other employees' files
- Encryption of files and email
- Rights of privacy
- Responsibilities for correctness of data
- Suspected malicious code
- Physical emergencies, such as fire and flood

Security Policies (continued)

Issue-specific policies contain contingency planning, risk management, and implementation of new regulations or laws.

3. **System-specific policies** focus on decisions taken by management to protect a particular system, such as application systems and network systems (i.e., management controls). Components of system-specific policies include security objectives and operational security rules. System-specific policies are often implemented through the use of logical access controls. They contain access control lists (ACLs) for a specific system, training users, and email/fax security policy. Examples of system-specific policies, which both functional management and information security management work together to develop, include:

   - Creating a gold disk (i.e., a master disk) in configuration management
   - Modem usage policy
   - Wireless security policy for planning, deploying, and configuring wireless access points to prevent war-driving attacks

4. **Acceptable use policies** require that a system user, an end user, or an administrator (e.g., system, security, and network administrator) agrees to comply with such policies prior to accessing computer systems, internal networks, and external networks (the Internet). Acceptable use is based on authorized access.

Security Policies (continued)

> For example, in a cloud computing environment, subscribers ensure that all subscriber personnel read and understand the provider's acceptable use policy and negotiate an agreement for resolution of agreed-upon policy violations in advance with the provider. The agreement also includes a process for resolving disputes over possible policy violations.

In addition to security policies, rules of behavior and rules of engagement must be considered to exact proper behavior from employees and outside contractors and vendors.

Rules of behavior describe the rules established and implemented concerning use of, security in, and acceptable level of risk of the system. Rules will clearly delineate responsibilities and expected behavior of all individuals with access to the system. The organization establishes and makes readily available to all information system users a set of rules that describes their responsibilities and expected behavior with regard to information system usage.

A rules-of-behavior document:

- Defines scope of coverage, including work at home; dial-in-access; connection to the Internet; use of copyrighted work; unofficial use of organization equipment; assignment and limitations of system privileges and individual accountability in using passwords; searching databases; and divulging information.
- Delineates responsibilities, expected use of system, and behavior of all users.

Security Policies (continued)

- Describes appropriate limits on interconnections of systems.
- Defines service provisions and restoration priorities.
- Clarifies consequences of behavior not consistent with rules of behavior

Rules of engagement provide detailed guidelines and constraints regarding the execution of information security testing. The rules of engagement are established before the start of a security test. The rules give the test team authority to conduct the defined activities without the need for additional permissions. Rules of engagement are aimed at outside contractors and vendors before performing their work for an organization.

Security Impact Analysis

An impact in an information system is the magnitude of harm that can be expected to result from the consequences of unauthorized disclosure of information, unauthorized modification of information, unauthorized destruction of information, loss of information, or loss of information system availability.

Impact levels are categorized as high, moderate, or low, which classify the intensity of a potential impact that may occur if the information system is jeopardized or compromised.

- A high-impact system is an information system in which at least one security objective (i.e., confidentiality, integrity, or availability) is assigned a potential impact value of high.
- A moderate-impact system is an information system in which at least one security objective (i.e., confidentiality, integrity, or availability) is assigned a potential impact value of moderate, and no security objective is assigned a potential impact value of high.
- A low-impact system is an information system in which all three security objectives (i.e., confidentiality, integrity, or availability) are assigned a potential impact value of low.
- A potential impact considers all three levels of impact regarding the loss of confidentiality, integrity, or availability. It could be expected to have (a) a limited adverse effect (low), (b) a serious adverse effect (moderate), or (c) a severe or catastrophic adverse effect (high) on organizational operations, systems, assets, individuals, or other organizations.

Security Impact Analysis (continued)

The security management analyzes changes to the information system to determine potential security impacts prior to change implementation. Security impact analysis is conducted by internal employees with information security responsibilities (e.g., system administrators, security officers, security managers, and security engineers). Individuals conducting these security impact analyses must have the appropriate skills and technical expertise to analyze the changes (e.g., system upgrades and modifications) to information systems and the associated security ramifications.

The scope of these security impact analyses includes:

- Reviewing information system documentation, such as the security plan, to understand how specific security controls are implemented within the system and how the changes might affect the controls.
- Assessing risk to understand the impact of the changes and to determine if additional security controls are required.
- Relating the amount of analysis to the impact level (i.e., a system with high impact requires more analysis).

In addition, security management analyzes new software in a separate test environment before installation in an operational environment, looking for security impacts due to flaws, weaknesses, incompatibility, or intentional malice.

After the information system is changed, security management checks the security functions to verify that the functions are implemented correctly, operating as intended, and producing the desired outcome with regard to meeting the security requirements for the system.

KEY CONCEPTS TO REMEMBER: Information Security

To provide reasonable security mechanisms over computer systems and networks:

- Implement access controls, firewalls, routers, sensors, hardware and software guards, and demilitarized zones to protect computer systems and networks from attacks.
- Build security into a system, do not add it on. Security principles, standards, policies, procedures, controls, safeguards, and mechanisms must be integrated into all phases or processes of a system development life cycle (from beginning to the end).
- Keep security as simple as possible. Complexity leads to design, development, and implementation problems, thus making a system unusable, unstable, unmanageable, uncontrollable, and even vulnerable to threats.
- Avoid single-point-of-failure situations, which are security risks due to concentration of risk in one place, system, process, or person. Causes leading to these situations include:
    - Placement of web services, and domain name system (DNS) servers in a company's network

Security Impact Analysis (continued)

- Use of primary telecommunication services without backups
- Use of centralized identity management
- Use of central certification authority
- Password synchronization problems
- Use of single sign-on systems
- Use of firewalls
- Use of Kerberos
- Use of converged networks with voice and data
- Use of cloud storage services
- Roles of system administrators and security analysts

Security Impact Analysis (continued)

- Fix security problems and issues correctly and as soon as possible. Practice separation of duties, whether manual or electronic. Require mandatory vacations for all employees. Practice rotation of job duties. Practice the principle of least privilege with secure defaults. Fail securely in a known, safe, and secure state. The efficiency and effectiveness of access control policy and its implementation depends on the system state and secure state the system is in at any point in time and the use of fail-safe defaults. A secure state is a condition in which no subject can access any object in an unauthorized manner.
- Implement system hardening techniques to make computer systems and networks more robust. These techniques include: removing all nonessential and unnecessary computer programs and their associated utility programs to prevent or eliminate backdoor or trapdoor attacks; and implementing security engineering principles.
- Implement secure coding principles, which include:
    - Minimizing attack surfaces
    - Establishing secure defaults

Security Impact Analysis (continued)

  - Implementing the principle of least privilege
  - Deploying defense-in-depth principle
  - Failing securely in a known system state
  - Avoiding security by obscurity
  - Keeping security simple
  - Minimizing programming errors that lead to software vulnerabilities
  - Implementing secure coding standards
- Balance the costs, risks, and benefits equation, because $10 should not be spent on controls to protect an asset, information, or a risk costing $1. Costs should not exceed benefits.
- A trade-off exists in security: Pay now or pay later.

Firewalls

A **firewall** is a network connectivity device that mediates all traffic between two computer networks and protects one of them or some part thereof against unauthorized access. Generally, the protected network is a private, internal network. A firewall may permit messages or files to be transferred to a high-security workstation within the internal network, without permitting such transfer in the opposite direction.

Many enterprise networks employ firewalls to restrict connectivity to and from the internal networks used to service more sensitive functions, such as accounting or personnel. By employing firewalls to control connectivity to these areas, an organization can prevent unauthorized access to its systems and resources. Inclusion of a proper firewall provides an additional layer of security. Organizations often need to use firewalls to meet security requirements from regulatory mandates.

Enclave boundary protection takes the form of firewalls and VPNs. While these technologies offer perimeter and access controls, authorized internal and external (remote) users can attempt probing, misuse, and malicious activities within an enclave. Firewalls do not monitor authorized users' actions, nor do they address internal (insider) threats. Firewalls also must allow some degree of access, which may open the door for external vulnerability probing and the potential for attacks.

Configuration management activities can be extended to firewalls using a firewall ruleset, which is a table of instructions that the firewall uses for determining how network packets or data packets should be routed between firewall interfaces.

Firewall management

Managing the firewall solution involves maintaining firewall architecture, policies, software, and other components of the solution chosen to be deployed, as discussed next.

- Test and apply patches to firewall devices.
- Update policy rules as new threats are identified and requirements change, such as when new applications or hosts are implemented within the network. Rules also should be reviewed periodically to ensure they remain in compliance with security policy.
- Monitor the performance of firewall components to ensure that potential resource issues are identified and addressed before components become overwhelmed.
- Monitor logs and alerts continuously to identify threats—successful and unsuccessful—that are made to the system.
- Perform periodic testing to verify that firewall rules are functioning as expected.
- Back up the firewall policies and rulesets regularly.
- Conduct penetration testing to assess the overall security of their network environment. This testing can be used to verify that a firewall ruleset is performing as intended by generating network traffic and monitoring how it is handled by the firewall in comparison with its expected response. Penetration testing should be employed in addition to, rather than instead of, a conventional audit program.

Encryption

Encryption or cryptography is a method of converting information to an unintelligible code. The process can then be reversed, returning the information to an understandable form. The information is encrypted (encoded) and decrypted (decoded) by what are commonly referred to as cryptographic keys. These keys are actual values used by a mathematical algorithm to transform the data. The effectiveness of encryption technology is determined by the strength of the algorithm, the length of the key, and the appropriateness of the encryption system selected.

Because encryption renders information unreadable to any party without the ability to decrypt it, the information remains private and confidential, whether transmitted or stored on a computer system. Unauthorized parties will see nothing but an unorganized assembly of characters. Furthermore, encryption technology provides data integrity assurance as some algorithms offer protection against forgery and tampering. The technology's ability to protect information requires that authorized parties properly manage the encryption and decryption keys.

Methods of encryption

In general, the encryption mechanism effectively seals the information within an object inside an additional (logical) container. Used primarily to provide confidentiality, general encryption can be used to ensure the detection of integrity violations and to otherwise hinder integrity attacks. Encryption is not absolute protection, as the sealing process may be only as safe as the encryption key. Also, encryption of an object does not in and of itself prevent damage to its integrity. However, encryption does provide an additional level of protection that must be circumvented in order to violate protection policies or to succeed at making violations without detection. Distinct advantages of encryption are its flexibility of use, meaning its ability to be used either as blanket protection or as on-demand protection, and its applicability to a wide array of object types. For example, digital signatures are intended to produce the desired effect as a real signature, an unforgeable proof of authenticity.

Cryptography and Data Protection

Data can be protected at different places, such as data at rest, data in transit, and data in storage. The scope of data at rest, data in storage, or data on a hard drive includes protecting the confidentiality, integrity, and availability of data residing on servers, workstations, computers, storage/disk arrays (e.g., redundant array of independent disks [RAID]), network-attached storage appliances, disk drives, tape drives, and removable media, such as flash, thumb, and pen drives.

Adding encryption to data at rest poses some challenges, such as changing the application code, data compression problems, slow response time, user unfriendliness, complexity, and additional cost to storage systems.

Storage encryption can be applied as a part of a data-at-rest solution in several places, such as encryption in the:

- Application
- File system or operating system
- Device driver or network interface
- Network
- Storage controller

Cryptography and Data Protection (continued)

- Storage device using a single-factor authentication (e.g., password, user ID, or, hardware token) and multiple-factor authentication (e.g., password, user ID, smart card, or cryptographic token)

The scope of data in transit, data in flight, or data on the wire includes protecting the confidentiality, integrity, and availability of data as they are transferred across the storage network, the LAN, and the WAN.

Cryptographic mechanisms in controlling data in transit through remote access to an information system include:

- Using encryption with a strong key in relation to the security categorization of the information.
- Restricting execution of privileged commands.
- Using standard bulk or session layer encryption, such as Secure Shell (SSH) and VPNs with blocking mode enabled.
- Routing all remote accesses through a limited number of managed access control points.
- Not using Bluetooth and peer-to-peer networking protocols because they are less secure.

Alternatives to Cryptography

There are at least three alternatives to cryptography to hide information: steganography, digital watermarking, and reversible data hiding.

Steganography (concealed writing) deals with hiding messages and obscuring who is sending or receiving them. It is the art and science of writing hidden messages in such a way that no one, apart from the sender and intended recipient, suspects the existence of the message and is a form of security through obscurity.

Steganography includes the concealment of information within computer files. In digital steganography, electronic communications may include steganographic coding inside of a transport layer, such as a document file, image file, program, or protocol.

The advantage of steganography over cryptography alone is that messages do not attract attention to themselves. Plainly visible encrypted messages—no matter how unbreakable—will arouse suspicion and may be incriminating in countries where encryption is illegal. Therefore, whereas cryptography protects the contents of a message, steganography can be said to protect both messages and communicating parties. Media files are ideal for steganographic transmission because of their large size and because changes are so subtle that someone not specifically looking for them is unlikely to notice them.

Digital watermarking, the process of irreversibly embedding information into a digital signal, is a type of marking that embeds copyright information about the copyright owner.

Alternatives to Cryptography (continued)

Steganography is sometimes applied in digital watermarking, where two parties communicate a secret message embedded in the digital signal. Annotation of digital photographs with descriptive information is another application of invisible watermarking. While some file formats for digital media can contain additional information called metadata, digital watermarking is distinct in that the data is carried in the signal itself.

A digital watermark is called robust with respect to transformations if the embedded information can reliably be detected from the marked signal even if it is degraded by any number of transformations. Typical image degradations are Joint Photographic Experts Group (JPEG) compression, rotation, cropping, additive noise, and quantization. For video content, temporal modifications and Moving Picture Coding Experts Group (MPEG) compression are often added to this list.

A digital watermark is called imperceptible if the cover signal and marked signal are indistinguishable with respect to an appropriate perceptual metric. In general, it is easy to create robust watermarks *or* imperceptible watermarks, but the creation of robust and imperceptible watermarks has proven to be quite challenging. Robust and imperceptible watermarks have been proposed as a tool for the protection of digital content, for example, as an embedded "no-copy-allowed" flag in professional video content.

Reversible data hiding is a technique that enables images to be authenticated and then restored to their original form by removing the watermark and replacing the image data with overwritten data. This technique would make the images acceptable for legal purposes.

SUMMARY OF ENCRYPTION METHODS THAT EXIST FOR DIFFERENT PURPOSES

- In link encryption, all data including addresses flowing on links can be encrypted. Data communications service providers generally perform the link encryption.
- In end-to-end encryption, a message is encrypted and decrypted only at endpoints by hardware and software techniques. End-user organizations generally perform the end-to-end encryption.
- Bulk (trunk) encryption is simultaneous encryption of all channels of a multichannel telecommunications trunk. No bulk encryption is needed when a public key cryptographic is used to distribute keys since the keys are generally short.
- Session encryption is used to encrypt data between applications and end users. It is effective in preventing eavesdropping attacks from remote access to firewalls. A secure server supports server authentication and session key encryption.
- Stream encryption encrypts and decrypts messages of arbitrary sizes.
- Line encryption protects data in transfer, which can be used to achieve confidentiality.
- File encryption protects data in storage. It is the process of encrypting individual files on a storage medium and permitting access to the encrypted data only after proper authentication is provided.

Alternatives to Cryptography (continued)

- Field-level encryption is stronger than file-, record-, and packet-level encryption.
- Folder encryption is the process of encrypting individual folders on a storage medium and permitting access to the encrypted files within the folders only after proper authentication is provided.
- Full (whole) disk encryption is the process of encrypting all the data on the hard drive used to boot a computer, including the computer's operating system, and permitting access to the data only after successful authentication with the full disk encryption product is made.
- Virtual disk encryption is the process of encrypting a container, which can hold many files and folders, and permitting access to the data within a container only after proper authentication is provided.
- Volume encryption is the process of encrypting an entire volume and permitting access to the data on the volume only after proper authentication is provided.
- Multiple (e.g., triple) encryption is stronger than single encryption, but costs may increase and system performance may decrease.
- NULL encryption is used when integrity protection is required for an IPsec system, not for confidentiality.

Alternatives to Cryptography (continued)

- Super-encryption is a process of encrypting information that is already encrypted. It occurs when a message, encrypted offline, is transmitted over a secured, online circuit, or when information encrypted by the originator is multiplexed onto communication trunks and then bulk encrypted. In other words, super-encryption is encryption plus encryption.
- Between authentication and encryption steps, encryption should be done first and authentication is done later (i.e., encrypt-then-authenticate), which provides the most secure approach.
- Encryption requires the use of either passwords or passphrases.

Risks and Threats in Systems Development and in Operational Systems

When a computer system is being developed or operated, it is subjected to several risks and threats from insiders (i.e., current employees and previous employees) and outsiders (i.e., hackers, adversaries, contractors, suppliers, and vendors) with different threat sources and threat objectives. These risks and threats are divided into three categories.

Categories of malware inserted during software development and maintenance work

Malware is malicious software or malicious code that is designed to deny, destroy, modify, or impede the software's logic, configuration settings, data, or program library routines. Malware can be inserted during software development, preparation for distribution, deployment, installation, and/or update. It can be planted manually or through automated means, and it can also be inserted during a system's operation. Regardless of when in the software life cycle the malware is embedded, it effectively becomes part of the software and can present substantial dangers and risks. Malware has become the most significant external threat to most systems, causing widespread damage and disruption and necessitating extensive recovery efforts within user organizations.

Malware is likely to be inserted during software development or maintenance in several ways: through backdoors or trapdoors, time bombs, logic bombs, or software holes. This malware is introduced into a system due to unnoticed, forgotten, or neglected functions or when unnecessary functions are disregarded, and can be discovered through tabletop reviews, periodic assessments, war-dialing, war-driving, wireless-scanning, and penetration testing. Not having a source code escrow is a risk by itself.

Categories of malware inserted during software development and maintenance work (continued)

Backdoors are hidden software mechanism used to circumvent the system's perimeter defenses and security controls, often to enable an attacker to gain unauthorized remote access to the system.

Trapdoors are hidden software or hardware mechanisms that can be triggered to permit circumvention of system protection mechanisms. Trapdoors are activated innocently (e.g., a special random key sequence at a terminal). Software developers often introduce trapdoors in their code to enable them to reenter the system and perform certain functions. Note that both backdoors and trapdoors are undocumented ways of gaining access to a computer system, and both are potential security risks to user organizations as they completely circumvent perimeter defenses. The terms **backdoor** and **trapdoor** are used synonymously.

One frequently used backdoor method is inserting a malicious program that listens for system commands on a particular TCP or User Datagram Protocol (UDP) port. Usually, both backdoors and trapdoors are introduced through software maintenance hooks because they are special instructions in software that allow easy maintenance and additional feature development. These hidden methods are not clearly defined during system access or design specification and are not documented. Maintenance hooks often allow entry into the code at unusual points or without the usual checks, so they are a serious security risk if they are not removed prior to live implementation.

Time bombs are resident computer programs that trigger an unauthorized or damaging action at a predefined time.

Logic bombs are resident computer programs that trigger an unauthorized or damaging action when a particular event or state in the system's operation is realized (e.g., when a particular packet is received).

Categories of malware inserted during software development and maintenance work (continued)

Software holes penetrate through lack of perimeter defenses, which is risky due to potential entry points in a computer system or network. Software holes can reside on any of the three layers (i.e., networking, operating system, or application), and software vendors or developers should provide security mechanisms to mitigate the risks. Defending the perimeter requires installing appropriate security controls at all entry points into the network, including the Internet connection. Defending the perimeter requires installing appropriate security controls at all entry points into the network, including the Internet connection. Testing the perimeter to identify backdoors and software holes requires tabletop reviews, periodic assessments, war-dialing, war-driving, wireless scanning, and penetration testing.

Source code escrow can be risky, as it is an arrangement with a third party (e.g., a bank) to hold the software under its custody and make it available to user organizations in unusual business circumstances. This arrangement is applicable to vendor-developed applications software packages either purchased or leased by user organizations. Usually vendors do not give the source code to user organizations for proprietary reasons; only the object is provided with the package. Vendors have the obligation to ensure that the escrowed source code is an exact copy of the production source code. The concept is similar to cryptographic key escrow.

The purpose of software escrow is to provide user organizations access to the source code under unusual business circumstances, such as when the vendor is going out of business or being merged with or acquired by another organization. In the absence of an escrow arrangement, user organizations may not be able to access the source code when needed. There should be a written contract for escrow arrangements signed by vendors and reviewed by an attorney specializing in such contracts.

Categories of malware planted on operational systems

Malware can be planted on operational systems in a number of ways, including viruses, worms, Easter eggs, Trojan horses, zombies, cross-site scripts, botnets, rootkits, cookies, adware, spyware, active content, electronic dumpster diving, and buffer overflow.

A **virus** is a self-replicating computer program (i.e., make copies of itself) that runs and spreads by modifying other programs or files and distributes the copies to other files, programs, or computers. A virus may attach itself to and become part of another executable program to, for example, become a delivery mechanism for malicious code or for a denial-of-service attack. It can replicate by attaching a copy of itself to other programs or files and can trigger an additional payload when specific conditions are met. Different types of viruses exist, including these:

- Boot sector viruses, which infect the master boot record of a hard drive or removable disk media (e.g., thumb drives and flash drives)
- File infector viruses, which attach themselves to executable programs such as word processing, spreadsheet applications, and computer games
- Macro viruses, which attach themselves to application documents, such as word processing files and spreadsheets, then use the application's macro programming language to execute and propagate
- Compiled viruses, which have their source code converted by a compiler program into a format that can be directly executed by the operating system

Categories of malware planted on operational systems (continued)

- Interpreted viruses, composed of source code that can be executed only by a particular application or service
- Multipartite viruses, which use multiple infection methods, typically to infect both files and boot sectors
- Morphing viruses, which change as they propagate, thus making them extremely difficult to eradicate using conventional antivirus software tools because their signature is constantly changing

Some examples of virus behaviors are listed next.

- Increase in file size
- Change in update timestamp
- Sudden increase of free space
- Numerous unexpected disk accesses
- Gradual loss of available storage space
- Unusual screen activity

Categories of malware planted on operational systems (continued)

Install antivirus software, which is a program that monitors a computer or network to identify all major types of malware and prevent or contain malware incidents. This software detects malicious code, prevents it from infecting a system, and removes malicious code that has already infected the system. Some drawbacks associated with antivirus software tools include the fact that virus-specific software may fail to detect other viruses, and detection software may fail to detect some viruses resident in memory when the software is loaded.

A **worm** is a computer program that copies itself (i.e., self-replicating) from system to system via a network and is self-contained and self-propagating. It exploits weaknesses in the operating system or inadequate system management. The release of a worm usually results in brief but spectacular outbreaks, shutting down entire networks. Most worms infect computers as a result of a user directly executing the worm (i.e., by clicking on it). It is unrealistic to assume that users will become cautious about executing unknown files. Countermeasures against worms include:

- Identification and authentication controls.
- Configuration review tools.
- Checksum-based change detection tools.
- Intrusion detection tools
- Wrapper programs to filter network connections.
- Firewalls to protect an organization's network from other networks.

Categories of malware planted on operational systems (continued)

Easter eggs trigger when a program code is placed in software for the amusement (fun) of developer. They are nuisances to users.

A **Trojan or Trojan horse** is a nonreplicating program that appears to be benign (i.e., looks innocent) but actually has a hidden malicious purpose. When the program is invoked, so is the undesired function whose effects may not be immediately obvious.

A **zombie** is a program that is installed on one computer system with the intent of causing it to attack other computer systems in a chainlike manner.

Cross-site scripting (XSS) is an attack technique in which an attacker subverts a valid website, forcing it to send malicious scripting to an unsuspecting user's browser. XSS is a delivery technique for malicious code.

A **robot (bot)** is an automated software program that executes certain commands when it receives a specific input. Bots are often used to implement Trojan horses, logic bombs, backdoors, and spyware.

Botnet is a term for a collection of software robots (bots) that run autonomously. A bot's originator can control the group remotely, usually through Internet relay chats and usually for nefarious purposes. Botnets can comprise a collection of infected computers running programs (usually referred to as worms, Trojan horses, or backdoors) under a common command-and-control infrastructure. Botnets are often used to send spam emails and to launch denial of service, phishing, and virus attacks.

A **rootkit** is a collection of files installed on a system to alter its standard functionality in a malicious and stealthy way. After gaining root-level access to a host computer, an attacker uses a rootkit to conceal his or her

Categories of malware planted on operational systems (continued)
activities on the host and to maintain root-level access to the host. Some protection methods against botnets and rootkits are listed next.

- Use and maintain antivirus software.
- Install a firewall.
- Use strong passwords.
- Update software with patches.
- Take precautions when using email and web browsers not to trigger an infection.

Cookies are small computer files that store information for a website on a user's computer. This information is supplied by a web server to a browser, in a response for a requested resource, for the browser to store temporarily and return to the server on any subsequent visits or requests. Cookies may contain information about the websites a user visited or may even contain credentials for accessing the website. Cookies are designed to be readable only by the website that created them, meaning cookies are unique to each website. Cookies can be used to uniquely identify all visitors of a website, which some people consider a violation of privacy. If a website uses cookies for authentication, then an attacker may be able to acquire unauthorized access to that site by obtaining the cookie.

Categories of malware planted on operational systems (continued)

Cookies have two mandatory parameters—name and value—and have four optional parameters: expiration date, path, domain, and secure parameters. Four types of cookies exist: encrypted, persistent, session, and tracking cookies. Some websites create **encrypted cookies** to protect the data from unauthorized access. **Persistent cookies** are stored on a computer's hard drive indefinitely so that a website can identify the user during subsequent visits. These cookies are set with expiration dates and valid until the user deletes them. Hence, persistent cookies pose a higher risk than session cookies because they remain on the computer longer. **Session cookies** are temporary cookies that are valid only for a single website session; they are cleared or erased when the browser is closed, and they are stored in a temporary memory. **Tracking cookies** are cookies placed on a user's computer to track the user's activity on different websites, creating a detailed profile of the user's behavior.

Adware is any software program intended for marketing purposes such as to deliver and display advertising banners or pop-ups to the user's computer screen or to track the user's online usage or purchasing activity. Adware tracks a user's activity and passes it to third parties without the user's knowledge or consent. **Click fraud** is possible with adware because it involves deceptions and scams that inflate advertising bills with improper usage and charges per click in online web advertisements.

Spyware is adware intended to violate a user's privacy. It is placed on a computer to secretly gather information about the user and report it. Types of spyware include web bugs, which are tiny graphics on a website that are referenced within the hypertext markup language (HTML) content of a web page or email to collect information about the user viewing the website and tracking cookies, as described earlier. Install antispyware software, which is a program that specializes in detecting both malware and nonmalware forms of spyware.

Categories of malware planted on operational systems (continued)

Active content technologies allow code, often in the form of a script, macro, or other mobile code representation, to execute when the document is rendered. HTML and other related markup language documents, whether delivered via HTTP or other means, provide rich mechanisms for conveying executable content. Examples of active content include Postscript and Portable Document Format (PDF) documents, web pages containing Java applets and JavaScript instructions, word processor files containing macros, spreadsheet formulas, and other interpretable content. Active content may also be distributed embedded in email or as executable mail attachments. Countermeasures against active content documents include security policy, application settings, automated filters, software version control, software readers, and system isolation.

Applets are small computer applications written in various programming languages that are automatically downloaded and executed by applet-enabled Internet browsers. Examples include Active-X and Java applets, both of which have security concerns.

Electronic dumpster diving involves scanning and enumeration of systems and ports to discover passwords and to investigate open source intelligence using DNS lookups and web searches to discover the characteristics of the system being attacked and particularly to pinpoint any potentially exploitable vulnerabilities.

Categories of malware planted on operational systems (continued)

Buffer overflow is a condition likely to occur in a programming interface under which more input is placed into a buffer or data-holding area than the capacity allocated, thus overwriting the information. Attackers and adversaries can exploit such a condition to crash a system or to insert specially crafted code that allows them to gain control of the system. As a countermeasure, use appropriate security controls across operational, network, and host layers, and apply updated antivirus software and patches, install firewalls, practice secure programming techniques, install intrusion detection system (IDS) software, and monitor with security event management tools. In addition, use secure file transfer protocol (SFTP) or secure copy protocol (SCP) instead of regular file transfer protocol (FTP) or trivial file transfer protocol (TFTP), as shown:

FTP/TFTP ⟶ SFTP/SCP

Categories of nonmalware deployed on operational systems

Sometimes malware is combined with nonmalware deceptive practices, such as social engineering techniques, to accomplish complex attacks on unsuspecting users. Three major categories of social engineering attacks include spamming, phishing, or pharming.

Social engineering attacks occur in many ways when malware is combined with deceptive techniques to accomplish complex attacks on unsuspecting users. In some cases, deception is used to trick the user into downloading and executing malicious code. Phishing is also a deception technique, although it does not require malicious code. In other cases, malware is used to enable a deception, as in pharming.

Spamming is an unsolicited bulk email where recipients who click links in the spam message can put themselves at risk of downloading spyware, viruses, and other malware. Spamming is the abuse of an email system in the form of sending unsolicited bulk emails and junk emails. A countermeasure is to install spam filtering software, which is a computer program that analyzes email to look for characteristics of spam and typically places messages that appear to be spam in a separate email folder.

Phishing is the creation and use of fraudulent but legitimate-looking emails and websites to obtain Internet users' identity, authentication, or financial information or to trick users into doing something they ordinarily would not do. In many cases, perpetrators embed the illegitimate website's URLs in spam, which is unsolicited bulk email, in the hopes that curious recipients will click on those links and trigger the download of the malware or initiate the phishing attack.

Categories of nonmalware deployed on operational systems (continued)

Pharming is the redirection of legitimate web traffic (e.g., browser requests) to an illegitimate website for the purpose of obtaining private information. Pharming often uses Trojan horses, worms, or virus technologies to attack the address bar of an Internet browser so that the valid URL typed by the user is modified to that of the illegitimate website. Pharming may also exploit the DNS server by causing it to transform a legitimate host name into an invalid website's Internet Protocol (IP) address; this form of pharming is known as DNS cache poisoning.

Web and Mobile Analytics

This section presents two types of analytics: web analytics based on websites and the Internet and mobile analytics based on mobile operating systems and devices. Both types present metrics that should be measured and monitored to improve the performance of web and mobile platforms. In addition, five web generations are presented so readers can understand the evolution of the web.

Web Generations

The World Wide Web (www), the Internet, has been evolving at a rapid pace moving from web 0.0 to web 5.0 generations:

Web 0.0—The birth of the Internet and its development. In a way, web 0.0 is in the concept stage of innovation with a proof of concept.

Web 1.0—Basic web features, such as browsing, static web format, mostly read-only, owner-published content. Uses portals and directories, banner advertising, directories, homepages, page views, web forms, online shopping carts, and minimal interactive publishing. Technologies and programming languages used include HTTP, TCP/IP, HTML, XML, and XHTML. Threats include viruses, worms, phishing, and social engineering approaches.

Web 2.0—Read-write (writing and participating web), social media platforms, cloud computing networks, blogs, wikis, tweets, audio/video images, tweets, tagging, podcasts, collaboration, sharing content, connected devices, web applications (apps), mashups, search engines, mobile computing, and interactive advertising. All these features have increased attacks on networks, computers, and devices with malware, spyware, adware, capturing user keystrokes, cross-site scripting, and phishing attacks. Web 2.0 provides an expanded bandwidth and greater computing power.

Web Generations (continued)

Web 3.0—Personal and portable; executing web; content consolidation; represents smart applications such as artificial intelligence, robots, augmented/virtual reality, and the Internet of Things (IoT). Focuses on user behavior and engagement; promotes behavioral advertising and outsourced emails.

Web 4.0—Mobile web connecting all devices in the real world and virtual world in real time.

Web 5.0—Open connection, linked and intelligent web, and emotional web.

Web Analytics

Similar to business analytics, data analytics, and audit analytics, web analytics are quantitative measurements of a company's website performance, functioning of online computer systems and networks, and overall Internet performance. These web analytics, which can be called web metrics and web key performance indicators (web-KPIs), must be tracked and improved similar to any other business-related KPIs. As electronic commerce (ecommerce) is increasing at a fast rate, it is important to pay special attention to web analytics. As with any other KPIs, web-KPIs should be few in number, significant in size, and big in impact to be of any value.

Examples of web analytics are listed next.

- Number of online shopping cart abandonments per day, week, month, quarter, and year. Shopping cart abandonments are a reflection of a poorly designed company website for customer orders with limited features and functions, followed by difficult flow of web screens with poor description of product's features. Overall, the online order system is unattractive and uninviting to customers, resulting in loss of sales orders and lost profits.
- Number of website crashes or shutdowns per day, week, month, quarter, and year. Crashes are reflections of poor system design, development, and testing of software followed by lack of preventive and regular maintenance. They result in loss of sales revenues, bad reputation, and loss of customer goodwill. The computer systems could be legacy systems requiring redesign or replacement.

Web Analytics (continued)

- Number of online software glitches per day, week, month, quarter, and year. Software glitches are reflections of untested software containing processing flaws and file updating errors, requiring software patches and fixes.
- Number of data breaches (e.g., data destruction, data stealing, and data hijacking) from external hackers or internal employees per day, week, month, quarter, and year. Data breaches are reflections of lack of adequate security controls with antiquated security design principles and practices. They are proof that hackers know more about system security weaknesses than the internal IT security staff.
- Number of marketing emails opened or not opened by targeted customers for advertising and promotional programs. This metric is a reflection of an aggressive marketing email campaign that customers got turned off coming from the same company repeatedly. It could be that customers are being bombarded or overwhelmed by frequent and unnecessary mass emails.
- Number of marketing emails responded to or not responded to by targeted customers for advertising and promotional programs. This metric is a reflection that customers are not interested in purchasing the company's products and services. Busy customers will not waste their time responding, and silence is their answer.

Web Analytics (continued)

- Number of marketing text messages replied to or not replied to by targeted customers for advertising and promotional programs. The text messages could be annoying and irrelevant to customers and can turn them off.
- Number of browser clicks made on a marketing advertisement campaign. An abnormal number of clicks could be a sign of click fraud and web fraud perpetrated by a hired advertising company that is cheating its customers by hiring employees or using software bots for fraud-clicking. A control is to replace the hired advertising company and focus on the reputation of a company before hiring.
- Percentage of system uptime (e.g., 90%) and system downtime (e.g., 10%) per day, week, month, quarter, and year. System uptime represents robust and resilient computer systems and networks; system downtime represents the opposite. Frequent system downtimes and crashes could lead to lost sales and customers switching to competitors due to frustration, which may require backup computer systems and alternative computer processing sites to keep the customers with the company with little or no system downtime or crashes.
- Number of times system maintenance (whether preventive or scheduled) work is done in a time period. Infrequent system maintenance work could lead to a higher percentage of system downtime.
- Social media metrics, such as: revenue per pin (Pinterest), average time to respond on Twitter's customer feedback, percentage of Twitter customers' comments replied or ignored, and percentage of Facebook customers' comments answered or ignored.

Web Analytics (continued)

- Using email as a sales channel, email metrics relevant to email campaigns are click-through rates, email open rates, and revenue per email.
- The click-through rate is the number of times a website user clicks on a web page advertisement compared to the total number of users viewing the same advertisement. The higher the click-through rate, the greater the interest in an advertisement and the higher the possibility of larger dollar amounts converted to online sales revenue (i.e., click-through conversion amount). As the click fraud rate increases, the click-through rate increases, showing a direct relationship. However, a greater number of click-through rates may or may not increase online sales revenue, because the conversion depends on whether the clicks have actually turned into sales orders.

  Click-through rate = (Number of visitors clicked) / (Total number of visitors) × 100

- Click-to-conversion time for a product or service is the elapsed time between a number of browser clicks made, number of website navigation paths taken, and number of online advertisements read before a purchase decision was made. Comparisons can be made between different products and at different times to shorten the click-to-conversion time. The shorter the conversion time, the faster the sales revenue, and vice versa. Customer data is classified, stored, and analyzed to study purchasing trends and patterns. As the click fraud rate increases, the click-to-conversion time and the click-through-conversion amount decreases, showing an inverse relationship.

Mobile Analytics

Examples of mobile metrics for using mobile websites and mobile devices are listed next.

- Number of customer visits (traffic count) to a retailer's websites classified as new customers or repeat customers. This website traffic is similar to foot traffic into physical stores. The simpler the design of the website, the better attraction it is to the site and vice versa.
- Number of customers who purchased a product using a smartphone after visiting a site and after going to a physical store. This metric is a measure of the online customer conversion rate because the customer purchased a product after visiting a site.
- Number of customers who abandoned a shopping cart, expressed as a percentage of total customers who ordered online. The higher the abandoned rate, the more poorly designed the site is.
- Number of page views on a retailer's site, expressed as above average, average, or below average. This metric represents the proper use of relevant search terms in product listings, which can enhance or diminish the visibility of page views to customers. Using pictures, photos, and other graphics in product listings can draw customer attention better than an average page view full of text.

Mobile Analytics (continued)

- Number of bounced emails, classified as hard bounces and soft bounces. Hard bounces are messages that are permanently rejected due to an invalid email address or a blocked server. Soft bounces are messages that are temporarily rejected because a recipient's inbox is full or a server is down.
- System response time to reach a site's homepage and the size of the homepage. Average response time for the homepage should be three seconds or less, and average size of the homepage should be two pages or less.
- Volume of mobile device user traffic not going through a company's trusted Internet connection, the official communication channel.

Software Piracy Audit

A periodic audit of software licenses within an organization should be conducted to mitigate legal risks (i.e., lawsuits and negative reputation) and financial liabilities (i.e., fines and penalties) with software vendors who are the owners of the software. Ineffective and inefficient management of software license issues can lead to software piracy risks. Here, the major issue facing the user organization is violation of the U.S. Copyright Act because the software is copyrighted by its owner. Developing and monitoring a software inventory management system is an effective control to detect illegal use of copyrighted software.

Risks from illegal software include:

- Telecommuting employees may install illegal software on their home computer, which is also used for business purposes, and the illegal software that is not authorized by their employers.
- Regular employees may bring software from home to work that is not authorized by their employers.
- Disgruntled employees may report illegal copying and using of vendor-developed software to government officers, internal company's hotline reporting, software vendor representatives, software alliance, or external watchdog groups.

Software Piracy Audit (continued)

Software monitoring can be performed to determine illegal acquisition of software and unauthorized use of software. For example, vendor-provided audit software running on a user computer can detect illegal acquisition, which is using unofficially acquired software. This audit can be performed either manually or with automated tools. For example, an organization may audit systems for illegal copies of copyrighted software. This problem is primarily associated with PCs and LANs but can apply to any type of computer system or mobile devices. Another requirement is retention of business records to comply with legal, tax, audit, and regulatory authorities.

User organizations can use a **software metering program** to ensure that software is properly licensed, as required by the licensing agreement. System users are defined to the software metering product, and the product controls and monitors who is using the system and determines whether the user is authorized to use the system. Unauthorized users will be denied access to the system.

Physical Security Reviews

The audit scope of physical security review includes access controls (e.g., keys, cards, and biometrics), access restrictions (i.e., limited access to known people), camera surveillance with closed circuit television (CCTV), and safety audit. Specifically, it requires a review of physical access to storerooms, cash vaults, research laboratories, manufacturing plants and factories, and computer centers. Physical access controls include limiting unauthorized access using electronic keys and cards and biometric access devices (e.g., thumbprint, eye retina scans, facial recognition, and electronic signature verification). In addition, risks in radio frequency identification (RFID) systems and beacon technology are presented.

Primary Functions of a Physical Protection System

The primary functions of a physical protection system (PPS) include detection, delay, and response. Detection includes exterior/interior intrusion sensors, alarm assessment, alarm communication and display, and entry control systems. Delay includes access delay. Response includes protective/response force (first responders and security guards) and response force communications. The correct sequence of the primary functions of a physical protection system:

Detection → Delay → Response

Detection

A **detection** measure senses an act of aggression, assesses the validity of the detection, and communicates the appropriate information to a response force (e.g., a security guard). A detection system must provide all three of these capabilities to be effective. Detection measures may include access-control elements that assess the validity of identification credentials. These control elements may provide a programmed response (admission or denial), or they may replay information to a response force. Security guards serve as detection elements, detecting intrusion and controlling access. Equipment (alarms and sensors), entry control, and response force are elements of detection. **Entry control** refers to allowing entry to authorized personnel and detecting attempted entry of unauthorized personnel and material. The measures of effectiveness of entry control are throughout (number of authorized personnel allowed access per unit time), false acceptance rate (rate at which false identities or credentials are allowed entry), and false rejection rate (frequency of denying access to authorized personnel). Once an alarm is initiated and reported, assessment of the situation begins. The assessment includes whether the alarm is a valid alarm or a nuisance (false) alarm and details about the cause of the alarm (i.e., what, who, where, and how many). The probability of detection will decrease as assessment time increases, and detection is not complete without assessment.

Delay

Delay is the slowing down of adversary progress. Delay can be accomplished by response force, barriers, locks, and activated delays. Delay before detection is a deterrent and is of little or no value because it does not provide additional time to respond to the adversary. Detection must occur before delay. Detection is most effective at the perimeter and delay is more effective at the target.

Response

Response consists of the actions taken by the response force to prevent adversary success. Here, response actions include interruption to stop the adversary's progress, communication to the response force, and deployment of the response force to the adversary's location. Response effectiveness is measured as the time between receipt of a communication of adversary action and the interruption of that action. The effectiveness measure of deployment is the probability of deployment to the adversary location and the time required to deploy the response force. Another response action used in nonindustrial and high-security application is neutralization, which is a one-on-one confrontation between the response force and the adversary.

Secondary Functions of a Physical Protection System

The secondary functions of a PPS include deterrence, defense, and defeat in that order:

Deterrence → Defense → Defeat

Deterrence

A potential aggressor who perceives a risk of being caught may be deterred from attacking an asset. The effectiveness of deterrence varies with the aggressor's sophistication, the asset's attractiveness, and the aggressor's objective. Although deterrence is not considered a direct design objective, it may be a result of the design. The deterrence is not proved to be effectively working all the time.

Defense

Defensive measures protect an asset from aggression by delaying or preventing an aggressor's movement toward the asset or by shielding the asset from attacks. Defensive measures include: delaying aggressors from gaining access by using tools in a forced entry (these measures include barriers along with a response force); preventing an aggressor's movement toward an asset (these measures provide barriers to movement and obscure lines of sight to assets); and protecting the asset from the effects of tools and attacks.

Defensive measures may be active or passive. Active defensive measures are manually or automatically activated response to acts of aggression. Passive defensive measures do not depend on detection or a response. They include such measures as blast-resistant building components and fences. Security guards (response/protective force) may also be considered as defensive measures.

Defeat

Most protective systems depend on response personnel to defeat an aggressor. Although defeat is not a design objective, defensive and detection systems must be designed to accommodate (or at least not interfere with) response force activities.

Physical Security Threats and Risks

Five threats and risks exist in physical security, including interruptions in providing computer services, physical damage, unauthorized disclosure of information, loss of control over system integrity, and physical theft.

1. **Interruptions in providing computer services**
   An external threat may interrupt the scheduled operation of a system. The magnitude of the losses depends on the duration and timing of the service interruption and the characteristics of the operations end users perform.

2. **Physical damage**
   If a system's hardware is damaged or destroyed, it usually has to be repaired or replaced. Data may be destroyed as an act of sabotage by a physical attack on data storage media (e.g., rendering the data unreadable or only partly readable). If data stored by a system for operational use are destroyed or corrupted, they need to be restored from backup copies or from the original sources before the system can be used. The magnitude of loss from physical damage depends on the cost to repair or replace the damaged hardware and data as well as costs arising from service interruptions.

Physical Security Threats and Risks (continued)

3. **Unauthorized disclosure of information**
   The physical characteristics of the facility housing a computer system may permit an intruder to gain access to media both external to system hardware (such as diskettes, tapes, and printouts) and within system components (such as fixed disks), transmission lines, or display screens. All may result in loss or disclosure of sensitive information.

4. **Loss of control over system integrity**
   If an intruder gains access to the central processing unit, it is usually possible to reboot the system and bypass logical access controls. This can lead to information disclosure, fraud, replacement of systems and application software, introduction of a Trojan horse, and more. Moreover, if such access is gained, it may be very difficult to determine what has been modified, lost, or corrupted.

5. **Physical theft**
   System hardware may be stolen. The magnitude of the loss is determined by the costs to replace the stolen hardware and to restore data stored on stolen media. Theft may also result in service interruptions.

Physical Protection System

The physical protection system (PPS) focuses on protecting specific assets against well-defined threats to a targeted level of protection. Protection systems integrate physical protective measures and security procedures to protect assets against a threat. In designing and implementing physical protection systems, it is important to blend technology factors and human factors.

The characteristics or functions of integrated protection systems include deterrence, defense, defeat, detection, delay, and response. A PPS must accomplish its objectives by either deterrence or a combination of detection, delay, and response. The last three primary functions (detection, delay, and response) must be performed in this order and within a length of time that is less than the time required for the adversary to complete his task.

The order is important because there must be awareness that there is an attack (detection) and slowing of adversary progress to the targets (delay), thus allowing the response force or protective force enough time to interrupt or stop the adversary (response). The total time for detection, delay, and response must be less than the adversary's actual time to attack a critical asset.

Physical Security Countermeasures

Deterrence is the preferred method to deal with attacks against property, whether criminal or not. If attacks are not deterred, access to selected areas or properties should be denied. If attacks are not denied, attacks that occur should be detected. If attacks are not detected in time, they should be delayed to allow time for response by authorities.

Physical Security Countermeasures (continued)

Physical security controls or countermeasures (e.g., locks and keys) are the first line of defense against potential risks and exposures and are mostly hardware related. People (employees) are the last line of defense by questioning strangers and others unfamiliar to them.

Physical security protective measures can be divided into three types: preventive measures, corrective measures, and detective measures. **Preventive measures** reduce the likelihood of a deliberate attack, reduce impact, introduce delays, reduce vulnerabilities, or cause an attack to be unsuccessful. Examples of preventive measures include physical deterrents, such as fences, lighting, physical barriers, access controls, locks, visitor controls, and window grilles, and psychological deterrents, such as CCTV cameras, employee screening, employee supervision, and visible security officers (protective/response force).

Corrective measures reduce the effect of an attack and restore the facility to normal operation. The corrective action should be in line with the identified threats. Examples of corrective measures include procedures for monitoring the protection system, assessing the information produced by alarms, and dispatching an appropriate response either through protective force or law enforcement authorities, or a combination.

Detective measures help discover attacks and activate appropriate preventive or corrective measures. Examples of detective measures include intrusion detection systems, identification badges, access controls, visual surveillance through CCTV, searching equipment by metal detectors, and investigation by protective force. Note that access controls such as doors, keys, and locks are both preventive and detective measures.

Design and Measurement of PPS

The design goals of a PPS must be based on sound engineering principles of protection in depth, minimum consequence of component failure, and balanced protection. The design process must be based on performance criteria, not on feature criteria. The feature-based criterion focuses on external and uses checklists to determine whether a feature is present or absent. The feature criterion does not look at internal factors. The performance-based criterion looks at measures and procedures and is more inclusive, as it is internal.

The performance measures for the detection function are listed next.

- Probability of detection
- Time for alarm communication and assessment
- Frequency of nuisance alarms

The performance measure for the delay function is time-to-defeat obstacles.

Design and Measurement of PPS (continued)

The performance measures for the response function are listed next.

- Probability of accurate communication going to response-force
- Time taken for accurate communication to response-force
- Probability of response force deployment to adversary location
- Time to deploy
- Response force effectiveness

Analytical techniques to analyze a complex PPS system can include identifying system deficiencies, evaluating improvements, performing trade-off analysis of cost versus performance, and making comparisons.

Memory Cards, Smart Cards, Hardware Tokens, Physical Tokens, and Biometrics

This section highlights the importance of memory cards, smart cards, hardware tokens, physical tokens, and biometrics in improving the overall physical security posture.

Memory Cards

Memory cards are data storage devices. These cards allow storage of information used for personal authentication, access authorization, card integrity, and applications. The card does not process information but serves as a repository of information. The data can be written to a magnetic stripe, bar code, or optically stored on the integrated circuit chip. When a smart card is used as a repository of information without requiring the cardholder to input a PIN or present a biometric reference sample, the smart card is used as a memory card. This method is often used for touch-and-go access and does not provide a high level of assurance since wireless transmissions can be intercepted easily.

If a user presents a memory card to a reader and enters valid PIN using a keypad or keyboard, then a two-factor authentication is employed. If the access control application determines that the PIN is valid and corresponds to the memory card presented, then the user is allowed access privileges based on something the user has and something that the user knows.

Smart Cards

A **smart card** has one or more integrated chip circuits and can also store data using memory chips. The difference between a smart card and a memory card is that the smart card processes data like a simple computer. Communications with a smart card can be via contact or contactless (proximity) interfaces. At an access control point, the smart card is presented to the reader. Many applications require cardholders to enter a valid PIN to enable smart card and cardholder authentication and subsequent establishment of a secure communication channel. This type of access represents two-factor authentication comprised of something a user has (a smart card) and something the user knows (a PIN).

Hardware Tokens

Hardware tokens (also called hard tokens or eTokens) are hardware devices with computing capability integrated into the device. As with biometrics systems, these devices can be integrated into either physical or logical access control solutions depending on the technology implemented on the token. For example, validation of the possession of a valid token can be used for access when low assurance is adequate for physical access; storing a user's private key on a token increases the overall assurance because the adversary now needs an additional item (the token) to breach the system.

Hardware Tokens (continued)

These hardware token devices include smart cards and USB cryptographic tokens. Use of hardware tokens, which contain tamper protections such as zeroization of contents and tamper detection switches, is essential. Entering a PIN with a hardware token represents a two-factor authentication: something a person has and something a person knows. USB key chain tokens that generate a passcode simply by pushing a button on the device represent single-factor authentication, something the user has. Tokens come in various shapes, sizes, and technologies and can perform various functions. Not all cryptographic modules are in separate hardware tokens. Some are implemented in software, called software modules. Many applications and operating systems have software modules, which unfortunately do not provide as high a degree of security as hardware.

Physical Tokens

Physical tokens consist of keys and unique documents, such as hand-carried orders. Access control methods used for single-factor personal authentication include simple physical keys, three-plane (complex) physical keys, and hand-carried orders. These physical tokens are authorized for the protection of non-mission-critical, unclassified, and nonsensitive assets. Like PKI, physical tokens represent something the user has. Unlike PKI, they provide a low level of assurance and are suitable for use only when protecting IT assets with a low risk and low confidentiality level.

Simple physical keys provide minimal protection and assurance, as they are highly susceptible to copying or theft, and locks controlled by simple keys are relatively easy to compromise.

A three-plane key is one of the more secure key systems since the keys themselves are more complicated to copy, blank key stocks are not readily available to adversaries and are more difficult to counterfeit, and the locks controlled by three-plane keys are more difficult to compromise.

Biometrics

Biometrics is becoming a popular physical security measure with unique features that often cannot be defeated or compromised. The term "biometrics" usually refers to technologies for measuring and analyzing human body characteristics, such as voice and facial pattern recognition (e.g., voice print, facial image, and eye retina or iris image) and hand measurements (e.g., fingerprints, handwriting, hand geometry, wrist veins, and thumb impressions). Unfortunately, equipment used in biometrics can lead to two types of errors: Type I and Type II. In practice, it is generally necessary to adjust the equipment for a compromise between false rejections of correct individuals (Type I error) and false acceptances of imposters (Type II error). The goal is to obtain low numbers for both types of errors. An equal error rate (crossover error rate) occurs when false rejection rates and false acceptance rates are equal. Biometrics can act as a strong security control mechanism in a multifactor authentication process.

Internal Physical Security Systems

This section presents topics such as security guards and dogs, keys and combination locks, door control devices, motion detectors, and mantraps and turnstiles.

Security Guards and Dogs

Physical protection measures, physical barriers, and intrusion detectors depend ultimately on human intervention. Security guards, whether fixed post or roving patrol, can help in this area. A guard may be assigned to a fixed post, such as a lobby, entrance door, truck dock, entrance gate, or security control desk. The guard's post orders may include:

- Checking entrant credentials and use of the sign-in log
- Issuing and recovering visitor badges
- Monitoring intrusion and fire alarm systems and dispatching personnel to respond to alarms
- Controlling movement of materials into and out of the building and enforcing property pass systems
- Enforcing rules and regulations established for the building
- Accepting registered mail

Keys and Combination Locks

The objective of entrance door controls is to screen entrants, deny entrance where appropriate, and control the flow of materials into and out of the building.

Screening can be done in two ways: by a guard's personal recognition of the entrant or acceptance of credentials or by the entrant's possession of a suitable device to unlock a door. Screening by a guard is by far the most positive method when applied conscientiously but costs more than use of electronic or mechanical devices. Electronic or mechanical devices can accomplish entrant screening. Authorized entrants may use a key (conventional or electronic), enter the combination of a push-button lock, or be screened by a device that compares an entrant characteristic (hand geometry, fingerprint, or voice characteristics) with stored information about authorized entrants.

Access control that depends on a key lock or screening device rather than a guard has several shortcomings. Keys or combinations can fall into the wrong hands. An intruder may enter immediately behind an authorized entrance (often referred to as tailgating or piggybacking). Skilled intruders may defeat locks. Although these shortcomings can be managed (careful key control, security-conscious employees, burglar-alarmed doors, etc.), computer security planners should be aware of these problems and not fall into the trap of accepting blanket

Keys and Combination Locks (continued)

statements like "This door is always locked" or "This key cannot be duplicated." Each entrance door should be capable of resisting forced or covert entry up to the level of effort likely to be applied. This type of entry requires careful consideration of door hardware and installation. Where appropriate, heavy-duty lock sets, reinforced strike plates and door frames, tamper-resistant hinges, and break-resistant glass in vision panels can be used. In addition to utilizing reinforced doors, companies can also connect critical doors to a perimeter alarm system to signal a security guard when a door is opened. This can be done for electric strike-equipped doors in such a way that an alarm is not sounded when normal entry is made but forced entry will cause an alarm.

Door Control Devices

At least five door control devices exist, including conventional keys and lock sets, pick-resistant lock sets, electronic key systems, electronic combination locks, and mechanical push-button combination locks.

1. **Conventional keys and lock sets** have low cost per cylinder, and almost any door can be equipped. However, keys are easily duplicated, and locks can be picked. A key holder can enter at any time. There is no control over entrance and exit of materials.

2. **Pick-resistant lock sets** cost about two or three times more than conventional locks, keys are much more difficult to duplicate, and locks are much harder to pick. Other characteristics are the same as conventional locks.

3. **Electronic key systems** use specially encoded cards to actuate an electronic door strike. Depending on features and installation, both key and cards can be expensive. Simple systems perform as pick-resistant lock sets. Higher-cost systems can include the ability to lock out specified cards, limit access to specified times, log all entrances and exits, and control a group of doors such that access to each door in the group can be specified for each card.

Door Control Devices (continued)

4. **Electronic combination locks** typically have electronic push buttons into which users key the combination to actuate an electric strike. Costs and features are generally similar to electronic key systems except users need not carry a card. Some allow users to use a special code when under duress, which will open the door but at the same time sound a remote alarm.

5. **Mechanical push-button combination locks** retract the bolt and allow users to open the door after they press the correct combination. These locks do not offer the special features described for electronic locks, but their cost is much lower.

Motion Detectors

There exist several technological means of determining access to or occupancy of critical areas during periods when the areas should be vacant. Two popular systems are light beams and CCTV systems.

An important caution is that CCTV systems are best used only for a determination of an area's status after there has been an alert from some other, more positive intrusion detector. There are at least four distinct technologies for detecting the presence of an intruder.

1. **Photoelectric systems** are passive systems that detect a change in an area's light level due to added sources of light. Since these systems are sensitive to ambient light level, they may be used only in windowless areas or areas in which the windows have been covered.

2. **Motion-detection systems** are based on the Doppler effect. When the source of a sound or electromagnetic signal, or a reflector of such a signal, moves toward or away from a receiver, the frequency or pitch of the signal received will be higher or lower, respectively. In a room having a source of wave energy and a receiver and if a body moves within that room, the motion can be detected from the change in frequency of received waveforms. The receiver will pick up the source frequency strongly but also detects a slightly different frequency at a much lesser strength.

Motion Detectors (continued)

3. **Acoustical-seismic detection systems (audio)** employ microphone-type devices to detect sounds that exceed the ambient noise level of the area under protection. A nuisance alarm is possible due to sounds from rain, thunder, aircraft, construction, and others. Seismic (vibration) systems utilize the same principle as audio detection systems except that highly sensitive and specialized microphones are attached directly to objects such as safes, filing cabinets, windows, walls, and ceilings.

4. **Proximity detection systems** detect the approach or presence of an object or an individual. In principle, a proximity system employs an electrical field that, when upset by a foreign body, causes an alarm. The field may be set up around a cabinet, or it may simply surround a wire. The field could be electromagnetic or electrostatic.

   Proximity systems are designed to be supplemental and are not effective as primary systems because they are susceptible to nuisance alarms caused by electric supply fluctuations and by the presence of items placed near them. Animals and birds can trigger alarms if systems are too sensitive. Therefore, proximity systems should be backed up by other security systems.

Mantraps and Turnstiles

Both mantraps and turnstiles are examples of physical security access controls.

Mantraps can provide an additional security at the entrance to high-risk areas. The outermost door may be opened inward with the use of access control cards. However, the inner door may be opened inward only, and the outer door may be opened outward only by security personnel from inside a room. Thus, an intruder who got past the outer door with the use of false identification would be trapped in front of the inner door. For highly sensitive areas, mantraps require a biometric measure, such as fingerprints combined with the weight of the person entering the facility.

Turnstiles decrease everyday piggybacking or tailgating by forcing people to go through a turnstile one person at a time. Turnstiles cannot be outer-wall perimeter devices unless they are enclosed to maintain environmental continuity within the building (i.e., heat and air conditioning).

Optical turnstiles communicate to users via visual/audible annunciation. Detection, scanning, and control electronics located within the bollards ensure that only one individual per valid access card presented is granted access, thus preventing tailgating. Any attempt to enter without a valid card trips an alarm replay output that can trigger any number of responses to prevent further access. These responses include alerting security personnel, switching CCTV cameras, and locking down interior doors and elevators. In addition to preventing tailgating, optical turnstiles can track employee time, attendance, and location and resolve issues regarding employee security, safety, theft, and accountability.

Perimeter Security Systems

This section discusses various perimeter security systems, such as physical intrusion detection sensors and alarms; physical and cyber-access to equipment; physical perimeter access; manual override control; and intra-perimeter communications.

Physical Intrusion Detection Sensors and Alarms

Intrusion detection devices, commonly referred to as burglar alarms, are used to detect and signal unauthorized entry or attempted entry. Doors, windows, and other movable coverings of openings in perimeter barriers must be equipped with magnetic contacts or vibration-detecting devices. All alarm-system circuits must be supervised to detect any interruption in electric power or tampering. Intrusion alarms must have emergency power or another direct current (DC) power source. Auxiliary power must provide for longer periods of operation (e.g., 120 hours) for intrusion alarms.

An intrusion detection system (IDS) must be fail-safe, have a backup power source, must resist and detect tampering, and must be linked to a security guard force. The basic triggers for operation of IDS include breaking an electrical circuit, interrupting a light beam, detecting sound, detecting vibration, and detecting a change in capacitance due to penetration of an electrostatic field.

Alarms are to be placed in the secure mode by a member of the staff after the workforce leaves. A primary and an alternative staff member should be designated in writing to activate the alarm system at the close of business. Personnel at all remote monitoring locations must have an up-to-date list of persons authorized to arm systems and place them in the open mode at the beginning of the workday. The security office monitoring the alarms should have the names of the primary and alternative contact points to notify during nonbusiness hours if an alarm signal is received. All alarm systems must be properly maintained and tested as recommended by the manufacturer or installer.

The perimeter of buildings must be checked for other possible entry points, such as windows, transformer vaults, air conditioning louvers, roof hatches, and the like. Each point that represents a potential intruder route should be appropriately secured physically or added to the perimeter alarm system. For example, exposed windows can be glazed with break-resistant glass or plastic. Louvers can be protected with heavy-gauge screens.

The most common causes of false alarms are user negligence, poor installation/servicing, and faulty equipment. The basic parts of an alarm system include a sensor or triggering device, a circuit that carries messages to the signaling equipment, and a signaling system or device (annunciator).

There are two types of alarm systems: electromechanical and volumetric. Electromechanical alarms include metallic foil, magnetic switches, wire lacing, and pressure mats. Volumetric alarms include vibration, microwave, ultrasonic, passive infrared, photoelectric, and capacitance.

Physical Intrusion Detection Sensors and Alarms (continued)

The electromechanical type of IDS is in widest use today. It consists of a continuous electrical circuit so balanced that a change or break in the circuit will set off an alarm. Examples of systems that use a continuous electrical circuit are listed next.

- Foil strips on a window that will break if the window is broken
- Magnetic or contact switches on doors
- Mercury switches on opening that tilt
- Vibration detectors to detect breaking through walls
- Screens and traps that consist of fine wires embedded in breakable dowels or in the walls, ceilings, and floors

Intraperimeter Communications

Mechanisms within the perimeter may rely on intraperimeter communication to ensure secure operation. The communication medium may consist of a physical, electrical (fly-by-wire), or wireless connection. Security concerns often overlook intraperimeter communications. Access to the intraperimeter communication medium constitutes access to the function or device itself with the potential for exploit and damage. The communication path must be physically secured to the same level as the components.

The length and complexity of the communication channel to be protected should be minimized. The communication channel and access ports should also be hidden from view, out of reach, and/or behind layers of perimeter security if possible. A conduit may be placed around the communication medium to provide additional resistance to tampering. Wireless communication should not be detectable or accessible outside the perimeter.

Safety Audit

The scope of a safety audit includes review of safety policies and procedures and accident statistics and investigations. Internal auditors need to make sure that corrective actions to safety problems are proper and timely and that all applicable labor laws are complied with. Internal auditors need to coordinate safety audit activities with other internal assurance functions, such as quality, health, security, and industrial engineering. Possible areas of coordination include sharing work plans and schedules, conducting periodic meetings, exchanging reports, developing work statistics, providing control training, and participating in investigations and corrective actions.

Summary of Entry Control Guidelines

The entry control perimeter should be under visual control at all times during working hours to prevent entry by unauthorized personnel. Security guards or monitored video surveillance systems should be in place.

A list of entry control guidelines is presented next.

- Limit the number of entrances to the computer facility to a minimum. There should be coordination of this measure with those responsible for fire protection and building security. Doors should be of sufficient strength to resist forced entry.
- Install a screening device at every entrance, be it a guard, a badge reader, an electronic lock, a TV camera manned by a guard in another location, or a physical lock. Maintain entry logs wherever possible. Monitor closely all items moving into or out of the facility, whether expected or not (e.g., scheduled deliveries).
- If there is an extensive perimeter requiring protection, consider use of exterior lighting, TV cameras, roving patrols, and intrusion detection devices. However, such protection requires coordination with building security staff.
- Secure all openings through which an intruder could gain entrance or receive material.

Summary of Entry Control Guidelines (continued)

- Control the use of badges to permit entry. They should not be issued in such quantity that guards cannot verify badge holders. When people leave the employ of the facility, whatever the reason, all keys and badges issued to them must be retrieved. Visitors should be issued temporary badges differing in appearance from employee badges.
- In case of any unusual diversions, such as power outages, bomb threats, or false fire alarms, make a thorough search of the facility to prevent or uncover loss or destructive activity that might have taken place during any confusion. Entry logs or other records of facility activity should be consulted; they might reveal any unusual occurrence that could serve as a clue to the perpetrator's identity.
- Provide adequate protection of remote terminals, data libraries, and trash areas (to prevent dumpster-diving attacks) that are both within and outside the confines of the computer facility. **Dumpster diving** refers to going through a company's trash and garbage containers to find valuable proprietary and confidential information that was discarded carelessly and using that information against the company for personal and/or financial gain.

Summary of Storage and Handling Protection Guidelines

Protection of sensitive and classified assets must include classified storage, proper security marking, transportation, destruction, and incident handling. Classified information (e.g., top secret or secret) must be guarded and/or alarmed 24x7. Intrusion alarms must be implemented and monitored with response times appropriate to the classification of the materials protected. To gain access at the access control perimeter of facilities or workplaces processing classified information, a two-factor authentication is required. This requirement can be met using visual monitoring by an attendant or through use of an automated entry system. Either automated or manual classified access logs should also be maintained to ensure accountability.

A list of storage and handling protection guidelines is presented next.

- Devise fire protection plans with data storage media in mind. Consider the risks that firefighting imposes on stored data. Tape and disk library vaults (safes) can be certified to have a particular protection rating and design that keeps contents safe from steam and water damage as well as from heat and flame. These ratings should be considered in evaluating and selecting storage facilities.
- Include protective measures in planning for disaster response. Disaster recovery procedures should be periodically tested and exercised. Arrangement should be made for the removal to a place of safekeeping of storage media, computer printouts, records of disclosure, and source material before a disaster. If potential threats of looting and pilfering exist, security guards should be posted; if data are vulnerable to water damage, protective plastic covers should be available.

Summary of Storage and Handling Protection Guidelines (continued)

- To ensure that protection of data is adequately maintained, conduct frequent unscheduled security inspections. Check for unlocked doors, doors propped open, locks that do not latch, and fire and intrusion alarms that have been turned off because they are too easily activated.

In summary, physical security measures are the first line of defense against the risks that stem from the uncertainties in the environment and the unpredictability of human behavior. Frequently, they are the simplest safeguards to implement and can be put into practice with the least delay. Naturally, not all physical security measures are required at any one installation; rather, a judicious selection should be made that provides a realistic overall coverage for the lowest expenditure.

Retail Physical Security Technologies

This section presents two physical security topics related to retail industry, RFID technology and beacon technology.

Radio Frequency Identification Technology

An RFID system is a form of automatic identification and data capture (AIDC) technology that uses electric or magnetic fields at radio frequencies to transmit information, such as in optical scanning of bar codes, text labels, and holograms. An RFID system can be used to identify many types of objects, such as manufactured goods, retail products, and people. Each object that needs to be identified has a small RFID tag affixed to or embedded within it. The tag has a unique identifier and may also hold additional information about the object. RFID readers wirelessly communicate with the tags to identify the item connected to each tag and possibly read or update additional information stored on the tag. This communication can occur without optical line of sight and over greater distances (both indoors and outdoors) than other AIDC technologies. RFID technologies support a wide range of applications—everything from tracking of physical assets to security access control, making automated payments in retail, tracking of a patient's chart in a hospital, and tracking of products in a supply chain from manufacturer to retail customer purchase to product recalls.

WHICH TECHNOLOGY IS WHAT?

- Bar code technology is basic, simple, old, and static.
- RFID technology is advanced, complex, new, and dynamic.
- Bar code technology can act as a backup or fallback system to the RFID technology.

RFID Risks

For RFID implementations to be successful, organizations should effectively manage four types of risks:

1. **Business process risk** includes:
    a. Failure of part or all of the RFID system leading to loss of critical business or operational records
    b. Human actions (e.g., either benign or malicious)
    c. Location of RFID technology
    d. Lack of robustness of business continuity planning
    e. Cloning of tags and attacks on enterprise subsystem networks
2. **Business intelligence risk** involves threats and vulnerabilities that could permit unauthorized parties to gain access to sensitive or proprietary information. A competitor or adversary can gain information from the RFID system in a number of ways, including eavesdropping on RFID transactions, reading tags, and gaining access to RFID-related databases. The risk of unauthorized access is realized when the entity engaging in the unauthorized behavior does something harmful with that information. In some cases, the information may trigger an immediate response, such as breaking into a container holding valuable goods. In other cases, data may also be aggregated over time to provide intelligence related to an organization's customers, operations, business strategy, or proprietary methods.

RFID Risks (continued)

3. **Privacy risk** results from a compromised RFID system when it uses a personal information for a purpose other than originally intended or if a third-party uses the presence of tagged items to profile individuals. In the case of the latter, the primary privacy risk is likely borne by the consumer, not the organization that implemented the RFID system. Nevertheless, the RFID implementing organization still has privacy-related risks, including penalties from noncompliance with existing privacy regulations, legal liability, and the reaction of consumers, employees, public interest groups, and other stakeholders.

4. **External risk** for an enterprise subsystem includes successful attacks on networked hosts and critical applications. Computer network attacks can involve malware or attack tools that exploit software vulnerabilities and configuration weaknesses to gain access to systems, perform a denial of service, or cause other damages. The impact of computer network attacks can range from performance degradation to complete compromise of a mission-critical application.

   Because external risk by definition involves risks outside of the RFID system, it is distinct from both business process and business intelligence risks; external risks can be realized without having any effect on RFID-supported business processes or without revealing any information to adversaries. Two examples of external risks include hazards of electromagnetic radiation and computer network attacks.

Beacon Technology

Beacons are electronic sensors equipped with Bluetooth signals and are installed in a retailer's physical stores at the entrance doors. Sensors are small plastic transmitters that are mounted on store walls near the entrance. Beacons know who is walking into the store and their smartphone number because they connect the customers' name to their phone number.

Beacons send push alerts and notifications to customers' mobile devices about upcoming sales, promotions, price discounts, coupons, rebates and rewards, and special deals to make a purchase at a future date or immediately. Beacons also deliver recipes for customers who choose to opt in to the program.

Personalized marketing is possible with beacon technology using a Wi-Fi connection combined with location-based (proximity-based) marketing; it is also called targeted marketing. Beacon technology is most applicable to a consumer-packaged goods (CPG) retailer selling goods such as wine and spirits, dry or frozen food, snacks, soft drinks, condiments, soups, soaps, shampoos, over-the-counter medications, and deli food items.

Beacon Technology (continued)

Examples of Applications of Beacon Technology

- Simon, a retail real estate company, is creating "smart malls" by installing beacon networks in more than 200 of its shopping malls in the United States. The goal is to enhance the shopping experience and to increase customer traffic in stores of its malls. It shows which retailer is having special sales and promotions.
- Various retailers have launched the beacon technology in their stores.
- Walgreens, a drugstore retailer, launched beacon technology to send digital incentives to the smartphones of shoppers inside its stores. Shoppers who opt in can be reminded of loyalty rewards or special offers.
- Barneys New York, a fashion retailer, is installing the beacon technology, which connects the offline and online channels and knows customer preferences, to help sales associates better service customers using the retailer's mobile app. Customers receive relevant content in the form of videos, lookbooks, and designer interviews. The app also delivers personalized notifications when a customer nears a product contained in their mobile shopping bags or wish lists.

Privacy Audits

Privacy is the right of an individual to limit access to information regarding him- or herself. The term "privacy" refers to the social balance between an individual's right to keep information confidential and the societal benefit derived from sharing information, and how this balance is codified to give individuals the means to control personal information. The term "confidentiality" refers to disclosure of information only to authorized individuals and entities.

Privacy also means that the rights of the accused (suspect) cannot be violated during an investigation. The accused can use protective orders if his or her privacy rights are ignored or handled improperly. If accused persons can prove that evidence brought against them would do more harm to them than good, courts will favor the accused in suppressing the presentation of such evidence.

- Organizations can protect themselves from privacy and confidentiality problems by developing a policy statement and by showing the amount of damage done by the accused. A policy statement is a prerequisite to handling privacy issues properly and legally. An incomplete or unclear policy could result in legal action against the organization by employees (suspects) when they find out that their privacy rights are violated. A basic privacy policy or rule to protect an individual's privacy right is to provide a simple opt-in and opt-out choice for web services on the Internet and company websites, including the social media platforms.

The organization must show that a perpetrator actually broke into a computer system and violated the organization's proprietary rights to the system, and must show the extent of damage caused. Organizations should have controls such as passwords, encryption, access controls, hidden files, and warning banners to establish

Privacy Audits (continued)

proprietary rights to a computer system. A policy statement should define this area. In general, internal auditors are concerned about accidental or intentional disclosure of confidential data and about collection and use of such data. Legal requirements mandate the collection, disclosure, and use of data, both in public and in private sectors. Internal auditors must understand that there is a trade-off between the level of protection (security) and the cost of that protection and that there is no absolute (perfect) security.

Threats to security come from individuals who already have authorized access to a computer system as well as from those who are unauthorized to have access. Internal auditors need to make sure that known threats, exposures, and risks are addressed during system design, that proper controls are established, and that established controls are working effectively on a continuing basis. Privacy laws affecting the public sector include the U.S. Privacy Act of 1974, the Freedom of Information Act, and the Health Insurance Portability and Accountability Act of 1996 (HIPAA). Privacy laws affecting the private sector include SEC requirements, the Foreign Corrupt Practices Act (FCPA), and others.

Most, if not all, of these privacy laws require establishing appropriate safeguards (controls) to ensure the confidentiality and integrity of personal or corporate records and to protect against anticipated threats that could result in substantial harm to individuals or corporations.

Internal auditors should be concerned not only with actual compliance with privacy laws but also with how such compliance can be proved to authorities, should questions arise. Documentation, in the form of manuals, should provide such proof, as documentation contains work rules, standard operating procedures, controls, and references to laws and regulations.

Performance Audits

Performance audits, also called value-for-money audits, mainly focus on public sector programs, activities, and functions, although they can be applied to private sector business functions as well. The audit scope can contain some elements of operational, compliance, financial, and information systems audits. Performance audits can assess a program's or a function's effectiveness; economy; efficiency; internal control systems; and compliance with laws, rules, and regulations (LRRs) and provide prospective analysis on how to handle future events based on current information.

MANAGEMENT APPROACHES TO IMPROVE EFFICIENCY

Management approaches to improve efficiency include:

- Restructuring outmoded business functions and operations
- Implementing business process improvement methods
- Deploying technology improvement methods
- Implementing a strategic approach to spending using spend analysis

A return-on-value (ROV) metric can be computed as annualized savings in operating costs divided by annual total operating costs. The resulting fraction is multiplied by 100 to yield a percentage. Here, value refers to savings. The goal is to increase the ROV metric every year.

Value-for-Money Audits

As a part of performance audits, the business goal and audit goal of value-for-money (VFM) audits are to realize several benefits, such as to: decrease operating costs through cost savings, increase sales and revenues, increase profits, increase market share and stock market price, and gain a competitive advantage in the marketplace.

In order to realize these benefits, auditors need to:

- Identify overlapping, duplicating, and fragmented business functions, departments, and divisions; and then streamline them or eliminate them.
- Identify fraud, waste, and abuse of valuable resources. An example of fraud involves making improper payments to suppliers, vendors, customers, business partners, employees, directors, officers, executives, managers, and others. An example of waste is using a company's money to buy things (e.g., computer) and not using them. An example of abuse is using a company's purchase card or credit card to purchase personal things and an employee padding travel and expense reports.

VFM audits are special audits with a specific issue or problem to solve with major outcomes. As such, these audits focus on factors such as economy, efficiency, effectiveness (i.e., 3*E*s), and quality. Because of the potential for big savings, companies should require a fundamental reexamination and reassessment of all business functions, departments, and divisions and their programs.

Value-for-Money Audits (continued)

VFM audits require auditors to wear an industrial engineer's hat and focus on the 4*M*s—men, machines, money, and materials. Industrial engineers are often called efficiency experts. Expertise drives the economy, efficiency, and effectiveness (3*E*s). Note that economy and efficiency are directly related with "resources" being the common factor. At the same time, economy and efficiency are indirectly related to effectiveness where the latter is achieving the stated objectives. For example, an employee can be efficient at work (i.e., increased production with fewer resources) but may not be effective due to misguidedness of that employee's work (i.e., did not achieve the stated objective).

Key Performance Indicator Reviews

KPIs are a type of metrics that show whether a business activity or function is achieving its stated objectives, established milestones, or performance targets. KPIs are warning mechanisms or red flags because they can signal or alert when an actual outcome deviates much from the targeted outcome or expected outcome. KPIs should be few in number because they should represent key measurements. They must be reliable, valid, appropriate, and meaningful to be of any use. Dashboards are often used to show the periodic progress of KPIs requiring management attention. Some companies combine the KPIs with metrics due to their similarity in function and focus. Therefore, both management and employees should focus on a few significant KPIs.

Some KPIs or red flags in an IT function are listed next.

- Computer system reports indicate unauthorized disclosures of customer information and/or lapses of security practices in protecting customer privacy information.
- Computer system reports are not timely or are incomplete, inconsistent, or inaccurate.
- Computer system reports lack relevance and are too detailed for use as an effective decision-making tool.
- Computer systems do not have a fully tested and ready business continuity plan.
- Computer system problems are attributed to integration of systems when merged with a new company's computer systems. These problems include system failures and unreliable systems as they do not keep pace with new technologies.
- Computer systems are exposed to fraudulent activities due to lack of built-in preventive and detective controls.

Key Performance Indicator Reviews (continued)

Computer systems are not audited frequently or have many unresolved control deficiencies. Some KPIs in a production plant safety operation are listed next.

Number of:

- Safety inspections conducted in a month, quarter, and year
- Factory equipment tested and calibrated in a month, quarter, and year
- Factory operations observed for safety conditions in a month, quarter, and year
- Safety accidents investigated and reported in a month, quarter, and year
- Accidents reduced from month to month, quarter to quarter, and year to year

Amount of:

- Machine downtime reduced resulting from reduced accidents in a month, quarter, and year
- Workers' compensation insurance premiums reduced resulting from reduced accidents

Internal auditors need to be aware that some employees may manipulate and distort KPIs to survive and may distort performance results to receive larger bonuses and promotions. Therefore, auditors should compare KPIs with industry norms as well as with the same company data from period to period. Also, auditors should be careful in analyzing both KPIs that look too good and KPIs that do not meet standards.

Balanced Scorecard Reviews

Most businesses have traditionally relied on organizational performance based almost solely on financial or accounting-based data (e.g., ROI and earnings per share) and manufacturing data (e.g., factory productivity, direct labor efficiency, and machine utilization). Unfortunately, many of these indicators are inaccurate and stress quantity over quality. They reward the wrong behavior; lack predictive power; do not capture key business changes until it is too late; reflect functions, not cross-functional processes; and give inadequate consideration to difficult-to-quantify resources such as intellectual capital. Most measures are focused on cost, not so much on quality.

Robert Kaplan and David Norton of Harvard Business School coined the term "balanced scorecard" in response to the limitations of traditional financial and accounting measures. They recommend that key performance measures should be aligned with strategies and action plans of the organization. They suggest translating the strategy into measures that uniquely communicate the vision of the organization. Setting targets for each measure provides the basis for strategy deployment, feedback, and review.

The balanced scorecard system is a comprehensive management control system that balances traditional financial measures with nonfinancial measures (e.g., customer service, internal business processes, and the organization's capacity for innovation and learning). This system helps managers focus on key performance measures and communicate them clearly throughout the organization.

Balanced Scorecard Reviews (continued)

Kaplan and Norton divided the strategy-balanced scorecard into four perspectives:

1. The **financial perspective** looks back.
2. The **internal business process perspective** looks from inside out.
3. The **customer perspective** is looks from outside in.
4. The **innovation and learning perspective** looks ahead.

Contract Audits

Business Contract Defined

A **contract** is a legal document with several benefits and costs accruing to all parties involved in the contract. In a business environment, these contract names are used often:

- Employment contract
- Sales contract
- Purchase contract
- Supply-chain contract
- Construction contract
- Systems development contract
- Third-party service provider contract
- Network integration contract

Business Contract Defined (continued)

By definition, business contracts have seven built-in risks:

1. Huge investment of money in a project or program
2. Too many fail points, resulting from too many contracting parties involved (i.e., too many hand-offs)
3. Conflicting objectives between and among the contracting parties
4. Unforeseen roadblocks and delays
5. Poor-quality work products
6. Missed deadlines and goals
7. Missed business opportunities due to delays

Requirements of a Contract

In most cases, an oral contract is binding and enforceable. However, there are a limited number of instances requiring the contract to be in writing. Moreover, there must be an absence of invalidating conduct, such as duress, undue influence, misrepresentation, or mistake, for the contract to be valid. It is always a good practice for a contract to be in writing because it avoids miscommunications and misunderstandings.

The parties can be principals or qualified agents. The parties cannot engage in any fraudulent activities. The use of force or coercion to reach an agreement is not acceptable in signing a contract because both parties must enter into the agreement of their own free will. Both parties must indicate a willingness to enter into the agreement and be bound by its terms. A promise meeting all of these requirements is contractual and legally binding. However, if any requirement is unmet, the promise is noncontractual.

The five basic requirements of a contract include:

1. Mutual assent (agreement by offer and acceptance)
2. Consideration (either express or implied mutual obligation)
3. Legality of object and subject matter (must be for a legitimate purpose, not for criminal and tortuous purposes, or not against the public policy). If the purpose is illegal, the resulting contract is null and void.
4. Capacity (only competent parties can have the full capacity to contract; adjudicated incompetents have no capacity to contract; and minors, incompetent persons, and intoxicated persons have limited capacity to contract).
5. Formality (i.e., in writing).

Developing a Business Contract

Although corporate legal staff members are involved in drafting and finalizing business contracts, internal auditors have a specific role and responsibility to ensure that the contracts describe potential risks and exposures from not executing the agreed-on contractual terms and conditions. The auditor's employer organization could be violating the contractual terms and conditions similar to other parties participating in the contract, thus creating risks to the organization. This means that all parties in a contract could be in violation of contractual terms and conditions.

A major concern of internal auditors performing contract audits is to ensure that the contract language is simple to read, easy to understand, and easy to implement by frontline or functional department's staff, supervisors, and managers because these are the ones who execute and implement contracts. Generally, contract implementation efforts fail because people who are implementing a contract do not understand its legalese, and this lack of understanding is a source of noncompliance with the contract. Other internal auditor concerns include contract failures, such as contractual defaults, breach of contracts, remedies for breaches, and curing defaults with reperformance or damages. Internal auditor review of contracts is a part of compliance audit, which in turn is a part of assurance audit engagements.

Internal Audit Review of Contracts

An internal auditor's roles and responsibilities in reviewing business contracts are listed next.

- Identify all legal risks and reputation risks associated with the noncompliance with contracts after considering the risk profiles of each contracting party.
- Ensure that each contract contains a right-to-audit clause or provision so internal auditors or others can review the contract status during precontract, contract, and postcontract periods. This right also requires that internal auditors receive management reports from the contractor and subcontractors directly for monitoring purposes.
- Take a sample of recently completed large-size contracts and review them for these items:
  - **Performance standards**, which involves establishment and monitoring of performance standards for products, services, processes, people, and technology.
  - **Confidentiality and security of information,** which means protecting confidential and sensitive information of user organizations with proper security and privacy controls.

Internal Audit Review of Contracts (continued)

- **Ownership and license issues**, regarding who owns the data generated by service providers, what user organization data a service provider can use, and whether a software escrow agreement is available for purchasing software from service providers.
- **Indemnification**, which involves relieving the user organizations of any claims filed against them resulting from the service provider's gross negligence. Indemnification specifies the possible damage types.
- **Default and termination**, which include:
  - Defining what constitutes a default
  - Acceptable remedies and opportunities for curing default
  - Contract termination and notification procedures
  - Preservation and timely return of user organization's data, records, and materials
  - Remedies for not meeting performance standards with damages paid
- **Limits on liability**, which are established by service providers to ensure those limits are in line with the assumed risks.

Internal Audit Review of Contracts (continued)

   - **Insurance**, proof of which service providers and contractors are required to provide. They also must notify the contracting company when there is a material change to insurance coverage.
   - **Customer complaints and resolution**, which involves tracking and monitoring of dispute resolution in terms of speed and satisfaction.
   - **Business resumption and contingency plan**, which discusses a service provider's responsibility to back up data; develop, maintain, and test contingency plans; and submit the test results to user organization

- Issue an audit report describing all the major findings and recommendations with "lessons learned" to the board, senior management, and legal counsel. Ensure that legal staff members conduct training classes to all employees, supervisors, and managers of the business function so past mistakes are not repeated and contract practices are improved.

Other Legal Matters

Four other legal matters discussed in this section include letters of intent, product review comments posted by customers, contracts requiring customers not to sue a company, and product warranty reviews.

A **letter of intent** drawn between two or more parties could be a binding contract depending on how it is written. If the letter is very detailed and specific with names, dates, action plans, and locations, it could be binding. If the letter is too general and vague, then it is not binding.

Regarding **product reviews**, before the U.S. Congress passed the Consumer Review Fairness Act, a company might sue customers who wrote honest but negative reviews on a company's product or service or claimed they had to pay much more than the advertised price for the product. The Consumer Review Fairness Act made such suits illegal. This act states that businesses cannot use contracts that prevent customers from writing truthful comments or penalize customers for writing negative reviews. If a business, including an online one, uses contract terms or conditions that limit a customer's right to comment, it is breaking the law. Two ethical questions that can arise include: (1) whether a seller (company) can buy a positive post-sale feedback (i.e., product reviews) from a buyer (customer) for a gift or discount on future purchases; and (2) whether the product reviewer is a real customer, a ghost customer, or a software bot.

Other Legal Matters (continued)

A **contract requiring customers** not to sue a company during their lifetime for any reason in exchange for a gift card, a small cash amount, or other token reward is illegal and unenforceable.

Regarding **product warranty reviews**, internal auditors must ensure that a company is adhering to the Magnuson-Mass Warranty Act of 1974, which governs consumer product warranties. The act requires manufacturers and sellers of consumer products to provide consumers with detailed information about warranty coverage. In addition, it affects both the rights of consumers and the obligations of warrantors under written warranties.

Financial Audits

The scope of financial audit engagement can include financial statement audits and financial statement analysis. Financial statement audits focus on the full and fair representation of the financial condition of an organization; financial statement analysis focuses on identifying trends and patterns in an organization's financial performance. External auditors perform financial statement audits, and internal auditors conduct financial statement analyses either as stand-alone audits or as part of other operational audits.

Financial Statement Audits

External auditors establish the scope of a financial audit in different ways, such as by (1) reviewing balance sheet accounts only (called balance sheet audit), (2) auditing the financial statements, (3) auditing internal controls over financial reporting, and (4) an integrated audit covering items 2 and 3.

A **financial audit** is defined as determining whether financial statements present fairly the financial position and results of operations. More specifically, financial auditing provides reasonable assurance about whether the financial statements of an audited entity present fairly the financial position, results of operations, and cash flows in accordance with generally accepted accounting principles (GAAP). Balance sheet and income statements are the focus; balance sheets provide the financial status of an entity at the end of an accounting period, and income statements report income earned during an accounting period.

During financial audit, auditors obtain a sufficient understanding of the entity's internal control structure to plan the nature, timing, and extent of tests to be performed and to assess the control risk associated with the control environment and the control risk associated with control procedures for safeguarding assets that the auditors conclude are vulnerable to loss or misappropriation. For example, external auditors would most likely detect an unreported disposal of a fixed asset due to the audit objective.

Financial Statement Analysis

Financial statement analysis requires a comparison of the firm's performance with that of other firms in the same industry, with its own previous performance, and/or both. Three major parties who analyze financial statements from their own perspectives are managers of the firm to gauge performance, potential investors who want to invest in the firm by purchasing stocks and bonds, and creditors and lenders (e.g., bankers) who analyze data in financial statements to assess the firm's financial strength and its ability to pay interest and principal for the money it has been lent. Investors use data in financial statements to form expectations about future earnings and dividends and about the riskiness of these expected values. The real value of financial statements is in their predictive power about the firm's future earnings potential and dividends payment strength.

Different stakeholders look at the financial statements in different ways:

- Investors look for earnings and dividends, and this is reflected in security values. Therefore, cash flows are the major basis for security values.
- Creditors look for asset strength and the ability to pay off the debt.
- Financial statements report accounting profits.
- High accounting profits generally mean high cash flows and the ability to pay high dividends and debt payments.

Four types of measures that are used to analyze a company's financial statements and its financial position are common size analysis, trend analysis, comparative ratios, and single ratios.

Limitations of Financial Statement Ratios

Because ratios are simple to compute, convenient, and precise, they are attractive and as such a high degree of importance is attached to them. Since these ratios are only as good as the data upon which they are based, the next limitations exist.

- The use of ratio analysis could be limiting for large, multidivisional firms due to their size and complexity—two conditions that mask the results. However, ratio analysis might be useful to small firms.
- Typically, financial statements are not adjusted for price-level changes. Inflation or deflation can have a large effect on the financial data.
- Since transactions are accounted for on a cost basis, unrealized gains and losses on different asset balances are not reflected in the financial statements.
- Income ratios tend to lose credibility in cases where a significant number of estimated items exist, such as amortization and depreciation.
- Seasonal factors affect and distort ratio analysis; these distortions can be minimized by using average figures in calculations.

Limitations of Financial Statement Ratios (continued)

- Beware of “window dressing” and “earnings management” techniques used by firms to make them look financially better than they really are. In these cases, management manipulates the financial statements to impress credit analysts and stock market investors (i.e., management fraud).
- Certain off-balance-sheet items do not show up on the financial statements. For example, leased assets do not appear on the balance sheet, and the lease liability may not be shown as a debt. Therefore, leasing can improve both asset turnover and debt ratios.
- It is very difficult to attain comparability among organizations in a given industry, since different organizations utilize different accounting procedures. These different accounting procedures require identification of the basic differences in accounting from organization to organization and adjustment of the balances to achieve comparability.
- Do not take the ratios on their face value since a “good” ratio does not mean that the company is a strong one nor a “bad” ratio that the company is weak. Ratios should be evaluated and interpreted using judgment and experience and considering the firm’s characteristics and the industry’s uniqueness.

Operational Audits

Operational audits are mostly performed within a company as they are the core assurance audits. The economic events and business transactions of an entity are usually classified into several cycles for convenience of grouping similar and related activities and in order to manage the audit work more effectively and efficiently. For example, typical cycles for a manufacturing organization can include:

- Revenue
- Expenditure
- Production/conversion
- Treasury (financing/investing)
- Financial reporting (external)

The production/conversion cycle is the only one that is different between manufacturing and nonmanufacturing organizations. Regardless of the nature of the organization, an internal control structure must meet several detailed internal control objectives to prevent, detect, and correct errors, omissions, fraud, and irregularities during the handling of business transaction cycles.

Information Technology Audits

IT audits are a part of assurance audits. Over the years, significant progress has taken place in auditing computer-based information systems and operations. This includes new audit methodologies and new techniques, such as participating in systems development projects, getting involved in the implementation of new information technologies, and more auditing through the computer instead of auditing around the computer.

Compliance Audits

The scope of compliance audits can include a review of compliance with laws, rules, and regulations and compliance with an organization's policies and procedures.

Understanding Relevant Laws and Regulations

Auditors may obtain an understanding of laws and regulations through review of relevant documents and inquiry of attorneys. Generally, more audits of compliance with laws and regulations take place in the public sector than in the private sector. For example, understanding relevant laws and regulations can be important to planning a performance audit because government programs are usually created by law and are subject to more specific rules and regulations than the private sector. What is to be done, who is to do it, the goals and objectives to be achieved, the population to be served, and how much can be spent on what are usually set forth in laws and regulations. Thus, understanding the laws establishing a program can be essential to understanding the program itself. Obtaining that understanding may also be a necessary step in identifying laws and regulations that are significant to audit objectives.

Testing Compliance with Laws and Regulations

Auditors should design the audit to provide reasonable assurance about compliance with laws and regulations that are significant to audit objectives. Doing this requires determining if laws and regulations are significant to the audit objectives and, if they are, assessing the risk that significant illegal acts could occur. Based on that risk assessment, auditors design and perform procedures to provide reasonable assurance of detecting significant illegal acts.

Compliance with Laws, Rules, and Regulations

Compliance with LRRs is a major concern to the board, senior management, and internal auditors alike. Internal auditors should determine whether the board and senior management have established adequate policies and procedures for ensuring compliance with applicable LLRs.

Specifically, internal auditors should:

- Determine the frequency of testing and reporting for compliance with LRRs by reviewing:
  a. Audit schedules, scope, and reports.
  b. Minutes of board committees.
  c. The payment of any fines, penalties, or legal liabilities arising from litigation cases against the organization or its employees, officers, directors, and executives.
- Determine whether appropriate attention and follow-up are given to violations of LRRs. Consider:
  a. The significance and frequency of the violations.
  b. Management's willingness and ability to prevent reoccurrence.
  c. The inclusion of "lessons learned" from the violations of LRRs into employee and management training and development programs.

Compliance with Laws, Rules, and Regulations (continued)

An example of using an internal control questionnaire to determine compliance with the U.S. Foreign Corrupt Practices Act of 1977 is presented next. The FCPA prohibits all U.S. domestic concerns from bribing foreign governmental or political officials to obtain business or licenses in foreign countries.

1. Has the organization adopted written policies that prohibit the offering or payment of improper or illegal payments, bribes, kickbacks, or loans to or from foreign government officials? (The same question holds true for officials of a foreign government instrumentality; a foreign political party; a foreign party official; a candidate for foreign political office; or a person that the organization's employee believes will give such money to those foreign officials.)
2. Has the policy been communicated to all employees of the organization?
3. If an allowable payment is made, did the organization properly record the transaction without trying to conceal the activity?
4. Does the allowable payment consist only of a payment made to expedite or secure the performance of a routine governmental action by a foreign official, foreign political party, or foreign party official?

Compliance Management Audit Program

The key concern when conducting a compliance management audit is the cost of noncompliance (e.g., fines, penalties, imprisonment, and fees) and not so much of cost of compliance (e.g., cost of implementation, cost of training, and cost of reporting). This is because negative reputation of a company depends on noncompliance with the LRR and the cost of noncompliance. The higher the noncompliance rate is, the higher the noncompliance costs, and the greater the negative reputation costs (or the greater the loss of reputation). The compliance audit management program requires this three-step process:

1. Understand relevant LRRs.
2. Test compliance with LRRs.
3. Develop action plans to comply with LRRs.

The compliance audit can be performed by functional business analysts, independent consultants, contractors, or internal/external auditors. Based on the audit report, management should develop action plans showing the timetables and resources required to conform to the missed LRRs. A checklist describing who should do what and when would help management in implementing the action plans.

Compliance Costs and Benefits

Corporate management says it costs a significant amount of resources to comply with the often confusing and duplicating LRRs in terms of recordkeeping and monitoring activities. Management does not readily see a direct and positive benefit from compliance. Regulators, however, say these LRRs are developed with a purpose for the benefit of the entire society and that the cost of compliance should be treated as a cost of doing business. The debate is never-ending, but in the end, the government wins due to its constitutional power. A trade-off analysis should be performed between the cost of compliance and the cost of noncompliance.

Total Cost of Compliance

The total cost of compliance is both compliance costs and noncompliance costs.

Compliance costs are a combination of costs of: planning; new equipment, installation, software, and hardware; hiring and training the compliance staff; subject matter expert consulting; compiling compliance data; implementing the compliance system; reporting; continuous monitoring; and overall administrative and management supervision and follow-up efforts.

Noncompliance costs are a combination of: government fines and penalties; legal fees; court costs; case preparation costs; legal expert consulting fees; nonquantified loss of image and reputation costs resulting from negative publicity in news media and public's rejection of purchase and use of the affected company's products and services. In a way, noncompliance costs are data evidence costs incurred to show a proof-of-evidence to government regulators and authorities.

Quality Audits

Quality audits are a part of assurance audits. The audit objective is to ensure that quality department management and senior management have appropriate policies, procedures, practices, tools, and techniques to ensure the quality of products and services. Most organizations view quality of a product or service as a competitive weapon. Quality can increase revenues and sales, decrease costs, and increase profits. The internal audit scope of quality function includes review of the charter, organization chart, quality policies and procedures, quality control tools, quality costs (cost of quality), quality management tools, quality standards, applicable laws and regulations, and six-sigma metrics.

CONSULTING ENGAGEMENTS

Consulting engagements are advisory in nature with great insights provided to audit clients. These engagements solve problems and make recommendations to improve a client's operations and processes by making changes. The nature and scope of these services are agreed with the client in advance and are intended to add value and improve an organization's governance, risk management, and control processes without the internal auditor assuming management responsibility. Consulting audits are boundaryless work with freely defined scope leading to flexible and customized scope of work (e.g., strategic management reviews and agile audits). Consulting auditors should not design, implement, or approve any operating policies or procedures resulting from their recommendations made during the consulting work. Moreover, they should not be involved in asset valuation activities and other management functions such as decision making.

From a higher-level perspective, consulting audits can be viewed from three different time horizons: past, present, and future.

Retrospective reviews are look-backward and postmortem reviews focusing on the past. The objective review results show "lessons learned" from adverse events that occurred in the past such as fraud, bribes, cyberattacks, and data breaches. They move from Present ⟶ Past.

Prospective reviews are look-forward and before-the-fact reviews focusing on the future. The limited review results show how a company is prepared and ready to handle new changes, new products, new services, new regulations, and new technologies. They move from Present ⟶ Future.

CONSULTING ENGAGEMENTS (CONTINUED)

Hindsight reviews are look-afterward and "what went wrong" reviews focusing on the past. The subjective review results show how control weaknesses have occurred, why the three-lines-of-defense mechanisms did not work, and how control features have failed. They move from Present ⟶ Past.

Contemporary reviews are look-now and "what can go wrong" reviews focusing on the present. The customized review results show how unforeseen and unexpected crisis situations are happening today and how to react quickly to handle and control those conditions (e.g., agile audits). They move from Past ⟶ Present.

Consulting services may include counsel, advice, facilitation, and training, which are nonassurance services. An internal auditor's role in consulting engagements is different from that of assurance engagements due to different objectives and outcomes, meaning auditors wear different hats and play different roles. Under these conflicting situations, the best audit practice is not to assign the same auditor performing the assurance engagement and consulting engagement on the same audit area of interest. The consulting engagement steps consist of defining problems, developing alternatives, selecting the best alternative, and implementing the best alternative.

Specifically, consulting engagements can include 18 topics:

1. Strategic management reviews
2. Agile audits
3. System design and development reviews
4. Due diligence reviews

CONSULTING ENGAGEMENTS (CONTINUED)

5. Business process reviews
6. Benchmarking studies
7. Balanced scorecard reviews
8. Control self-assessments
9. Internal control assessments
10. Business process mapping reviews
11. Internal control training
12. Big-data audit
13. Big-data modeling
14. Data-quality audit
15. Outsourcing reviews
16. Conflicts of interest reviews
17. Code of ethics reviews
18. Workplace safety audit

Each consulting engagement is discussed next.

Strategic Management Reviews

Consulting auditors can conduct strategic management reviews at a higher-level scope than the traditional assurance auditors in order to provide insight and advice for strategic objective setting, the strategic decision-making process, governance structures, and risk management processes. The main reason for focusing on the higher-level scope of work is that the audit-clients for consulting services are the high-level management such as board members and senior management. However, consulting auditors do not establish the organization's strategic policies or make business decisions; these are the rights and responsibilities of company management. However, consulting auditors can influence company management by asking the right questions about the strategic objectives and their underlying assumptions. Note that consulting auditors should not second-guess decisions of company management. Consulting auditors have a duty to report deficiencies in the strategic management process and can make recommendations for improving the process. If consulting auditors do not conduct strategic management reviews, inappropriate and incorrect strategic decisions could be made, leading to operational risks, which are contrary to the organization's risk appetite. Operational risks result from ineffective and inefficient policies, procedures, practices, processes, and controls that consulting auditors did not review. In other words, strategic management reviews could have prevented these operational risks from occurring.

Strategic Management Reviews (continued)

Possible topics in the strategic management review can include reviews of:

- Mergers, acquisitions, and divestitures plans
- Corporate restructuring and reorganization strategies
- Corporate transitional activities
- Due diligence
- New product and services introductions
- Capital investment plans and projects
- Deployment of new technologies
- Impact of new laws and regulations

Tools to Use During Strategic Management Reviews

Consulting auditors have several tools at their disposal during the review of strategic management processes, including SWOT analysis, market-opportunity matrix analysis, fit-gap analysis, force-field analysis, and scenario analysis.

- Strengths, weaknesses, opportunities, and threats (SWOT) analysis focuses on internal and external environments of a company. Specifically, it focuses on strategies; competitors; core competencies of products, services, and employees; and government laws.
- Market-opportunity matrix analysis focuses only on the external environment. Specifically, it focuses on customers, products, and markets.
- Fit-gap analysis focuses only on the internal environment. Specifically, it focuses on what fits and what does not fit (gap). It is also known as gap analysis.
- Force-field analysis identifies all inhibiting and facilitating forces or positive and negative variables acting on a specific situation at hand, whether those situations are internal or external to an organization. This is a problem-solving tool.
- Scenario analysis provides different outputs (strategic outcomes) for different inputs (strategy variables) using different strategic scenarios, such as best scenario, most likely scenario, and worst scenario.

Agile Audits

Agile audits are based on audit intelligence gathered by auditors during their previous routine audit work combined with business intelligence. Auditors take on a specific current issue facing their company to review and report the results to the board and senior management. Agile audits are audit-initiated projects without any special requests from the board and senior management. Agile audits focus on anticipating and predicting problems, issues, and adverse events before they happen (i.e., like wearing management's hat and keeping eyes and ears open).

Basically, agile audits focus on crisis situations (e.g., product contamination, product recalls, cyber-attacks, data security breaches, ransomware demands, management scandals, plant shutdowns and strikes, service breakdowns, and website crashes) and critical issues (e.g., legal, ethical, and social matters facing the company such as corruption, bribery, and pollution scandals). Agile audits require internal auditors to be adaptable, flexible, and resourceful, with proactive thinking and forward-looking attitudes.

Agile Auditors ⟶ Anticipate Plus Respond Plus Improve

Doing this requires that the speed of the audit work matches the speed of the business work, and the scope and size of the audit work changes as the risks to the business change.

Scope of Agile Audits = Audit Intelligence + Business Intelligence

Agile Audits (continued)

Agile audits concentrate on two major things: threats and opportunities. Doing this requires internal consulting auditors and external consultants to identify immediate and current threats facing an organization and major business opportunities available to the organization and to seize them in a timely manner. Agile audits occur only rarely but have big impact, either positive or negative, that can increase or decrease the reputation risk facing the organization. The impact can be felt in strategic and operational areas of the company. These threats and opportunities are further detailed next.

MAJOR THREATS TO AN ORGANIZATION

Major threats are crisis situations. Examples follow.

- A company is experiencing product recalls due to products causing serious accidents and customer deaths.
- A company is experiencing product contaminations causing health-related problems and customer deaths.
- A company is experiencing product hazards causing accidents and customer deaths.
- Corporate scandals have arisen due to insider trading deals by the board of directors, CEO, and senior management.
- Major new regulations have been introduced that can increase the costs of compliance.

Agile Audits (continued)

- Excessive regulatory fines and penalties have been announced for violating LRRs.
- There are lawsuits due to mishandled or mistreated customers, suppliers, and employees during the course of day-to-day work.
- Sudden natural disasters, such as cyclones, hurricanes, tornadoes, wildfires, and mudslides, displace the labor workforce and result in unoccupied business facilities.
- There is increased online shopping cart abandonment for retailers and nonretailers, resulting in lost sales and lost profits.
- Lawsuits have been filed due to bid rigging and price discrimination.
- Frequent website crashes and shutdowns are creating inconveniences to customers and lost sales to companies.
- Lawsuits have been filed for data breaches from hacking, stealing, and selling customers' personal and financial data.

Agile Audits (continued)

Opportunities: Major Opportunities for an Organization

Major opportunities are strategic and operational situations. Examples follow.

- Major deregulations have been announced that can decrease the costs of compliance with LRRs.
- Reduced corporate tax rates lead to new investments in new goods, new services, and new facilities (e.g., offices, warehouses, and plants).
- Competitors have exited current market segments.
- A company's R&D department has discovered a new product with big projections in revenues and market share.
- New mergers and acquisitions that can reduce operating costs and increase operating income have been announced.
- New sales leads and deals, new markets, new products, new services, and new business partners have been announced.
- A competitor is experiencing product recalls, contaminations, and hazards that are open to further exploration and analysis so useful lessons can be learned.

Agile auditors are resourceful and competent with known expertise. They can take on a very challenging work that is important to the board of directors, CEO, and senior management of a company.

System Design and Development Reviews

IT consulting engagements can vary from organization to organization and may include several projects, such as IT strategic planning, computer capacity planning, business and IT continuity planning, customer service, and system design and development reviews.

Auditor Role

Regarding system design and development project, the internal auditor should find out first whether a system development methodology is in place. A methodology can improve the quality of systems, decrease system development and maintenance costs, and increase user service levels and satisfaction. Once a methodology is in place, the internal auditor must ensure the proper application of such a methodology. Another area of focus for the auditor is project control to reduce time delays and cost overruns. Internal auditors should refrain from designing and installing any computer system for their organizations. However, they can consult, review, and evaluate any computer system.

During a system development consulting engagement, the internal auditor should:

- Determine whether the IT steering committee approves major system development and maintenance projects as part of its charter.

Auditor Role (continued)

- Review the user's system service request to determine the need for a new system development or maintenance project. Understand the business need for the project.
- Review the feasibility study report for understanding of technical, functional, and economic requirements. Determine whether time and budget estimates are achievable.
- Review general system design to ensure complete coverage of user business needs. Determine whether design of controls is adequate.
- Review detailed system design for inputs (transactions with volumes, input screen formats), process (logic and flow), and outputs (report layouts, output screen formats, and file contents).
- Review system conversion and test plans to determine their adequacy and timing.
- Review system training plans to determine whether appropriate user parties will be trained to do their job properly with the new system.
- Review system implementation plans to determine whether the new system will be implemented all at once or with a phased approach.

Application Design and Development

Timely participation of auditors in the application system development process is based on the belief that early detection and correction of inadequate and incomplete controls planned during the system design phase will save time and money in the long run. This is because of the expensive nature of bringing up inadequate controls to an acceptable level at a later stage when the same system is put into operational status. Ideally, controls should be built in rather than built on.

The auditor's participation in the system development and maintenance project may take the form of continuous or intermittent reviews and tests. It is important to note that the application systems development and maintenance process should be reviewed against IT standards or methodology.

The degree of auditor participation really depends on the audit staff's time availability and required skills and on the riskiness of the phase and the application system. Some phases are considered to be more critical from the standpoint of the auditor's contribution to the system development process. The auditor should participate in the early phases where critical decisions are made regarding system requirements, control/security requirements, design approaches, and software testing plans and approaches. The auditor should also participate during file/system conversion and postimplementation reviews.

Due Diligence Reviews

Due Diligence Defined

Due diligence is a legal concept that means exerting proper care in all important matters of interest in business situations. Basically, it contains three legal terms: due diligence, due care, and due regard. At least two parties are involved in a due diligence review or investigation. The first party reviews the performance of the second party before agreeing to do new business between these two parties. A due diligence review is a process by itself, but it does not suggest how that process needs to be carried out (i.e., no guidance on methods, tools, and techniques). Note that due diligence reviews can be conducted either by internal employees or by external third parties. The three legal concepts of due diligence, due care, and due regard are similar to the prudent-man or reasonable-person concept or the reasonable-basis requirement.

Due diligence involves preassessment, examination, analysis, and reporting on major activities with due care before they are finalized or approved by management. Its purpose is to minimize potential risks from undertaking new businesses and ventures and participating in mergers, acquisitions, and divestitures. Due diligence requires organizations to develop and implement an effective system of controls, policies, and procedures to prevent and detect violation of policies and laws. It requires that organizations have taken minimum and necessary steps in their power and authority to prevent and detect violation of policies and laws. In other words, due diligence is the care that a reasonable person exercises under the circumstances to avoid harm to other persons or to their property. A **due diligence defense** is available to a defendant in that it makes the defendant not liable if the defendant's actions are reasonable and are proven.

What Is Due Diligence Anyway?

Due diligence is exercising due care, normal care, usual care, reasonable care, possible care, or ordinary care. It also means meeting or satisfying minimal standards expected of others (i.e., standard of care or required care).

Due diligence is *not* exercising abnormal care, unusual care, unreasonable care, impossible care, extraordinary care, or absolute care.

Due diligence is *not* exercising more care or less care, only just care or right care.

Due diligence is *not* exercising gross negligence or wrong care.

Scope of Due Diligence Reviews

The scope of due diligence reviews can include performing investigations such as before:

- Selecting a new supplier, vendor, distributor, dealer, wholesaler, or sales agent
- Entering into a contract with a third party
- Buying a new franchise business
- Opening a new account in a bank

Scope of Due Diligence Reviews (continued)

- Acquiring a new company
- Merging with an existing company
- Divesting a part or whole of a company
- Hiring a new external service provider such as a third-party firm, outsourced vendor, audit quality assessor, or audit consultants
- Hiring or selecting a new business partner
- A securities issuer offers asset-backed securities
- A securities broker-dealer sells securities to investors
- An investment advisor selects alternative investments, such as hedge funds, private equity, venture capital, and private funds
- Hiring a new employee with proper background checks or hiring a new executive with an employment contract
- Contracting into new/current markets with new/current products and services

Why Perform Due Diligence Reviews?

In a way, due diligence reviews can be viewed as precautionary reviews, check-it-out procedures, or compatibility tests before getting into new business ventures. Compatibility tests determine whether the business models and management styles of two separate companies fit together. The goal is to make sure the two companies' technology is proper, people are good, management has integrity, and that people, facilities, and products and services meet expectations. Due diligence reviews can also be viewed in terms of insurance policies, meaning the reviews will protect the insured when needed. If due diligence reviews are not performed in a timely and proper manner, the company may be exposed to various types of risks (e.g., governance, strategic, operational, compliance, reputation, and legal risk), financial losses, litigation cases, and loss of reputation due to people's unexpected behaviors. Hence, the more complete the due diligence review, the better the chances that potential risks for both companies will be reduced. Due diligence reviews are needed only for major projects, not for everyday routine work.

Due Diligence Review Approach

The due diligence review approach includes:

- Reviewing plans and contracts for mergers, acquisitions, and divestitures activities.
- Analyzing request for proposal and request for services documents when hiring external service providers and external assessors to evaluate audit quality; reviewing major and complex contracts with third parties (e.g., new marketing agents, dealers, distributors, and suppliers).
- Reviewing outsourced vendor contracts, facilities, and systems (e.g., outsourcing of human resources, supply chain, manufacturing, logistics, finance, accounting, internal audit, legal, and tax services).
- Any other special projects.

Due diligence audits provide a safety valve to management that is planning to acquire, manage, or consolidate with other businesses. Joint ventures and environmental audits are also subject to due diligence audits. These audits are the minimum managerial requirements to ensure that all applicable laws and regulations are met and that risks and exposures are minimized. For example, due diligence audits are a risk management tool for banks, land buyers, and lending agencies when a buyer is purchasing land or accepting it as a gift. Here the buyer wants to minimize the potential legal liability resulting from the land acquisition.

Due Diligence Review Approach (continued)

Due diligence audits are a team-based effort with internal auditors, external auditors, lawyers, engineers, IT staff, and other specialists. These audits consist of three phases: information gathering (phase 1), information analysis (phase 2), and information reporting (phase 3). Information gathering involves collecting information through document reviews, interviews, and meetings. Information analysis may include analytical reviews, including ratio analysis, regression analysis, and other quantitative techniques. Information reporting includes writing a balanced report based on facts with an executive summary. In addition to writing reports, oral reports can be used for immediate response and clarification of issues and findings.

However, due diligence reviews do not guarantee a business success, and they do not discover all actual and potential risks because people, who have their own built-in limitations, conduct these reviews. Not doing a due diligence review at all is pure gross negligence.

Business Process Reviews

The scope of business process reviews includes two topics, business process reengineering (BPR) and business process improvement (BPI).

Business Process Reengineering

In an effort to increase revenues and market growth, organizations are conducting business process reviews. The idea behind business process reviews, whether for a production process or a service process, is to streamline operations and eliminate waste. The result is increased efficiencies, which can lead to greater effectiveness. A proven technique is BPR, which requires big thinking and making major, radical changes in the business processes. Work flow analysis is a part of BPR.

BPR is one approach for redesigning the way work is done to support the organization's mission and reduce costs. BPR starts with a high-level assessment of the organization's mission, strategic goals, and customer needs. Basic questions are asked, such as: Does our mission need to be redefined? Are our strategic goals aligned with our mission? Who are our customers? An organization may find that it is operating on questionable assumptions, particularly in terms of the wants and needs of its customers. Only after the organization rethinks *what* it should be doing does it go on to decide *how* best to do it.

Within the framework of this basic assessment of mission and goals, reengineering focuses on the organization's business processes: the steps and procedures that govern how resources are used to create products and services that meet the needs of particular customers or markets. As a structured ordering of work steps across time and place, a business process can be decomposed into specific activities, measured, modeled, and improved. It can also be completely redesigned or eliminated altogether. Reengineering identifies, analyzes, and redesigns an organization's core business processes with the aim of achieving dramatic improvements in critical performance measures, such as cost, quality, service, and speed.

Business Process Reengineering (continued)

Reengineering recognizes that an organization's business processes are usually fragmented into subprocesses and tasks that are carried out by several specialized functional areas within the organization. Often no one is responsible for the overall performance of the entire process. Reengineering maintains that optimizing the performance of subprocesses can result in some benefits but cannot yield dramatic improvements if the process itself is fundamentally inefficient and outmoded. For that reason, reengineering focuses on redesigning the process as a whole in order to achieve the greatest possible benefits to the organization and its customers. This drive for realizing dramatic improvements by fundamentally rethinking how the organization's work should be done distinguishes reengineering from BPI efforts that focus on functional or incremental improvement.

Reengineering is not a panacea. There are occasions when functional or incremental improvements are the method of choice, as when a process is basically sound or when the organization is not prepared to undergo dramatic change. When there is a need to achieve order-of-magnitude improvements, reengineering is the method of choice.

Business Process Improvement

BPI should be continuous, not discrete, and it tends to be more of an incremental change that may affect only a single task or segment of the organization. The concept of fundamental or radical change is the basis of the major difference between BPR and BPI. Quite often BPI initiatives limit their focus to a single existing organizational unit. This in itself breaks one of the tenets of BPR, which is that BPR must focus on redesigning a fundamental business process, not existing departments or organizational units. While BPR seeks to define what the processes should be, BPI focuses more on how to improve an existing process or service.

Through BPI, organizations can achieve significant incremental improvements in service delivery and other business factors (e.g., increase in employee's productivity). The expected outcomes of BPI are not as dramatic as those associated with BPR initiatives, but the process is also not as traumatic as in achieving the radical changes seen with BPR. In many cases, incremental changes may be achieved in situations lacking the support necessary for more radical changes.

BUSINESS PROCESS REENGINEERING VERSUS BUSINESS PROCESS IMPROVEMENT

- BPR focuses on achieving dramatic improvements.
- BPI focuses on achieving incremental improvements.

Benchmarking Studies

Benchmarking Defined

Benchmarking is the selection of best practices implemented by other organizations. **Best practices** are the best ways to perform a business process. Organizational change and improvement are the major elements of benchmarking. Benchmarks are the result of a study of organizational processes and performance through internal comparisons (i.e., between and among a company's business units and divisions) and external comparisons (i.e., between two or more outside organizations). The first-level, basic processes that define a company's operations are listed next.

- Understanding markets and customers
- Designing products and services
- Marketing and selling those products and services
- Producing what customers need and want
- Delivering products and services
- Providing service to customers

Benchmarking Defined (continued)

Supporting these basic processes, management and support processes maximize the value with the use of human resources, information technology, and financial/physical resources.

The best way to practice benchmarking is to:

- Analyze business processes (inventory major business processes, conduct documentary research, and attend conferences to understand new developments).
- Plan the benchmark study (define scope, request site visits, and develop a methodology for capturing the new data).
- Conduct the benchmark study (analyze best practices and identify performance gaps).
- Implement the benchmark results (incorporate best practices into business processes and reevaluate the business processes).

Types of Benchmarking

Two types of benchmarking exist: business process benchmarking and computer system benchmarking. Business process benchmarking deals with BPI and BPR to reduce costs and to improve quality and customer service. Computer system benchmarking focuses on computer hardware/software acquisition, computer system design, computer capacity planning, and system performance. Each has its own place and time.

Business benchmarking is an external focus on internal activities, functions, or operations in order to achieve continuous improvement. The objective is to understand existing processes and activities and then to identify an external point of reference, or standards, by which that activity can be measured or judged. A benchmark can be established at any level of the organization in any functional area, whether manufacturing or service industries. The ultimate goal is to attain a competitive edge by being better than the best.

Value creation is the heart of organizational activity, whether in a profit or a nonprofit entity. Benchmarking provides the metrics by which to understand and judge the value provided by the organization and its resources. Benchmarking focuses on continuous improvements and value creation for stakeholders (i.e., owners, customers, employees, and suppliers), utilizing the best practices to focus improvement efforts.

Benchmarking targets the critical success factors for a specific organization. It considers the mission of an organization, its resources, products, markets, management skills, and others. It requires an identification of customer(s), whether internal or external to the organization. Benchmarking is an early warning system of impending problems and is not a onetime measurement. Benchmarking can focus on improving organization structures, analyzing managerial roles, improving production processes, and developing strategic issues.

Sources of Information for Benchmarking

Benchmarking can be done by using published materials, insights gained at trade association meetings, and conversations with industry experts, customers, suppliers, academics, and others.

The Right Time for Business Process Benchmarking

Benchmarking should be undertaken when "triggers" are present. These triggers can arise internally or externally in response to information needs from some other major project or issue or problem in the company. Examples of these triggers include quality programs, cost reduction programs, new management, new ventures, and competitive moves. Benchmarking should be done as needed, without any preconceived notions.

Reasons for Business Process Benchmarking

A company should benchmark for three reasons:

1. It wants to attain world-class competitive capability.
2. It wants to prosper in a global economy.
3. It simply wishes to survive (desperation).

Reasons for Business Process Benchmarking (continued)

A company can benchmark in six distinct ways:

1. Internal benchmarking
2. Competitive benchmarking
3. Industry benchmarking
4. Best-in-class benchmarking
5. Process benchmarking
6. Strategic benchmarking

Internal benchmarking is the analysis of existing practices within various departments or divisions of the organization, looking for best performance as well as identifying baseline activities and drivers. Drivers are the causes of work: the trigger that sets in motion a series of actions or activities that will respond to the requests or demands by the stockholders.

In doing internal benchmarking, management is looking downward, examining itself first before looking for outside information. Significant improvements are often made during the internal analysis stage of the benchmarking process. Value-added activities are identified and non-value-adding steps are removed from the process. Internal benchmarking is the first step because it provides the framework for comparing existing internal practices

Reasons for Business Process Benchmarking (continued)

to external benchmark data. Internal benchmarking focuses on specific value chains or sequences of driver-activity combinations.

Competitive benchmarking looks outward to identify how other direct competitors are performing. Knowing the strengths and weaknesses of competitors provides good input for strategic and corrective actions.

Industry benchmarking extends beyond the one-to-one comparison of competitive benchmarking to look for trends. It is still limited in the number of innovations and new ideas it can uncover because every company is following every other company in the industry. At best, industry benchmarking can help establish the performance baseline or can give an incremental gain. It gives a short-run solution and a quick fix to an existing problem. However, it does not support quantum leaps or breakthroughs in performance since the comparison is limited to one industry.

Best-in-class benchmarking looks across multiple industries in search of new, innovative practices, no matter what their source. Best-in-class benchmarking is the ultimate goal of the benchmarking process. It supports quantum leaps in performance and gives a long-run competitive advantage.

Process benchmarking centers on key work processes, such as distribution, order entry, or employee training. This type of benchmarking identifies the most effective practices in companies that perform similar functions, no matter in what industry.

Strategic benchmarking examines how companies compete and seeks the winning strategies that have led to competitive advantage and market success.

Reasons for Business Process Benchmarking (continued)

WHICH BENCHMARKING DOES WHAT?

- Internal benchmarking looks downward and inward.
- Competitive benchmarking looks outward.
- Industry benchmarking looks for trends. It provides a short-run solution and a quick fix to a problem.
- Best-in-class benchmarking looks for the best all around. It provides a quantum jump in improvement.
- Process benchmarking is specific.
- Strategic benchmarking is broad with big impact.

Balanced Scorecard Reviews

Most businesses have traditionally relied on organizational performance based almost solely on financial or accounting-based data (e.g., ROI and earnings per share [EPS]) and manufacturing data (e.g., factory productivity, direct labor efficiency, and machine utilization). Unfortunately, many of these indicators are inaccurate and stress quantity over quality. They reward the wrong behavior; lack predictive power; do not capture key business changes until it is too late; reflect functions, not cross-functional processes; and give inadequate consideration to difficult-to-quantify resources such as intellectual capital. Most measures are focused on cost, not so much on quality.

Kaplan and Norton of Harvard Business School coined the term "balanced scorecard" in response to the limitations of traditional financial and accounting measures. They recommend that key performance measures should be aligned with strategies and action plans of the organization. They suggest translating the strategy into measures that uniquely communicate the vision of the organization. Setting targets for each measure provides the basis for strategy deployment, feedback, and review.

The balanced scorecard system is a comprehensive management control system that balances traditional financial measures with nonfinancial measures (e.g., customer service, internal business processes, and the organization's capacity for innovation and learning). This system helps managers focus on key performance measures and communicate them clearly throughout the organization.

Balanced Scorecard Reviews (continued)

Kaplan and Norton divided the strategy-balanced scorecard into four perspectives or categories:

1. **Financial perspective.** The financial strategy focuses on matters from the perspective of the shareholder. It measures the ultimate results that the business provides to its shareholders, including profitability, revenue growth (net income), ROI, economic value-added, residual income, costs, risks, and shareholder value. Financial measures are lagging measures (lag indicators); they report on outcomes, the consequences of past actions. They tell what has happened. The financial perspective is looking back.

2. **Internal business process perspective.** The internal business process focuses on strategic priorities for various business processes, which create customer and shareholder satisfaction. It focuses attention on the performance of the key internal processes that drive the business, including such measures as quality levels, efficiency, productivity, cycle time, production and operating statistics such as order fulfillment or cost per order. Internal process measures are leading measures (lead indicators); they predict what will happen. The internal process theme reflects the organization value chain. The internal process (operations) perspective is looking from the inside out.

3. **Customer perspective.** The customer strategy is aimed at creating value and differentiation from the perspective of the customer. It focuses on customer needs and satisfaction as well as market share, including service levels, satisfaction ratings, loyalty, perception, and repeat business. The customer perspective is looking from the outside in.

Balanced Scorecard Reviews (continued)

4. **Innovation and learning perspective.** The innovation and learning strategy sets priorities to create a climate that supports organizational change, innovation, and growth. It directs attention to the basis of a future success—the organization's people and infrastructure. Key measures might include intellectual assets, employee satisfaction and retention, market innovation (new product introductions), employee training and skills development, research and development (R&D) investment, R&D pipeline, and time to market a product or service. Innovation and learning perspective is looking ahead.

Measures should include both financial and nonfinancial. Financial measures include ROI, residual income, EPS, profit, cost, and sales. Nonfinancial measures include customer measures, internal business process measures, innovation and learning measures, and manufacturing measures. Customer measures include satisfaction, perception, and loyalty. Internal business process measures include efficiency, quality, and time. Innovation and learning measures include R&D investment, R&D pipeline, skills and training for employees, and time to market a product or service. Manufacturing measures include factory productivity, direct labor efficiency, and machine utilization.

A good balanced scorecard system contains both leading and lagging indicators and both financial and nonfinancial measures. For example, customer survey (performance drivers) about recent transactions might be a leading indicator for customer retention (a lagging indicator); employee satisfaction might be a leading indicator for employee turnover (a lagging indicator); and so on. These measures and indicators should also establish cause-and-effect relationships across the four perspectives. The cause-and-effect linkages describe the path by which improvements in the capabilities of intangible assets (people) get translated into tangible customer satisfaction and financial outcomes.

The balanced scorecard provides graphical representation on strategy maps and provides a logical and comprehensive way to describe strategy. They communicate clearly the organization's desired outcomes and describe how these outcomes can be achieved. Both business units and their employees will understand the strategy and identify how they can contribute by becoming aligned to the strategy.

WHICH SCORECARD PERSPECTIVE IS WHICH?

- The financial perspective is looking back.
- The internal process perspective is looking from inside out.
- The customer perspective is looking from outside in.
- The innovation and learning perspective is looking ahead.

Strategy Scorecards

Kaplan and Norton recommend that key performance measures should be aligned with strategies and action plans of the organization. They suggest translating the strategy into measures that uniquely communicate the vision of the organization. Setting targets for each measure provides the basis for strategy deployment, feedback, and review.

They divided the strategy-balanced scorecard into four perspectives or categories as follows:

1. **Financial perspective.** It measures the ultimate results that the business provides to its shareholders, including profitability, revenue growth (net income), ROI, economic value added, residual income, and shareholder value. Financial measures are lagging measures (lag indicators); they report on outcomes, the consequences of past actions. They tell what has happened. The financial perspective is looking back.

2. **Customer perspective.** It focuses on customer needs and satisfaction as well as market share, including service levels, satisfaction ratings, loyalty, perception, and repeat business. The customer perspective is looking from the outside in.

Strategy Scorecards (continued)

3. **Internal perspective.** It focuses attention on the performance of the key internal processes that drive the business, including such measures as quality levels, efficiency, productivity, cycle time, production and operating statistics such as order fulfillment or cost per order. Internal process measures are leading measures (lead indicators); they predict what will happen. The internal process theme reflects the organization value chain. The internal process (operations) perspective is looking from the inside out.

4. **Learning and growth perspective.** It directs attention to the basis of a future success—the organization's people and infrastructure. Key measures might include intellectual assets, employee satisfaction and retention, market innovation (new product introductions), employee training and skills development, research and development (R&D) investment, R&D pipeline, and time to market. Learning and growth perspective is looking ahead.

Strategy scorecards provide graphical representation on strategy maps and a logical and comprehensive way to describe strategy. They communicate clearly the organization's desired outcomes and describe how these outcomes can be achieved. Both business units and their employees will understand the strategy and identify how they can contribute by becoming aligned to the strategy.

Control Self-Assessments

Control self-assessments (CSAs) deal with evaluating the system of internal control in any organization. CSAs are a shared responsibility among all employees in the organization, not just internal auditing or senior management. The examination of the internal control environment is conducted within a structured, documented, and repetitive process. The formal assessment approach takes place in workshop sessions with business users as participants (process owners) and internal auditors as facilitators (subject matter experts) and non-facilitators (note takers). The purpose of the sessions is conversation and mutual discovery and information sharing.

Two types of people conduct internal audit engagements: internal auditors and noninternal auditors. Auditors conducting audit engagements are based on an audit plan and include assurance audits, consulting audits, and compliance audits.

The work of nonauditors performing audit-related work includes self-assessments of risks and controls, which are proactive in nature, meaning nonauditors are reviewing, assessing, and evaluating their own work. These self-assessments, although not traditional audits, are conducted by audit clients (functional employees and managers of business unit), consultants, and process owners. Usually process owners are a part of audit clients.

Self-assessments mean self-reviews, self-examinations, self-tests, self-evaluations, self-rating, self-ranking, self-grading, self-certifications, and self-reporting of a business function, department, operation, process, or system, which are conducted by nonauditors after they are trained and are facilitated by internal auditors, using questionnaires, templates, and checklists. Note that internal auditors do not prepare or develop the questionnaires; do not conduct the self-assessments; and do not write the self-assessment reports. Instead, nonauditors do this work. Here, internal auditors act as facilitators of self-assessments, not as regular auditors.

There are obvious benefits to audit clients and internal auditors from these self-assessments. Benefits to audit clients include (1) identifying strengths and weaknesses in their business functions, (2) establishing controls to minimize significant risks, (3) using them as an exercise of risk awareness, and (4) injecting control consciousness into them. Benefits to internal auditors are that the self-assessments can reduce the overall scope of audit to some extent and increase audit efficiency to some extent due to time and effort saved from prior work done by the audit clients during the self-assessments.

Participants in the self-assessments exercise with specific roles include:

- Audit client employees, supervisors, and consultants conducting self-assessments
- Process owners performing self-evaluations
- Audit client managers issuing self-certifications, similar to the CEO and CFO certifying their company's financial statements

Control Self-Assessments (continued)

- Internal auditors acting as trainers, facilitators, and subject matter experts on risks and control matters, including note takers (nonfacilitators) during training classes and workshops given to audit clients

Note that the original audit-clients who were trained by internal auditors can later train other employees (i.e., train the trainer) in either the same department or other departments. These specific roles are briefly presented next.

Audit clients conduct self-assessments (i.e., client-facilitated).

Process owners perform self-evaluations (i.e., client-facilitated).

Audit client managers issue self-certifications (i.e., client-facilitated).

Auditors act as trainers, facilitators, subject matter experts, and note takers during training classes and workshops and later review and use the self-assessment results only after independent validations and verifications (audit-facilitated).

Auditors should use professional skepticism and professional judgment when reviewing, understanding, and using the results of self-assessments prepared by audit clients due to their built-in bias of reviewing and evaluating their own work (i.e., a strong motive to look good). When audit clients conduct self-assessments,

Control Self-Assessments (continued)

two outcomes are possible due to their little or no experience in conducting risk and control assessments: false positive results and false negative results. A **false positive result** can occur when a business activity or control is rated as effective when it is ineffective. A **false negative result** can occur when a business activity or control is rated as ineffective when it is effective. Internal auditors need to understand the reasons for these ratings of effective or ineffective and proceed further with caution.

FALSE POSITIVE RESULT VERSUS FALSE NEGATIVE RESULT

- **A false positive result** can occur when a business activity or control is rated as effective when it is ineffective.
- A **false negative result** can occur when a business activity or control is rated as ineffective when it is effective.

Internal Control Assessments

An organization's internal control system should, with reasonable assurance, help prevent or detect:

- Inaccurate, incomplete, or unauthorized transactions.
- Deficiencies in the safeguarding of assets.
- Unreliable financial and regulatory reporting.
- Violations of laws or regulations.
- Deviations from an organization's own policies and procedures.

With so much at stake, the board and senior management can request consulting auditors to perform internal control assessments in one line of business or in all lines.

A suggested audit work program to perform internal control assessments is presented next.

- Determine whether policies and procedures exist to ensure that decisions are made with appropriate management approvals and authorizations for business transactions and activities.
- Determine whether business processes exist to ensure that:
  - Customer accounts are reconciled continually, independently, and in a timely manner and that outstanding items, both on balance sheet and off balance sheet, are resolved and cleared.

Internal Control Assessments (continued)

- Policy overrides are kept to minimum levels and that exceptions are reported to management.
  - Employees in sensitive positions or risk-taking activities do not have absolute control over their own work areas. This control goal is accomplished through segregation of duties, rotation of jobs, or vacation requirements for employees.
  - Restricting access to sensitive assets or records.
  - Implementing dual control or joint-custody policies over access to sensitive assets.
- Determine whether reporting lines within a line of business or functional area provide sufficient independence of the control function, such as the internal audit function, from the other functions through organizational structure and status and separation of duties.
- Determine whether operating practices conflict with established areas of responsibility and control in terms of unethical and illegal practices.
- Determine whether the internal audit function is sufficiently independent through proper organizational structure and status and reporting levels.
- Determine whether the company management unduly influences the timeliness of performing risk analysis and control evaluations and their reporting to the board.

Business Process Mapping Reviews

The scope of business process mapping review includes understanding the purpose of a business process and knowing how to use charts and graphs to map a business process, activity, or function with the goal of improving it.

Process maps include relationship maps, cross-functional process maps, and flowcharts.

Relationship maps show the customer-supplier relationships or linkages that exist between parts of an organization. These maps show the big-picture view that shows how the major functions of the business interact with each other. Relationship maps can also be used to show any individual function.

Cross-functional process maps show how an organization's major work processes cut across several functions. These maps show the sequence of steps that make up the work process as well as the inputs and outputs associated with each process step.

Process maps can be used in a variety of ways, such as to:

- Orient new employees.
- Organize work.
- Clarify employee roles and contributions.
- Identify improvement opportunities.

Business Process Mapping Reviews (continued)

- Reduce cycle time.
- Measure performance.

For example, cross-functional process maps and flowcharts can be used to reduce costs, reduce defects, conduct benchmarks, and reengineer a process. Similarly, relationship maps, cross-functional process maps, and flowcharts can be used to design performance measurement systems and to measure customer satisfaction.

Flowcharts are good to illustrate work processes since they help define, document, and analyze processes at the detailed level, especially about the individual performing the work or developing the work procedures step by step. Flowcharts are presented in more detail next.

Flowcharts

Flowcharts are most valuable in providing a summary outline and overall description of the process of transactions in a system. The objective of a flowchart is to present a clear and concise picture and description of a system or operation, whether manual or automated. This description provides a basis for an understanding of information flow and for subsequent audit work required in testing and evaluating internal controls. Usually flowcharts are supplemented by other forms of documentation, such as narratives, policies and procedures, internal control questionnaires, or interviews.

Flowcharts are used in business functions other than auditing. Flowcharts are increasingly the focus now due to TQM programs. Flowcharting is the most effective way to describe how a process works now, how to fix it when it does not work, and how it is going to be improved in the future. To improve a process, repetitive tasks or activities need to be looked at for streamlining, to improve consistency and quality, and to reduce confusion.

Another use of flowcharting is to improve and facilitate training. People learn more quickly with a flowchart because they can see and understand the process as a whole—a picture is worth 1,000 words.

Charts and Graphs

The basic purpose of a chart or graph is to give a visual comparison between two or more things. For example, changes in budget from one year to the next may be represented in a graph. One significant reason for visualizing a comparison is to reinforce its comprehension.

Charts and graphs are used to dramatize a statement, a fact, a point of view, or an idea. Visual aids assist in the quick comprehension of both simple and complex data, statistics, or problems.

A chart should explain itself in silence; it should be completely understood without the assistance of a caption. The caption must act only as reinforcement to its comprehension.

Various charts, such as tabular charts, column charts, bar charts, pie charts, line charts, layer charts, and radar charts are discussed briefly.

The **tabular chart** is used to represent items of interest. It requires a fair amount of study in order to grasp the full meaning of the figures. This is because it takes longer to digest the meaning of an itemization of compiled figures than if the same figures are presented graphically. The **column chart**, which is vertical, is most commonly used for demonstrating a comparison between two or more things.

The **Gantt chart,** a bar chart, is essentially a column chart on its side, and it is used for the same purpose. This horizontal chart is a tool that allows managers to evaluate whether existing resources can handle work demand or whether activities should be postponed. The Gantt chart is used for milestone scheduling where each milestone has start and completion dates. A milestone represents a major activity or task to be accomplished (e.g., design phase in a computer system development project).

Charts and Graphs (continued)

A Gantt chart is a graphical illustration of a scheduling technique. The structure of the chart shows output plotted against units of time. It does not include cost information but highlights activities over the life of a project and contrasts actual times with projected times using a horizontal chart. It gives a quick picture of a project's progress in terms of actual timelines and projected timelines.

The **pie chart** is used to represent a 100% total of two or more items. The **line chart** is exceptionally impressive when comparing several things but could present a visual problem if the comparisons are too many or too close in relation to one another. Advantages are that line charts are simple to draw. Disadvantages are that if the lines are close to each other, it is difficult to distinguish some of the plotted points.

The **layer chart** is linear in appearance but has a different representation than the other charts. It depicts the accumulation of individual facts stacked one over the other to create the overall total. This chart is more complex than the others, since it illustrates much more. In addition to showing the comparison of layers that add up to the total, layer charts also show how each group of layers relates to subsequent groups. Layer charts require more work to prepare than the other charts. More arithmetic is involved, and drawing the chart requires a good deal of concentration.

The **radar chart** is a visual method to show in graphic form the size of gaps in a number of areas, such as current performance versus ideal (expected) performance and current budget versus previous budget.

Internal Control Training

Internal auditors, other employees of the organization, and management at all levels need an understanding of internal control concepts. This is because internal control affects every employee of the organization in terms of policies, work rules, and procedures.

Internal control training should integrate individual and organizational goals because internal control focuses on people, processes, and objectives. Internal auditors can play both student and teacher roles in internal control training; they become students to satisfy the continuing education requirement, and they become teachers in educating and training other employees in internal control concepts.

An internal control training syllabus should include:

- Reviewing recommendations of the Treadway Commission regarding internal control framework.
- Understanding control objectives and control procedures in various functional areas of business.
- Explaining employee duties and responsibilities in promoting internal control in the organization.
- Discussing limitations of internal controls (what internal control can do and what it cannot do).

Big-Data Audit

In addition to asking traditional questions about data quality, data security, data sources, and data privacy during a big-data audit, internal auditors should ask new questions about data models, use of intellectual property assets, audit resources, and audit team structure. These new questions are consistent with rating the big data as a high-risk audit area and due to the popular saying "Garbage in, garbage out," especially in relation to data sources and data models.

Conducting a big-data audit is technical in nature. As such, it requires a mix of technical skills and competencies from internal and external sources. Internal audit management must ensure that the internal audit resources are in-sourced (audit staff), cosourced (nonaudit internal staff), or outsourced (external talent) with subject matter experts, consultants, and contractors for a successful completion of the audit project work. Nonaudit staff can include marketing, operations, and other internal staff. Internal audit management must ensure that the selection of data-analytics tools (i.e., software and hardware) by the data analytics team consists of legal staff, IT staff, and a statistician. For example, (1) legal staff can advise the team about the legal requirements to protect privacy of data or access to the external data; IT staff can help in developing data-analytic tools and to avoid duplicative software and hardware purchases; and (3) a statistician can help educate the team about the merits and applications of each type of statistical method.

Imagination is the only limit to audit applications of big data, data analytics, and data mining.

Big-Data Modeling

Consulting auditors are often asked to participate in planning, designing, and developing new data models to analyze and extract new big data that gives new insights that can facilitate new business opportunities in terms of increased revenues, decreased costs, and increased profits. These consulting auditors may request technical help from outside subject matter experts such as statisticians to draw statistical inferences, operations research staff to develop alternative data models, and computer systems development staff to actually build new data models. Consulting auditors need guidelines regarding model planning, model development, model testing, model implementation, and model termination.

Data Quality Audits

Because corporate data is a corporate asset and because corporate management makes decisions using the corporate data, the board and senior management have concerns about the quality of data they are using. As corporate decisions have major impacts on the entire corporation's success, the board and senior management can request consulting auditors to conduct data quality audits on major computer systems that are generating decision-support data for the board and senior management. Data quality can be a major problem in big data, as big data contains several sources with different quality levels.

Data Quality Audits (continued)

Data quality is a major problem, especially in legacy computer systems that were designed and developed using very old programing languages that are very difficult to change or modify, which have little or no built-in controls. Legacy computer systems are unstable in operation with marginal reliability due to software patches applied to hold them together and to keep them in a working order. In addition, legacy systems are difficult to integrate with other computer systems so data quality suffers.

In general, the data quality in database systems is better than in legacy systems because the design approaches and programming languages of database systems are flexible with built-in controls. Whether a computer system is a legacy or a database system, there are common and essential elements of data quality, including timeliness, accuracy, security, integrity, consistency, completeness, and relevance.

The real value of big data does not come from a mere collection of data from several sources. Instead, the real value comes from data usage and application, which can lead to major insights and better decisions. Because big data (data asset or strategic asset) is put to so many good uses and with so many benefits, a return-on-data (ROD) metric can be calculated for value-measuring purposes. ROD indicates how data assets of an organization are utilized effectively and efficiently (i.e., 10% or 40%).

Outsourcing Reviews

The term **outsourced service provider** broadly includes all entities or firms that have entered into a contractual relationship with a user organization (i.e., the company engaging the service provider) to provide business functions or operational activities. Examples of these functions or activities include accounting, internal audit, human resources, sales and marketing, procurement, tax and legal services, risk and insurance management, and IT. Outsourcing a business function does not mean abdication of management's responsibility. Instead, it means management is searching for the best alternative in an effective and efficient manner and knowing that management is always responsible for and accountable for all business functions, whether they are outsourced or not.

From a strategic viewpoint, user organizations should outsource only noncore functions and keep core functions in-house. Core functions are those that closely relate to and are vital to achieving a user organization's mission, vision, strategy, success, and growth. Note that core functions for each user organization could be different. For example, core functions for a manufacturing company are operations (i.e., production, supply chain, logistics, and inventory), marketing, and finance.

User organizations often outsource their business functions when:

- Senior management is managing too many internal functions with little time available.
- Skills and competency levels of internal employees are scarce.

Outsourcing Reviews (continued)

- Internal operating costs for managing business function are slowly increasing year after year.
- External vendors possess unique and specialized skills that internal employees do not have.
- Senior management can improve the performance of core functions better later, with more time.

Deciding on a wrong function to outsource has several negative consequences, such as:

- Changing business outcomes.
- Creating unknown problems.
- Increased operating costs.
- Noncompliance with LRRs.
- Delaying services to customers.

In summary, what function to outsource is a more important decision than when to outsource (time and conditions), where to outsource (domestic, foreign, local, and regional vendors), and whom to outsource to (known, unknown, old, or new vendors). The use of service providers and third parties to perform operational functions

Outsourcing Reviews (continued)

presents various risks to user organizations. Some risks are inherent to the outsourced activity itself, whereas others are introduced with the involvement of a service provider. If not managed effectively, the use of service providers may expose user organizations to risks that can result in regulatory action, financial loss, litigation cases, and loss of reputation.

A user organization should conduct an evaluation of and perform the necessary due diligence review for a prospective service provider prior to engaging the service provider. The depth and formality of this review will vary depending on three things: the scope, complexity, location, and importance of the planned outsourcing arrangement; the user organization's familiarity with prospective service providers; and the reputation and industry standing of the service provider. A user organization's financial team, technical consultants, operational experts, legal analysts, external consultants, and business staff must be engaged throughout the due diligence review and approval process.

Conflict-of-Interest Reviews

A **conflict of interest** means an individual's goals and objectives do not fit with the goals and objectives of that individual's organization. It is any relationship that is actual or appears to be actual and not in the best interest of the organization. Such a relationship would prejudice an individual's ability to perform duties and responsibilities objectively. A conflict-free mind-set requires a full disclosure of financial interests or other conflicting matters, such as working for competing firms or owning stock of competing firms. Other examples of conflict-of-interest situations include favoring:

- One executive over other executives.
- One contractor over other contractors.
- One company to merge with or acquire over other companies.
- One supplier over other suppliers.
- One employee over others in making hiring, promotion, demotion, transfer, and termination decisions.

Code of Ethics Reviews

After the board and senior management approves the written code of ethics or code of conduct document, it should encourage the timely and confidential communication of suspected fraud, misconduct, or abuse to a higher-level person within a company. Such a code is intended to foster a culture of integrity and accountability. An ethics officer or chief legal counsel can provide advice to all employees regarding ethics-related questions. The ethics officer performs annual review of the ethics policy and discusses ethics at all levels of the bank. Internal auditors monitor the effectiveness of the ethics program and whistleblower policy. Internal auditors should assess the corporate culture and ethics processes to identify any governance-related weaknesses. They should assure the board that suspected fraud and misconduct are promptly reported, investigated, and addressed.

Workplace Safety Audit

The scope of a workplace safety audit includes review of the safety department's policies and procedures and accident statistics and investigations. The internal auditor needs to make sure that actions to correct safety problems are proper and timely and that all applicable labor laws are complied with. The internal auditor needs to coordinate safety audit activities with other internal assurance functions, such as quality, health, security, building maintenance staff, and industrial engineering. Possible areas of coordination include sharing work plans and schedules, conducting periodic meetings, exchanging reports, developing safety statistics, providing control training, and participating in investigations and corrective action plans. Internal auditors should make sure that the safety statistics are accurate and proper and that they are not manipulated. Misreporting of safety statistics in the workplace can result from violations of safety and security rules, such as employee accidents, bodily injuries, exposure to chemicals, and work hazards—all related to poor working conditions in manufacturing factories, processing plants, warehouses, and distribution centers.

In 1970, the U.S. Congress enacted the Occupational Safety and Health Act (OSHA) to ensure a safe and healthful working environment for every worker. The act established the Occupational Safety and Health Administration to develop standards, conduct inspections, monitor compliance, and institute enforcement actions against those that are not in compliance. Internal auditors should make sure that the management of the safety department complies with OSHA.

COORDINATION BETWEEN INTERNAL AUDITORS AND OTHERS

Assurance Services

Several parties, both inside and outside an organization, provide assurance services to the board and senior management. **Assurance services** are objective examinations of evidence for the purpose of providing an independent assessment on governance, risk management, and control processes for an organization. Examples of these assurance services include financial, operational, performance, compliance, security, privacy, third-party, and quality engagements.

During assurance services, internal auditors coordinate with both internal and external assurance providers and with internal assurance requestors at different times to minimize duplication of work, to gain economies of effort, to reduce total audit costs and audit failures, to identify all possible risks, to minimize disruption to operational services, and to result in better-quality audit evidence. In addition to coordinating with assurance service providers, internal auditors must coordinate with internal assurance requesters, such as the board and senior management, for special projects of interest to them.

- **Internal assurance providers:** Internal auditors, control assessors, compliance officers, risk officers, ethics officers, legal counsel, quality auditors, environmental auditors, and nonaudit assurance providers such as frontline business managers

Assurance Services (continued)

- **External assurance providers:** External auditors, audit quality assessors, risk management consultants, technology consultants, accounting/finance/legal consultants, bank examiners, and regulatory auditors (e.g., tax agents, securities agents, insurance auditors, energy auditors, and other government agents)
- **Internal assurance requesters:** Board members, board-level committee members, CEO, and senior management

An **assurance map** is a powerful tool to document all the assurance work done by several parties. It becomes a reference document for various parties. Assurance maps are organization-wide and coordinated exercises involving mapping assurance coverage provided by multiple parties against key or significant risks facing the organization in each risk category so that duplicate efforts, missed risks, and assurance gaps can be identified and monitored. Assurance maps are developed around an organization's risk categories. An example of risk categories in manufacturing operations includes production capacity, service capacity, product quality, service quality, and supply-chain practices. The CAE, senior management, and the board need these assurance maps to ensure proper coordination among diverse risk activities.

Assurance gaps or coverage maps can occur when the number of actual, significant risks addressed or covered is not equal to the number of significant risks that were discovered or uncovered. An assurance gap is a sign of weakness in a risk analysis and risk assessment exercise. The gap indicates that the exercise does not measure the breadth and depth of risks inherent in all vertical and horizontal departments or functions.

Audit Reliance and Audit Assurance

Often, internal auditors work with several outside auditors, such as bank examiners, regulatory auditors, quality auditors, environmental auditors, and external auditors, who rely on the work performed by the internal auditors. In this regard, outside auditors can assess the key elements of internal audit, such as:

- The adequacy and independence of the internal audit function and the audit committee
- The independence, professional competencies, and quality of the internal audit staff
- The quality and scope of the audit methodology, audit plan, and risk assessment program
- The adequacy of audit program, audit testing, and workpaper standards

When outside auditors place a low reliance level on the work of internal auditors, their assurance levels to management will be low, and vice versa. Also, the amount of reliance by outside auditors on effective internal auditors depends on the risk-level of the audited area, as shown:

Low-Risk Areas → More Reliance on Effective Internal Auditors → No Additional Reviews or Tests Needed

High-Risk Areas → Less Reliance on Effective Internal Auditors → Additional Reviews or Tests Needed

Low Reliance = Low Assurance

High Reliance = High Assurance

Internal Auditors and External Auditors

The nature and extent of coordination between internal and external auditors can vary based on the timing, availability, experience, and competency of internal auditors who can assist external auditors. Internal auditors are often asked to coordinate their work with that of external auditors. For example, external auditors would keep the work of attesting to the fairness of presentation of cash position in the balance sheet. Shared audit work between these auditors would be to:

- Evaluate the system of controls over cash collections and other financially sensitive transactions.
- Evaluate the adequacy of the organization's overall system of internal controls.
- Review the system established to ensure compliance with a company's policies and procedures that could have a significant impact on company operations.
- Review the authenticity of third-party and related-party transactions using forward-tracing and backward-tracing techniques.
- Review the accounting journal entries with significant amounts and questionable entries.
- Review and reconcile depreciation and amortization schedules.

Internal Auditors and Regulatory Auditors

The nature and extent of coordination between internal and regulatory auditors may take the form of clarifying the content of new LRRs and implementation of such LRRs. Internal auditors should also find out if regulators have performed retrospective analysis and flexibility analysis for LRRs. If so, internal auditors should request copies of such analysis for a better understanding of the background behind the LRRs. Internal auditors should also find out if the organization's compliance managers have performed barrier analysis and cost-benefit analysis for LRRs. In addition, regulatory auditors often request copies of internal audit reports for their own monitoring purposes.

Internal Auditors and Control Assessors

The nature and extent of coordination between internal and control assessors can include reviewing complaints about control failures, control overrides, control breakdowns, and control deficiencies. Internal auditors need to find out how control-related training programs incorporate these control-related problems to make employees control-aware. Nonaudit assurance providers, such as frontline business managers, often perform control or management self-assessments. However, these frontline managers are not independent of their departments so their work needs to be tested and evaluated by independent internal auditors.

Internal Auditors and Compliance Officers

The nature and extent of coordination between internal and compliance officers can include understanding the reported violations of LRRs, including the associated fines, penalties, and punishments. Internal auditors need to find out how noncompliance issues are inventoried and incorporated into employee training programs so these violations are not repeated. Internal auditors should also find out if the organization's compliance officer has performed barrier analysis and cost-benefit analysis for LRRs. In addition, customers and suppliers often ask companies how their personal information in electronic commerce systems is secured and protected.

Internal Auditors and Risk Officers

The nature and extent of coordination between internal and risk officers deals with risks and controls. The risk management function and internal audit function will be more effective when they work together rather than separately, especially when there is a common understanding of each other's roles. Internal auditors can ask risk managers how they estimate the value-at-risk (VAR) amounts for major assets and how they reconcile the estimated VAR with the actual VAR. Four collaborative practices between risk officers and internal auditors can result in recognizable value, as follows.

1. Link the audit plan and the enterprise risk assessment and share other work products. It provides assurance that significant risks are being identified effectively.
2. Share available resources wherever and whenever possible. It allows for efficient use of scarce resources (e.g., money, staff, and time).
3. Cross-leverage each function's respective competencies, roles, and responsibilities. It provides communication depth and consistency, especially at the board and senior management levels.
4. Assess and monitor strategic risks. It allows for deeper understanding and focused action on the most significant risks.

Internal Auditors and Ethics Officers

The nature and extent of coordination between internal auditors and ethics officers can include several reported ethical complaints, such as:

- Employing child labor and sweat labor working in hazardous operating conditions receiving less than minimal pay in making garments, shoes, and other products in offshore factories, all resulting in deaths, accidents, and fires.
- Issues in implementing whistleblower policy in terms of management retaliation against employees reporting on management's illegal and unethical activities.
- Violation of the U.S. FCPA in terms of management receiving bribes or paying kickbacks to and from suppliers, contractors, and foreign entities. (The FCPA prohibits all U.S. domestic concerns from bribing foreign governmental or political officials to obtain business or licenses in foreign countries.)
- Violations of conflict-of-interest agreements, code of ethics principles, and insider trading rules.
- Misreporting of safety statistics in the workplace, such as employee accidents, bodily injuries, exposure to chemicals, and work hazards, all related to poor working conditions in manufacturing factories, processing plants, warehouses, and distribution centers.

Internal Auditors and Ethics Officers (continued)

- Manipulation of computer software inside automobiles to reduce pollution emissions. Later, automobile company managers were found guilty and were fined and imprisoned.
- A major bank's managers encouraged employees to open fake bank accounts, charged insurance premium amounts to customers who have car loans with the bank, and charged additional fees to customers on home mortgage loans, all without the consent and approval of the affected customers.

Internal auditors need to find out whether the ethics officer is planning to conduct ethics training for all employees at all levels about unethical practices and the ramifications of such practices on the company's reputation.

Internal Auditors and Legal Counsel

The nature and extent of coordination between internal auditors and legal counsel can include several legal complaints, such as:

- Lawsuits on illegal practices during mergers and acquisitions in violation of laws and regulations such as the U.S. Sherman Antitrust Act and the U.S. Clayton Antitrust Act. The Sherman Antitrust Act prohibits actions that are "in constraint of trade" or actions that attempt to monopolize a market or create a monopoly. Legal actions under this act typically involve price fixing or other forms of collusion among sellers. However, the law also prohibits reciprocity or reciprocal purchase agreements. The Clayton Antitrust Act makes price discrimination illegal and prohibits sellers from exclusive arrangements with purchasers and/or product distributors. The Clayton Act strengthens the Sherman Act by restricting such practices as price discrimination, exclusive dealing, tying contracts (i.e., two or more contracts linked to gain leverage), and interlocking boards of directors where the effect may be to substantially lessen competition or tend to create a monopoly.
- Price discrimination lawsuits that violate laws and regulations, such as the Robinson-Patman Act, which further addresses the issue of price discrimination established in the Clayton Act. It prohibits sellers from offering a discriminatory price where the effect of discrimination may limit competition or create a monopoly. It also includes a provision that prohibits purchasers from inducing a discriminatory price. While a seller may legally lower price as a concession during negotiations, the purchaser should not mislead or trick the seller, thus resulting in a price that is discriminatory to other buyers in the market.

Internal Auditors and Legal Counsel (continued)

- Bid-rigging practices during procurement activities in violation of the FTC Act, which authorizes the Federal Trade Commission to interpret trade legislation, including the provisions of the Sherman Antitrust Act that deal with restraint of trade. The act also addresses unfair competition and unfair or deceptive trade practices.
- Lawsuits by employees, customers, and suppliers in violation of employment laws, customer goodwill, and best business practices, respectively.
- Lawsuits by company against third parties and related parties in violation of trust and confidentiality requirements.

Internal auditors need to find out whether the legal counsel is planning to conduct executive briefings (training classes) to the board, CEO, and senior management about laws dealing with mergers, acquisitions, and price discrimination.

Internal Auditors and Quality Auditors

The nature and extent of coordination between internal auditors and quality auditors can include review of complaints about product recalls, product contaminations, product hazards, product liability suits, and product warranty claims. Internal auditors need to find out whether quality management is prepared to handle these complaints, including taking remedial action and plans. Quality auditors need to be familiar with the Magnuson-Mass Warranty Act, which governs consumer product warranties. The act requires manufacturers and sellers of consumer products to provide consumers with detailed information about warranty coverage. In addition, the act affects both the rights of consumers and the obligations of warrantors under written warranties.

Internal Auditors and Environmental Auditors

The nature and extent of coordination between internal auditors and environmental auditors can include lawsuits, fines, and penalties resulting from violation of environmental LRRs. Internal auditors need to find out whether the environmental management is prepared to control these lawsuits, including taking remedial action and plans. Environmental auditors need to be familiar with the federal and state-issued Environmental Protection Agency laws and regulations.

Internal Auditors and Board-Level Committee Members

All the board members or the board-level committee members can request internal auditors to perform special projects, such as data quality reviews and integrating financial metrics with nonfinancial ones. This is because quality of data is becoming a major concern to the board due to data mishaps and breaches and data usage in making decisions. Traditionally, boards focused on financial metrics only, not on nonfinancial metrics, where nonfinancial metrics are as important as financial metrics for ensuring long-term survivability and sustainability of a company. Data quality review is presented in the consulting engagements section of this domain. Board members on compensation, audit, ethics, and finance committees are very much interested in integrating financial metrics with nonfinancial ones. Integrating financial and nonfinancial metrics can also improve the long-term survivability and sustainability of a company because the company needs to focus on both metrics equally, not just on financial metrics at the expense of nonfinancial ones.

Sample lists of financial metrics and nonfinancial metrics are presented next.

Financial Metrics

Return on investment (ROI)

Return on equity (ROE)

Return on assets (ROA)

Internal Auditors and Board-Level Committee Members (continued)

Earnings per share (EPS)

Market price per share (MPS)

Return on sales (ROS)

Return on value (ROV)

Return on data (ROD)

Return on training (ROT)

Return on quality (ROQ)

Inventory turnover rates

Asset-to-liability ratio

Debt-to-asset ratio

Loss reserve ratio

Internal Auditors and Board-Level Committee Members (continued)

Nonfinancial Metrics

Workplace safety, security, and diversity record

Product and service quality record

Deployment rate of new and emerging technologies

Corporate sustainability record

Management and employee turnover rates

Regulatory compliance record

Customer acquisition, retention, and defection rates

Online shopping cart abandonment rates

Product recalls, product contaminations, and product hazards record

Management and board reputation record

Employee survey results

Customer satisfaction feedback results

Competitors' intelligence results

Pertinent Questions Regarding Metrics Integration Review

The next questions must be answered either before or during the integration of financial metrics and nonfinancial metrics:

- Are the nonfinancial metrics a part of risk assessment program?
- Are the nonfinancial metrics connected to a company's strategic and financial goals?
- Are the nonfinancial metrics a part of the CEO's annual performance reviews?
- Are the nonfinancial metrics a part of the senior management's and operational management's annual performance reviews?
- Are the nonfinancial metrics a part of the executives and officers compensation package?
- Are the nonfinancial metrics communicated to shareholders, corporate promoters, investors, owners, and regulators?

Internal Audit Plan

Executive summary reports or audit information packages should be a part of the communicating and reporting process and contain this information:

- Status reports on accomplishing the annual audit plan or schedule, including any adjustments in the plan or schedule, and activity reports on audits completed, in process, deferred, or canceled with reasons explained
- Information about audit staffing levels, auditor independence, auditor training and development, and auditors' professionalism, including professional certifications
- Discussion of significant accounting, financial, and regulatory issues related to internal audit, external audit, or internal controls
- Summaries of audits conducted and significant audit issues reported to audit clients resulting from these audits

Internal Audit Plan (continued)

- Summaries of IT audit findings (e.g., cybersecurity attacks and data breaches), fiduciary matters, and regulatory and company policy compliance audits
- Highlights of risk assessments performed by company's risk management staff, internal audit staff, or any external risk consultants
- Significant outstanding (open) audit and control issues, in the form of tracking reports that describe the audit issues, when the audit issues were discovered, department or person responsible for corrective action, promised date of correction, and status of corrective action (e.g., completed, in progress, or delayed)

Internal Audit Metrics and KPIs

In general, metrics are mostly quantitative measurements that provide a basis for comparison of progress. They provide a baseline against which progress can be compared and assessed. Metrics must:

- Align with the goals and objectives of an organization.
- Drive its effectiveness and efficiency.
- Be applicable (useful), actionable and controllable, practical (cost effective and acceptable), reliable (stable), and valid (accurate and appropriate).

The effective audit function will always look for continuous improvement regarding its scorecard or metrics reporting to the board and senior management (i.e., audit clients and audit stakeholders). It should shift from reporting traditional metrics to reporting new metrics to deliver what its audit clients and stakeholders are expecting.

Examples of Traditional Audit Metrics

- Percentage of the audit plan completed in a year (e.g., 95%).
- Percentage of audit recommendations accepted and implemented by audit clients in a year (e.g., 90%).
- Traditional audit metrics are auditor initiated and are useful to auditors for scorekeeping and recordkeeping purposes.

Internal Audit Metrics and KPIs (continued)

Examples of New Audit Metrics

- Did the audit function add value or reduce value?
- Did the audit function increase risks or decrease risks?
- Did the audit function act as a positive change agent or a negative change agent?
- Is the cost of the audit function in a year less than or equal to the total value of all assurance services and consulting services provided to all of its audit clients in a year?
- Are most audit clients satisfied? Do they continue to receive the audit services as before?
- New audit metrics are audit client initiated and are useful to audit clients for business improvement purposes.

Internal Audit Red Flags

A list of red flags to watch for within and around the internal audit function is presented next.

- The CAE is reporting to other than the board of directors or its audit committee.
- The CEO and senior management are trying to control or inhibit communications from the CAE to the board due to organizational politics.
- There are unexplained or unexpected changes in the CAE job or significant changes in the overall audit plans and programs.
- There is an increased turnover of internal auditors and decreased budget levels for the internal audit function.
- Internal audit reports do not address identified internal control weaknesses.
- Significant internal control deficiencies identified in audit reports have not been corrected.
- Internal audit management is not meeting the internal audit schedule or not adequately covering significant risk areas, thus increasing the residual risks.

Internal Audit Dashboards

The effective audit function develops and maintains an audit dashboard tool (i.e., audit reporting tool) to show various items of interest to management, as described next.

- An individual audit's progress from planning to completion stages (i.e., start to finish) showing audit objectives and audit scope of work
- Interim audit progress to show audit clients.
- Audit metrics and KPIs to show senior management and the board. Sources for these metrics and KPIs include audit standards, audit charter, audit mission, applicable laws and regulations, audit strategies, and audit plans.
- Reports to the audit committee comparing audit plan to actual work (i.e., budget versus actual) and budget variances.
- Effective communication tools that are easy to use, visualize, and understand.

Internal Audit Dashboards (continued)

- An audit intelligence mechanism where summaries of important historical audit work related statistics are gathered, stored, and reported. Examples of these statistics include:
  - Number of audits completed in a year
  - Audit budget and staff levels for a year
  - Auditors' proficiency, competency, and talent levels (i.e., education and experience)
  - Noteworthy accomplishments for the audit function or individual auditors
- Benchmarked audit data with similar or best-in-class audit functions. This data can include important audit metrics, KPIs, scorecards, and industry trends.

Audit Risk Indicators

Audit risk indicators are significant risks that an internal audit function is either knowingly or unknowingly facing in the eyes of the organization's board and senior management. Examples are listed next.

- Audit failures due to auditors' gross negligence and incompetence and not delivering a quality audit work
- Unqualified and inexperienced auditors assigned to audit engagements because they were transferred from a company's nonaudit functions to provide them employment when the company is going through massive employee layoffs
- Auditors with a low competency level assigned to high-risk and high-profile audits, which is a mismatching of resources with unaddressed risks
- Poor supervision in audit assignments due to excessive workloads for audit supervisors
- Use of inapplicable audit metrics and meaningless KPIs
- Auditors making false assertions or empty promises to audit clients to win their goodwill
- Auditors facing personal reputation risks in the eyes of audit clients due to their lack of credibility, honesty, and integrity, and above all independence and objectivity
- Auditors either knowingly or unknowingly exhibiting personal cognitive traps and biases, such as projecting, stereotyping, and stovepiping behaviors and attitudes

Audit Risk Indicators (continued)

- Auditors' failure to identify ethical lapses, such as bribes, corruption, and violations of conflict-of-interest rules and code of ethics principles
- Auditors' failure to identify fraudulent activities, such as not reporting known fraud incidents to management
- Auditors' failure to identify legal issues, such as violating LRRs and their associated, fines, penalties, punishments, and imprisonments
- Auditors' failure to identify cultural issues, such as workplace violent incidents, employee discrimination lawsuits, and sexual harassment cases
- The CAE does not identify governance failures, such as the board's inability to identify underperforming directors who are renominated or reappointed as directors.
- The CAE was disinvited to board meetings, and thus the CAE is in the dark and cannot effectively perform board-level audits.
- Nonaudit executives are assigned to the CAE job on a rotation basis and as a part of an executive development program. These nonaudit executives have no previous experience, no relevant education, and no professional certifications in internal auditing. Hence, the independence, objectivity, and competency of the CAE and staff can be questioned.

Domain 2: Planning the Engagement (20%)

This domain covers several major theoretical topics. It determines engagement objectives, evaluation criteria, and scope of the engagement. It plans the engagement to assure identification of key risks and controls. This domain completes a detailed risk assessment of each audit area. It determines engagement procedures and prepares the engagement work program. This domain determines the level of audit staff and resources needed for the audit engagement.

OBJECTIVES AND SCOPE OF AUDIT ENGAGEMENT

This section presents topics such as audit objectives, audit scope, considerations for audit scope, and audit scope impairments.

Audit Objectives

Audit objectives are what the audit project is going to accomplish. Clearly defining the audit assignment objective(s) is a must at the beginning of each audit since audit objectives guide the extensiveness of internal control assessment as well as the scope and methodology of the audit work. Audit assignments with broad objectives are generally more difficult to accomplish and require more staff resources and time than do assignments with specific objectives. Therefore, to the extent possible, audit objective(s) should be defined as precisely as possible to preclude unnecessary work while concomitantly meeting the assignment's purpose.

For example, this audit objective might require extensive data gathering based on a random statistical sample: "Determine what percentage of program recipients are ineligible for benefits." In this case, the total recipients, eligible recipients, and ineligible recipients must be determined. Statistical projections are required based on the sample results.

Audit Objectives (continued)

In contrast, this audit objective might be accomplished with less extensive statistical sampling: "Determine if the agency consistently uses reasonable controls to ensure that only eligible recipients receive benefits." In this case, the controls must be assessed using different methods (e.g., review of controls over beneficiary enrollment), in which a sampling procedure is a part of the audit procedures.

At the beginning of an audit, there should be a meeting of minds between auditor and auditee regarding the objectives in order to have a useful audit at the end. In all cases, the objectives, scope, and methodology section of the audit report should clearly describe the audit objectives, scope, and assumptions and basis for auditor conclusions.

Audit Scope

The scope of an internal audit is initially defined by the audit objectives. Preliminary survey, audit programs, audit project scheduling, and time estimates are driven by audit objectives. An example of an audit objective is evaluating whether cash receipts are adequately safeguarded.

What Is Audit Scope?

Audit scope can include anything from the mailroom to the shipping room or from the mailroom to the boardroom, meaning every and all functions and activities within an organization. However, audit scope should not include reviewing the strategic management process, assessing the quality of management decision making quantitatively and qualitatively, and reporting the results to the audit committee. Strategic planning and decision making are the core duties of senior management. Internal auditor should not second-guess senior management because the auditors may not be qualified to perform such reviews.

Scope is the boundary of the audit, meaning it says what is included in and excluded from the audit. Determining the scope of the audit is part of audit planning. It addresses such things as the period and number of locations to be covered. The audit scope should include financial, operational, and compliance audits. There are eight steps in determining the scope of the audit:

1. Considering the significance and the needs of potential users of the audit report

Audit Scope (continued)

2. Obtaining an understanding of the area to be audited
3. Considering legal and regulatory requirements
4. Considering internal control structure
5. Identifying criteria needed to evaluate subject matter of the audit
6. Identifying significant findings and recommendations from previous audits that could affect the current audit objectives (Auditors should determine if management has corrected the conditions causing those findings and implemented those recommendations.)
7. Identifying potential sources of data that could be used as audit evidence and determining the reliability of these data, including data collected by the audited entity, data generated by the auditors, or data provided by third parties
8. Considering whether the work of other auditors or of experts may be used to satisfy some of the auditors' objectives

Audit objectives, audit scope, and audit methodology are not determined in isolation. Auditors determine these three elements of the audit plan together, as the considerations in determining each often overlap.

Considerations for Audit Scope

Determining the audit scope normally involves matters such as the number of locations to be visited, time frames to be covered, and the type and depth of work needed to ensure that assignment objectives are accomplished and that all applicable audit standards are met. In establishing an audit scope, the audit team or the supervisor should consider these questions, among others:

- What elements of a finding are required? Is disclosing a particular condition enough, or is it necessary to establish cause and effect? Will it be necessary to evaluate the condition against criteria?
- Will assignment findings relate only to the samples or cases reviewed, or will it be necessary to generalize them to a larger universe?
- What are the relevant sources of data? Who/what holds the data (people, data tapes, and files)?
- Will the data be available? Are the data likely to be reliable?
- What kind of information will be required? For example, will a judgmental sample be acceptable, or will a statistically projectable random sample be required?
- When are audit work results (i.e., audit reports) required?

Determining scope may require trade-offs. For example, a narrower scope may result in a less powerful message. But it may be the best that can be done considering available resources and time. Is the narrower scope acceptable?

Considerations for Audit Scope (continued)

When establishing an audit scope and audit objectives for a specific audit engagement, internal auditors must consider the next guidelines to avoid potential audit risks, such as audit failures, audit false assurances, and negative audit reputation.

- Assign competent audit staff to conduct specific audit engagements.
- Perform the right audits using a risk assessment process.
- Test the real risks and the right controls at the right time.
- Consider the red flags and warning signals of fraud.
- Report the audit results to the right people at the right time.
- Apply professional skepticism and judgment when trusting management assurances and assertions rather than taking them on face value.
- Follow honesty, integrity, and due diligence principles so as not to create any negative image of auditors.

Audit Scope Impairments

During the audit engagement, auditors may find scope impairments. When factors external to the audit organization and the auditor restrict the audit scope or interfere with the auditor's ability to form objective opinions and conclusions, the auditor should attempt to remove the limitation or, failing that, report the limitation. For example, under the next conditions, an audit will be adversely affected and the auditor will not have complete freedom to make an objective judgment:

- Interference or influence that improperly or imprudently limits or modifies the scope or type of an audit
- Interference with the selection or application of audit procedures or the selection of transactions to be examined
- Denial of access to sources of information, such as books, records, and supporting documents, or denial of opportunity to obtain explanations by officials and employees of the organization or activity under audit
- Unreasonable restrictions on the time allowed to complete an audit competently

Audit Scope Impairments (continued)

KEY CONCEPTS TO REMEMBER: Audit Scope

- When faced with an imposed scope limitation, the director of internal auditing should communicate the potential effects of the scope limitation to the audit committee of the board of directors.
- When an internal auditor is auditing the financial operations of an organization, the audit scope does not include a review of the financial decision-making process. The scope does include:
  - Reviewing the reliability and integrity of financial information.
  - Reviewing systems established to ensure compliance with applicable policy, plans, procedures, and other types of authority.
  - Appraising economy, efficiency, and effectiveness of the employment of resources.
- Internal auditors should review the means of safeguarding assets from losses arising from exposure to the elements.

RISK ASSESSMENT FOR AUDITABLE AREAS

Two major topics discussed in this section include audit planning and planning materiality, including how to compute such materiality. It is suggested that audit plans are developed based on risk levels.

Risk Assessment Defined

A **risk assessment exercise** for an individual audit area (i.e., auditable activity) is a separate exercise based on the scope, objectives, and risk factors unique to that audit. However, this risk assessment for an individual audit is a subset of the total audit risk assessment exercise done by the internal audit department for the entire audit-plan year.

$$\text{Total audit risk assessment} = \text{Audit 1 risk assessment} + \text{Audit 2 risk assessment} + \text{Audit 3 risk assessment} + \text{Audit } N \text{ risk assessment}$$

Audit Planning

Internal audit management should establish and adhere to an audit plan that is periodically reviewed and updated, takes into account the organization's risk profile, emerging risks and issues, and establishes the frequency with which business functions or activities should be audited. An effective audit risk assessment methodology provides the internal audit management and the board with objective information to prioritize the allocation of audit resources properly. When the audit risk assessment indicates a change in risk, the audit plans should be reviewed to determine if planned audit coverage should be changed. A linkage between audit plan to audit cycles is shown next.

Audit Plan ⟶ Audit Coverage ⟶ Audit Plan Changes ⟶ Audit Universe ⟶ Audit Cycles

The **audit universe** (risk universe) consists of all auditable entities or areas, such as business units, functions, activities, operations, processes, or systems. The internal audit department can establish and maintain the audit universe file through several means, such as:

- Reviewing incorporation filings and bylaws.
- Listing business affiliates, subsidiaries, and holding companies.
- Reviewing previous audits completed.
- Collecting information from cost, profit, investment, data, and computer centers.

Audit Planning (continued)

- Analyzing business partners and strategic alliances, such as joint ventures.
- Reviewing the accounting general ledger.
- Reviewing mergers, acquisitions, and divestitures undertaken.
- Knowing new product or service approval processes.
- Understanding computer operating systems and computer-based major application systems.
- Reviewing business contracts with suppliers, outsourcing vendors, and third-party service providers.
- Reviewing significant laws and regulations.
- Reviewing internal audit's risk assessment, risk function's risk assessment, and the information security risk assessment.
- Reviewing risk-based control self-assessments and management's self-assessments.

Audit Planning (continued)

An **audit cycle** identifies the frequency of audits to be conducted (e.g., 12, 18, or 24 months), which are approved in advance by the audit committee. Audit cycles are usually driven by the risk scores of the business activities or areas in the audit risk assessment. The audit risk assessment process identifies both an inherent risk score and a residual risk score to each auditable entity. The residual risk score is most commonly used in determining how often the auditable area should be audited and in assigning the audit cycle frequency, after taking into account mitigating controls. It is not practical to audit each business area or activity due to lower risk levels and shortage of audit resources. In general, auditable entities with higher risk scores are assigned a shorter audit cycle frequency. Regardless of the risk scores and risk levels, the assigned and approved audit cycle should ensure compliance with laws, rules, and regulations. The link among audit work projects, risk scores, and audit cycle frequencies is shown next.

Audit Projects ⟶ Higher Risk Scores ⟶ Shorter Audit Cycle Frequencies

Audit Projects ⟶ Lower-Risk Scores ⟶ Longer Audit Cycle Frequencies

Specifically, two kinds of audit plans exist: staff plans and audit plans.

Staff Plans

Staff planning should include assigning staff with the appropriate skills and knowledge for the job, assigning an adequate number of experienced staff and supervisors to the audit (consultants should be used when necessary), and providing for on-the-job training of staff.

The availability of staff and other resources is an important consideration in establishing the objectives, scope, and methodology of an audit. For example, limitations on travel funds may preclude auditors from visiting certain locations or lack of expertise in a particular methodology may preclude auditors from undertaking certain objectives. Auditors may be able to overcome such limitations by use of staff from local offices or by engaging consultants with the necessary knowledge, skills, and expertise.

Audit Plans

A written audit plan should be prepared for each audit and is essential to the efficient and effective conduct of audits. The form and content of the written audit plan will vary among audits. The plan generally should include an audit program and a memorandum or other appropriate documentation of key decisions about the objectives, scope, and methodology of the audit and of the auditors' basis for those decisions.

Audit Plans (continued)

Documenting the audit plan is an opportunity for auditors to review the work done in planning the audit to determine whether:

- The proposed audit objectives are likely to result in a useful report.
- The proposed audit scope and methodology are adequate to satisfy the audit objectives promptly.
- Sufficient staff and other resources have been made available to perform the audit.

Written audit plans should generally include this information:

- **Introduction and background.** To the extent necessary, information should be provided about the legal authority for the audited organization, program, activity, operation, or function; its history and current objectives; its principal locations; and similar information needed by auditors to understand and carry out the audit plan.
- **Scope and objectives.** A clearly described scope and clearly stated objectives should indicate what the audit is to accomplish.

Audit Plans (continued)

- **Audit methods.** The audit methodology should be clearly described and should present suggested steps, procedures, and sampling plans, which should be included in the audit program. For coordinated audits, the audit organization planning the work should ensure that comparable audit methods and procedures are followed to ensure that the data obtained from participating locations will be complete. Auditors should design the methodology to provide sufficient, competent, and relevant evidence to achieve the objectives of the audit. Methodology includes not only the nature of the auditors' procedures, but also their extent (e.g., sample size).
- **Special instructions.** The auditors should clearly understand and reach early agreement on the responsibilities in each audit. This agreement is especially important when the work is to be directed by a central audit organization with work to be conducted at several different locations. This section of the plan may be used to list the responsibilities of each audit organization, such as preparing audit programs, conducting audit work, supervising audit work, drafting reports, handling auditee comments and questions, and processing the final report.
- **Report.** To the extent possible, the audit plan should set forth the general format of the audit report, cite the types of information to be included, and list the recipients of the report.

Planning the Audit Work

Planning and managing an audit assignment starts from developing work plans to completing the audit engagement. The majority of the audit work takes place in the fieldwork phase. In planning, auditors define the audit's objectives, scope, and methodology. Planning continues throughout the audit, and auditors should document their plan and changes to it. The most important task is to make sure that sufficient staff and other resources are available to do the audit work. The audit work can be done either at the headquarters (home office) and/or at the field offices. Exhibit 2.1 summarizes advantages and disadvantages of headquarters and field office work.

At headquarters	At field offices
Advantages	**Advantages**
More avenues to recruit new auditors.	Travel time and expenses are reduced.
Availability of qualified auditors due to location and ability to recruit auditors due to corporate name.	Auditors will be familiar with local operations and people.
Auditors with special skills can be hired.	
Disadvantages	**Disadvantages**
Headquarters and auditors are not familiar with field office operations and people.	More expensive to operate a separate office.
More travel time and expenses are required.	Lack of qualified auditors due to location.
Auditors will be away from home and family.	Lack of specific skills among the audit staff.
Auditors will feel burned out.	Auditors will not be familiar with the corporate culture.
	Auditors will not have management insight due to lack of ongoing contact.

Exhibit 2.1: Audit work at headquarters and field offices

Planning Materiality

Material errors, irregularities, and illegal acts will have a direct and material effect on financial statement amounts. **Materiality** is defined as the magnitude of a misstatement that would influence the judgment of a reasonable user of financial statements. Audit procedures must be designed to provide reasonable assurance of detecting material financial statement misstatements (i.e., material errors and irregularities). Thus, materiality refers to the level of precision (or accuracy) of the financial statements; the lower the materiality, the greater the precision and vice versa.

From an internal audit viewpoint, materiality refers not only to the financial statements but also to the business operations and computer systems.

- From a financial statement standpoint, materiality is to be evaluated in relation to the financial statements as a whole.
- From an operations standpoint, materiality is to be evaluated in relation to a specific operation under consideration as well as all other operations affected by it.
- From a computer system standpoint, materiality is to be evaluated in relation to a specific information system under consideration as well as all other interfacing systems affected by it.
- Material weaknesses in either business operations or computer systems may or may not directly affect the financial statements.

Planning Materiality (continued)

For example, heavy use of pirated software may become a sensitive and material issue if it was known to software vendors or other interested third parties (e.g., software auditors) that existed to monitor software piracy situations in companies. Subsequent fines and penalties imposed could be high, and the acquisition of software through official sources would cost money. In addition, loss of image and bad reputation are major factors to think about.

Similarly, unauthorized dissemination of product formulas, process knowledge, and secret recipes to competitors would have a material effect when competitors decide to take advantage of the newfound information. Another example is impact of poor-quality products and possible violations of environmental controls by the organization.

Material weaknesses in business operations and computer systems have a business risk. The risk of adverse publicity and injury to the organization's reputation is of concern here. Business risk (exposure risk) is different from audit risk. From an internal auditor's perspective, audit risk is best defined as the risk that the auditor may fail to detect a significant error or weakness during an examination and performance of an audit. Audit risk is the probability that an auditor will issue an unqualified (clean) opinion on financial statements that actually contain material misstatements. Audit risk is therefore the complement of the level of assurance; *the lower the audit risk, the greater the assurance and vice versa*. Since audits are performed on a test or sampling basis, audit risk cannot be reduced to zero except at prohibitive cost. The concepts of materiality and audit risk suggest that financial statements are accurate only within reasonable and practical limits.

Planning Materiality (continued)

In practice, decisions relating to materiality and the extent of audit testing are left to the professional judgment of the individual auditor. Increased audit testing would reduce both the business risk and the audit risk (and possibly the level of materiality) and at the same time would increase the cost of conducting the audit. This is because even small reductions in materiality and/or audit risk can result in disproportionately large increases in sample sizes and hence audit costs. *Short of 100% verification, audit risk cannot be reduced to zero.*

About 53% of respondents in a survey of government auditors indicated that they ordinarily attempt to quantify audit risk in determining the extent of audit testing. Audit risk and materiality are important considerations in planning an audit and evaluating its results. Materiality plays a major role in planning the scope of an audit and the extent of audit testing and in evaluating the sufficiency of audit evidence. As a practical matter, the materiality threshold is a gray area that separates what is very likely material from what is very likely not material.

Audit Planning and Evaluation

In planning the audit, the scope of the audit should be large enough so that possible errors will not exceed the materiality threshold at a reasonable level of assurance.

In forming the audit opinion at the evaluation stage of the audit, if possible errors exceed the materiality threshold, the auditor must either issue an adverse opinion or collect more evidence to reduce uncertainty.

Types of Errors

Three types of errors can exist: known errors, likely errors, and possible errors (see Exhibit 2.2). **Errors** are defined as financial statement misstatements that are either intentional or unintentional. Since audits are performed on a test or sampling basis, it is helpful to distinguish between three types of errors.

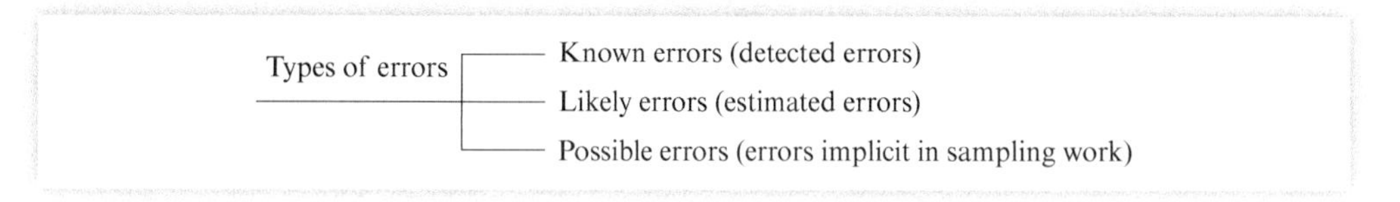

Exhibit 2.2: Types of errors

Types of Errors (continued)

Known errors are errors that have actually been detected by the auditor during substantive testing. Likely errors are estimated errors obtained by projecting to the population the same proportion of known errors observed in representative samples. **Likely errors** include known errors. **Possible errors** represent the amount of error at the upper limit of the confidence interval obtained in projecting sample results to the population. Possible errors are implicit in both statistical and nonstatistical sampling, although they can be quantified using only statistical sampling. Possible errors include both likely and known errors.

Who Should Set the Materiality Level?

The auditor and the auditee should arrive at an understanding about the levels of materiality and the assurance level to be applied in an audit. This understanding should be based on cost-benefit considerations.

A structured audit approach will be more effective in controlling audit risk and audit costs than an unstructured one. A structured approach is one that relies on statistical sampling and/or formal decision aids for integrating audit evidence.

Auditor judgment plays an important role in determining materiality, in determining the amount of audit work to be performed, and in evaluating the evidence that is collected. Providing formal guidance to auditors may increase judgment consensus.

What Is Material and Immaterial?

Due professional care requires that the auditor consider the relative materiality or significance of matters to which audit procedures are applied. Various studies suggest that the magnitude of an error as a percentage of income is the most important factor in determining its materiality; items that have a more than 10% effect on income would normally be considered material while items constituting less than 5% of income would normally be considered immaterial.

An auditor would most likely judge an error in an account balance to be material if the error involves a large percentage of net income. Least likely to be material are clerical mistakes that are unlikely to occur again, unverified routine transactions, and unusual transactions for the company. When a related party is involved, such as a major stockholder, an error would be considered material when the stockholder's receivables balance accounts for less than 1% of the company's receivables.

Other factors of materiality, besides income effect of the error, include effect on earnings trend, on working capital, and on total assets. Legal and political factors are important, and compliance with laws and regulations is also crucial.

As a practical matter, assurance level cannot be separated from materiality. Given the same sample size, an auditor with a lower materiality level established will have a higher level of audit risk; for audit risk to be comparable across auditors, the assurance level must be related to a materiality level.

Qualitative versus Quantitative Materiality

Sometimes qualitative materiality such as the nature of disclosure (sensitive or not) and the evidence of a desire to mislead (accidental or deliberate) is more important than the quantitative materiality, such as 50% or 60%. The auditor should pay more attention to human behavior, which is an example of a qualitative materiality.

Quantitative materiality is applicable during the planning stage of an audit. This is because it is not practical to plan the audit to detect qualitative misstatements during the planning stage, as it is too early.

In addition to quantitative materiality, the auditor should consider qualitative materiality. Qualitative materiality may include the cumulative effect of immaterial items or the needs of users.

The materiality threshold should vary for each audit project and for each audit type (i.e., operational audit, financial audit, compliance audit, information technology audit).

Legal and political factors and environmental factors may affect the determination of qualitative materiality. Irregularities, fraud, illegal acts, legal covenants, and account misclassifications would likely be considered qualitatively material.

The auditor needs to strike a balance between cost-effectiveness and preferences of user groups for financial statements completely free of errors.

How to Compute Materiality

Materiality is computed by taking a base and multiplying that by a percentage. The base, in declining order of importance, includes total revenues, total expenditures, total assets, retained earnings, and income. The percentage used can be a flat percentage or one obtained from a sliding scale. A flat percentage is based on the notion that materiality is completely relative; a sliding scale is based on the notion that some amounts are large enough to be always material.

In the government auditors' survey, it was noted that a majority (65%) of respondents used a flat percentage while 35% used a sliding scale to compute materiality.

ENGAGEMENT WORK PROGRAM

This section defines an audit work program, presents the essential elements of an audit work program, shows how to develop one, and compares a standardized audit work program with a customized audit work program. All audit work programs are based on risk levels.

Audit Work Program Defined

Audit work programs are sets of procedures used by auditors in performing assurance services, including automated audit processes using technology (e.g., computer-assisted audit techniques and big-data analytics). The audit work programs for each audit area should establish the scope and timing of audit procedures, the extent of testing (including criteria for selecting items to be tested, that is, sampling), and the basis for conclusions. Audit work programs help to ensure consistency in conducting audits, gathering evidential information, documenting procedures performed, arriving at conclusions, and issuing the audit reports.

Risk-Based Auditing ⟶ Risk-Based Audit Plan ⟶ Risk-Based Audit Work Program

Elements of an Audit Work Program

The chief audit executive (CAE) should ensure that the audit work programs are properly planned, designed, prepared, documented, and maintained and that controls are in place to ensure integrity, confidentiality, and availability. Internal audit work programs typically contain these essential elements as a guide to internal auditors:

- Review and evaluation of policies, procedures, and control systems
- Review of risk and control assessments
- Review of laws, rules, and regulations
- Selection of audit samples and results (sampling processes)
- Verification of selected transactions or balances through examination, confirmation, and inspection
- Controls over records selected for an audit

Regarding sampling processes, auditors need to document sampling objectives, define population, determine sample size, select a sampling methodology, evaluate sample results, and develop audit findings and recommendations.

Development of an Audit Work Program

Preparing an **audit program** is the next step after completing the preliminary survey work. An audit program serves as a roadmap for the auditor. It provides the auditor the necessary guidance to proceed with the detailed audit work in terms of audit procedures to be conducted and audit evidence to be collected during the audit. The audit program should focus on major activities and key controls within and around such activities.

Audit program development should take a structured approach where the audit project is broken down into phases, tasks, and steps. Audit programs provide a description of the methodology and suggested steps and procedures to accomplish the audit objectives, a systematic basis for assigning work to audit supervisors and staff, and the basis for a summary record of work.

Audit procedures are the detailed steps, instructions, or guidelines provided for the auditor for the collection and accumulation of a particular type of audit evidence during the audit. Audit procedures can be verbal or written; the latter are preferred and are developed by auditors and approved by audit supervisors. They should be clear to enable auditors to understand what is to be accomplished.

An example of an audit procedure might be: "Obtain physical inventory sheets, verify the accuracy of inventory extension by multiplying the quantity with cost/price figures. Note any exceptions." Usually audit procedures start with using action words, such as: *review, verify, look, observe, analyze, confirm, interrelate, construct, reconstruct, prove, read, identify, inquire, determine, reconcile, ascertain, examine, scan, foot, cross-foot, compute, recompute, compare, count, trace,* and *retrace.*

Development of an Audit Work Program (continued)

Written audit programs should not be used merely as checklists of steps to be conducted. Effective work on operational and performance audits requires that the staff understand audit objectives and use initiative and creativity in applying the audit program and in assessing the results of the work.

Two types of audit programs exist: standard audit programs and customized audit programs. Exhibit 2.3 compares each of these programs.

Standardized audit programs	Customized audit programs
Inexperienced auditors can execute the programs.	Experienced auditors required to execute the programs.
Do not require a great knowledge of the operating environment to develop the programs.	Much knowledge of the operating environment is required to develop good programs.
Not much work is required to develop the programs.	Significant amount of time and effort are required to develop the programs.
Appropriate for use in a simple and stable operating environment that changes minimally.	Appropriate for a complex or changing operating environment.
Appropriate for use in multiple locations with similar operations.	Cannot be used in multiple locations with dissimilar operations.
Useful in conducting repeat, routine audits.	Useful in conducting unique, nonroutine audits.
Not appropriate for a complex or changing operating environment.	Not appropriate for a simple or unchanging operating environment.

Exhibit 2.3: Standardized versus customized audit programs

KEY CONCEPTS TO REMEMBER: Audit Programs

- The primary role of an audit program is to serve as a tool for planning, directing, and controlling audit work.
- The primary purpose of developing a written audit program is to help ensure that the audit work is properly planned and documented.
- The audit program should be designed for each individual audit and should include audit steps and procedures to provide assurances that the objectives of the audit are met. To achieve established objectives of the audit department, each audit program should be tailored to meet the needs of the specific audit assignment.
- Essential criteria for developing audit programs include:
  - Description of the objectives of the audit client operations as agreed to by the auditee.
  - Specificity as to the controls to be tested.
  - Specificity as to audit work steps to be followed.

Development of an Audit Work Program (continued)

- Essential items in the preparation of an audit program:
  - The performance of a preliminary survey.
  - A review of materials from prior audit reports.
  - A review of performance standards set by management.

Preparation of a budget identifying the costs of resources needed is not essential during the audit program phase. It would be essential during the planning stage of the audit.

- Upon discovering that an audit area was omitted from the audit program, the auditor should evaluate whether completion of the audit as planned will be adequate.
- Audit programs that test internal controls should be tailored for the audit of each operation.
- Audit programs focus on audit objectives and related audit procedures required to achieve those objectives.
- Due professional care standards require that the auditor consider the relative materiality or significance of matters to which audit procedures are applied.

Development of an Audit Work Program (continued)

Examples

- *Audit objective*: Ensure that an update of a master file is performed accurately.
- *Related audit procedure:* Reconcile computer-generated totals with totals on the updating reports.
- *Audit objective*: Determine whether inventory stocks are sufficient to meet projected sales.
- *Audit procedure*: Observe the procedures used to identify defective units produced.
- *Audit objective*: Determine whether current company policies and procedures are sufficient to provide adequate control over employee additions and deletions to the payroll master file.

Due professional care standards require that the auditor consider the relative materiality or significance of matters to which audit procedures are applied.

AUDIT RESOURCES FOR AUDIT ENGAGEMENTS

Two kinds of plans exist: (1) staff plans and (2) audit plans where the former is derived from the latter. Audit staff planning should include assigning audit staff with the appropriate skills and knowledge for the audit work job, assigning an adequate number of experienced staff and supervisors to the audit (consultants should be used when necessary), and providing for on-the-job training of the audit staff.

The availability of staff and other resources is an important consideration in establishing the objectives, scope, and methodology of an audit. For example, limitations on travel funds may preclude auditors from visiting certain locations, or lack of expertise in a particular methodology (e.g., data mining) may preclude auditors from undertaking certain objectives. Auditors may be able to overcome such limitations by use of staff from local offices (co-source) or by engaging consultants with the necessary knowledge, skills, and expertise (outsource).

Audit Work Plan ⟶ Audit Staff Plan ⟶ Audit Resources

Audit Resources = In-Source + Co-Source + Outsource

AUDIT RESOURCES FOR AUDIT ENGAGEMENTS (CONTINUED)

The audit program should be supported by qualified audit staff. The chief audit executive (CAE) should ensure that qualified and independent auditors are assigned to execute the plan. Audit activities, including various audit types (e.g., operational, performance, assurance, and consulting), can be performed by a single auditor or team of auditors. The CAE should assign internal audit staff according to the expertise and skills needed to execute a particular audit such as information technology (IT) audit or consulting audit. In considering the qualifications of the internal audit staff assigned to a given audit, the CAE should look at the skills and expertise of the team collectively. Often, the lead auditor retains the required skills and is able to provide direction and oversight of other auditors. Internal audit position titles (job titles) may include requirements for education, professional certifications, and work experience levels that help to demonstrate qualifications.

Domain 3: Performing the Engagement (40%)

This domain focuses on several major theoretical topics. It conducts a preliminary survey of the audit engagement area using several information-gathering tools and techniques. It uses sampling methods and statistical analysis techniques in the audit engagement. It applies various audit analytics, such as computerized audit tools, data mining, big-data audit, and process mapping techniques, to analyze and evaluate data as part of performing the audit engagement. This domain explains the scope of audit evidence and legal evidence and the differences between them. It prepares audit workpapers as an official record of the audit work performed and to summarize the engagement results and conclusions. This domain identifies key activities required, such as review and comment on the workpapers as part of supervising the audit engagements.

INFORMATION-GATHERING TOOLS AND TECHNIQUES

Auditors use several information-gathering or data-gathering tools and techniques to obtain background information on the audit client's operations and to collect audit evidence and pertinent data for the audit purpose. For example, either statistical sampling or nonstatistical sampling methods can be used to collect audit evidence and to control risk based on quantified and scientific evidence. Several specific information-gathering tools and techniques are discussed here: interviews, questionnaires, checklists, focus groups, observations, unobtrusive measures, and anecdotal records, including several sources to collect data and information.

Interviews

Interviews are of two types: structured and unstructured (i.e., less structured). A **structured interview** is one in which auditors ask the same questions of numerous individuals or individuals representing numerous organizations in a precise manner, offering each interviewee the same set of possible responses. In contrast, an **unstructured interview** contains many open-ended questions, which are not asked in a structured, precise manner. With unstructured interviews, different auditors interpret questions and often offer different explanations when respondents ask for clarification. The structured interview technique is good to apply in an organization with multiple locations, units, or divisions. The less structured and less guided type of unstructured interview may be more useful to one-of-a-kind interviews.

Structured Interviews versus Unstructured Interviews

- Structured interviews are good for repetitive types of interviews.
- Unstructured interviews are good for one-of-a-kind interviews

Telephone interviews and, even more, face-to-face interviews enable interviewers to establish rapport with respondents. Individuals who would not answer certain questions on their own often can be persuaded to provide truthful answers in telephone or face-to-face interviews.

In comparison to telephone interviews, face-to-face interviews give interviewers the opportunity to observe as well as listen. More complex questions can be asked in face-to-face interviews than in telephone interviews. More questions can be asked in face-to-face interviews since the time can last up to an hour (optimum time) while 30 minutes is the usual limit for telephone interviews. In comparison with mail questionnaires, face-to-face and telephone interviews are much faster methods of gathering data.

A good preparation for an interview requires several dimensions, such as making sure that interview questions are appropriate (i.e., relevant to the audit—relevance), directed to the proper persons (i.e., selection of respondents), and easily answered (i.e., ease of response). If needed, ask sensitive questions in a mail questionnaire where confidentiality or anonymity can be granted. Also avoid questions that could cause unnecessary confrontation, causing interviewer and interviewee to take sides and do battle. Also avoid questions that have no answers and avoid questions that, if you attempt to ask them, produce unusable results. These are not to be confused with questions for which the legitimate answer might be "no basis to judge" or "no opinion."

Structured Interviews versus Unstructured Interviews (continued)

The order in which the questions are presented in an interview is important. Early questions, which set the tone for the data collection procedure and can influence responses to later questions, also help the auditor get to know the interviewee and to establish the rapport essential to a successful interview. Remember that the questions should hold the interviewee's attention; thus, the auditor must begin to introduce some "interesting" questions.

The questions should be presented in a logical manner, keeping the flow of questions in chronological or reverse order, as appropriate. It is good to avoid haphazardly jumping from one topic to another and to avoid introducing bias in the ordering of questions. There are ways to compose good interview questions and to fore-stall problems with comprehension or bias. The appropriateness and level of language used in the interview, the effects of qualifying language, and the importance of clarity are all important to consider. The auditor needs to be familiar with the various kinds of **bias** that can creep into the wording of interview questions and its effect on the validity of the audit results. Bias can appear in the stem (or statement) portion of the question or in the response-alternative portion. Bias may also result when a question carries an implied answer, choices of answer are unequal, "loaded" words are used, or a scaled question is unbalanced.

Questionnaires

Three phases occur in questionnaires: data design, data collection, and data analysis. A questionnaire is a data collection instrument, and auditors employ it for a number of reasons, including to ask auditees:

- For figures, statistics, amounts, and other facts
- About conditions and procedures that affect the work, organizations, and systems with which they are involved
- For their judgments and views about processes, performance, adequacy, efficiency, and effectiveness
- To report past events and to make forecasts
- To describe their attitudes and opinions
- To describe their behavior and the behavior of others

Questionnaires are popular because they can be a relatively inexpensive way of getting auditees to provide information. However, because questionnaires rely on people to provide answers, a benefit-risk consideration is associated with their use. People with the ability to observe, select, acquire, process, evaluate, interpret, sort, retrieve, and report can be a valuable and versatile source of information under the right circumstances. However, the human mind is a very complex and vulnerable observation instrument. *If we do not ask the right people the right questions in the right way, we will not get high-quality answers.*

Questionnaires (continued)

Questions must be clear, interesting, and easy to understand and answer. The answers to the questionnaires become input to audit report writing. Properly designed questionnaires can be seriously compromised if they are not presented in a format that is easy to read and understand by respondents. Formatting the questions is a design issue, and there are two types of formats: open-ended questions and closed-ended questions.

1. **Open-ended questions** are easy to write and difficult to interpret. They increase the response burden on respondents in terms of time to answer, respondents can leave out some important factors due to memory lapses, and the questionnaire results cannot easily be quantified or tabulated. Open-ended questions are easy for auditors to develop and difficult for them to interpret; they also are difficult for audit clients to answer.

   Content analysis can be used to analyze the descriptive answers provided to open-ended questions. During the content analysis, either the auditor or someone else reads and rereads the written responses a few times, identifies the major categories of themes, and develops rules for assigning responses to these categories. Open-ended questions are good to use when one is uncertain about criteria or when engaged in exploratory work. Also, answers to the open-ended questions can become an input to the closed-ended questions.

2. **Closed-ended questions** consist of yes/no, multiple-choice, free-choice, and fill-in-the-blank questions. Yes/no questions are good in dealing with measures that are absolute, such as black and white, and are dichotomous variables. They are not good for measures that span a range of values and conditions.

What Kinds of Questions Should Be Asked?

Three kinds of audit questions should be asked: descriptive, normative, and causal (impact). As the name implies, the answers to **descriptive questions** provide descriptive information about specific conditions or events and focus on "what is." An example is the number of people who received certain types of medical benefits in a given year.

The answers to **normative questions** compare an observed outcome to an expected level of performance and focus on "what should be." An example is the comparison between airline safety violations and the standard that has been set for safety.

The answers to **causal questions** (cause-and-effect with impact) help reveal whether observed conditions or events can be attributed to business operations. An example is determining the effect of changing a policy or a procedure.

Auditors should use these three kinds of questions in questionnaires since they are all relevant to most common audit situations. The best way to achieve the right balance is to see if each question can be labeled as one of the three kinds of questions. If a question does not belong to any of these types of questions, the auditors need to decide whether to drop the question or use it as a general background, information-gathering information.

Constraints in Using Questionnaires

- Time, cost, and staff expertise are examples of primary constraints while location and facilities are a secondary constraint in using and administering questionnaires. For example, if location and facilities are a constraint, use of a mail questionnaire or telephone interviews is advised compared to face-to-face interviews.
- If money is tight and the subject matter can be phrased intelligibly for the respondent population, use the mail.
- If time is tight and staff time is not, use the face-to-face or telephone interview methods.

Questionnaires versus Interviews

- Auditors should review the conditions and requirements of the data collection methods before deciding to use questionnaires and again before deciding the methods for administering the questionnaire.
- Mail questionnaires are a versatile, low-cost method of collecting detailed data. They are particularly adaptable to survey methods when the population is big, difficult to contact, likely to be inconvenienced, concerned about privacy, and widely dispersed. But mail questionnaires usually have a long turnaround time. Auditors must be willing to invest the time required to carefully design and test these questions. And respondents must be willing and able to provide unbiased answers.
- Interview methods, while much more expensive and more prone to bias, help ensure against respondent error, have less turnaround time if sufficient staff is provided, and can be used to provide some auditor verifications during the interviews.

Questionnaires versus Flowcharts

- The questionnaire is a data collection instrument—a means of gathering information about documents processed, forms used, procedures followed, record contents, program logic, and data editing details. However, questionnaires are not useful for document analysis and control evaluation purposes, which is a weakness.
- Flowcharts overcome this weakness.

Quality of Questionnaires

The quality of questionnaires can be checked by four methods:

1. Pretesting
2. Expert review
3. Peer review
4. Verification, validation, corroboration, and reliability criteria

The first three methods belong to the data design phase, while the fourth method is used in the data collection and data analysis phases. During the design phase, the questionnaire should be pretested (or pilot tested) on selected persons or departments that represent the range of conditions likely to influence the auditor's results. The questionnaires should also be sent out for review by experts who are familiar with both the issue area and the respondent group. In addition to expert reviews, peer reviews can be done by an auditor who worked on the auditable area before or a new auditor who never worked before in that area.

Criteria for Questionnaires

- The term "verification" refers to the accuracy of data.
- The term "validation" refers to the purpose of measure (shows that the observation measures what it is supposed to measure).
- The term "corroboration" refers to validation with multiple parties.
- The term "reliability" refers to the consistency of measures.

Verification versus Validation in Questionnaires

- Verification is different from validation.
- Verification is ideally conducted by testing a sample, which is time-consuming and expensive.
- Validation does not require sampling approaches.

Verification versus Reliability in Questionnaires

- The procedures for testing the reliability of answers are different from those for verifying answers.
- When information is verified, auditors usually go to a different source for the same information or use a different technique on the same source, such as observations or in-depth interviews.
- To test reliability, auditors have to administer the same test to the same source.

Checklists

Auditors are familiar with using checklists for various purposes. They are memory aids to ensure that all required steps or actions are completed. Checklists can be used in any phase of the audit, including planning, survey, fieldwork, report writing. Checklists are especially useful during workpaper review to ensure that all components of the quality assurance program are addressed properly.

Supervisors can use checklists to document their review comments when they look at the auditor's workpapers. Supervisors can later use the review comment sheet (also called point sheet) for follow-up to ensure that all points that were raised are cleared by the auditor who worked on the audit. There is no limit to the number of applications of checklists, and it really depends on the creativity of the auditor. Audit quality can be enhanced with the use of checklists since they provide a discipline and framework to work with by all parties involved in an audit. For example, checklists can be used during a peer review of workpapers to mark compliance with the requirements.

Focus Groups

The primary purpose of focus groups is to collect qualitative data, with quantitative data being the secondary purpose. Focus groups represent an important tool for discovery and exploration of ideas and opinions. They are a choice between individual interviews or focus group interviews when time is a constraint. Focus groups, which consist of 6 to 12 people, produce a rich body of data expressed in the respondents' own words and context.

Surveys ask for responses expressed on point rating scales or other constrained response categories. Surveys produce more artificial responses than focus groups due to absence of interaction among respondents. The data provided by focus groups is idiosyncratic and difficult to summarize. In surveys, the response categories may or may not be those with which the respondents are comfortable, although they may still be selecting answers.

Surveys versus Focus Groups

- Surveys produce artificial responses due to lack of interaction among respondents.
- Focus groups do not produce artificial responses due to interaction among respondents.

Some major advantages resulting from the focus groups are listed next.

- Focus groups provide data from a group of individuals much more quickly and at less cost than would be the case if each individual were interviewed separately. They also can be assembled on much shorter notice than would be required for a more systematic and larger survey.

Surveys versus Focus Groups (continued)

- The focus group interview process is objective and rigorous as it rests on an extensive body of empirical theory and research, as well as practice.
- Focus groups allow the moderator to interact directly with respondents. This provides opportunities for the clarification of responses, follow-up questions, and probing of responses. Respondents can qualify responses or give contingent answers to questions. In addition, it is possible for the moderator to observe nonverbal responses, such as gestures, smiles, and frowns.
- The open response format provides an opportunity to obtain large and rich amounts of data in the respondents' own words. It allows respondents to react to and build on the responses of other group members.

Some major disadvantages resulting from the focus groups are listed next.

- The results obtained in a focus group may be biased by a very dominant or highly opinionated group member. More reserved group members may be hesitant to talk.
- The open-ended nature of responses obtained in focus groups often makes summarization and interpretation of results difficult.
- The moderator may bias results by knowingly or unknowingly providing cues about what types of responses and answers are desirable.
- Each focus group really represents a single observation, although it is a group of people. Group consensus is possible here. Therefore, more than one focus group should be conducted on a specific topic.

Observations

Observation is a direct notice of things, events, and people's actions. It is the ability to see what is happening in an individual and/or within a group and to respond appropriately. Watching body language in addition to words and actions is an additional benefit of observation. In other words, body language says more than the words and actions of people.

Observation is considered a reliable audit procedure but one that is limited in usefulness. It is not sufficient to satisfy any audit assertion other than existence. Observation provides information on how transactions are handled at one particular point in time, not how they are processed throughout the period under study. It provides a snapshot of operations. The reason why observation is limited is that individuals can react differently when being observed.

Unobtrusive Measures

An **unobtrusive measure** is the one that is not readily noticeable to others. An auditor can use an unobtrusive measure, for example, to check to see if all hourly employees in a manufacturing plant are clocking in when they report to their workstation, as opposed to someone else clocking in for them. An auditor would stay in an area in an unobtrusive manner where employees clock in to determine their natural motions and actions. Compliance with procedure is the auditor's major objective here.

Another application is to determine whether security guards at a retail store are checking all bags and personal belongings of all employees when they leave the store building. An auditor would observe this in an unobtrusive manner so that the security guard would not notice the auditor. This is a test of control compliance with the store policy that all employee bags are checked every day at quitting time.

Anecdotal Records

Anecdotal records constitute a description or narrative of a specific situation or condition. For example, during the employee performance evaluation process, the appraiser writes down anecdotes that describe what the employee did that was especially effective or ineffective. The appraiser can be the immediate supervisor, peers, self-evaluation by the employee, or immediate subordinate(s).

Another example of use of anecdotal records is allowing a fraud suspect to make a narrative response concerning the incident after the interviewer has established rapport and sold the suspect on the need to cooperate in the interview.

Sources for Collecting Data and Information

Information is the heart of the problem-solving process. Decisions are made using the information to solve existing problems. For the information to be useful in so many ways, it has to meet certain quality attributes, such as availability, timeliness, accuracy, and relevancy.

Knowledge is power and is the result of information. The right kind of information a person has can make the difference between an informed decision and a guess, between success and failure. Knowledge is a synthesis of information. In this information age, knowing means winning. The more someone knows about something, the more control the person has over his or her own destiny. *Relevant information is needed not only to avoid present failures but also to maximize future opportunities and minimize potential future problems.*

As changes create a need for more information, the value of information will begin to increase significantly. The successful executives and professionals (e.g., auditors) will be those who have mastered the art of being information conscious. Information consists of facts, figures, rules, news, statistics, data, values, impressions—pieces of intelligence that singly or jointly increase awareness of the subject matter.

Information should be differentiated from assumptions. An assumption is a conclusion based on noninformation, which can be true or false. It has no evidence. Assumptions are made all the time. We make false assumptions, such as certain data are: easy to find when in fact they are difficult to find and the reverse; or inexpensive to buy when in fact they are expensive and the reverse.

Information can be obtained only by asking questions or searching for it. Information is an outcome of a process that involves fact gathering, data collection, measurement, interpretation, analysis, and forecasting.

Sources for Collecting Data and Information (continued)

Information can be said to be the result of data. Data consist of raw numbers and facts. Information consists of meaningful numbers and facts and involves the addition of a certain value to data through some level of selection, interpretation, or rearrangement.

Since management makes decisions and auditors use information, auditors need to know where the information is coming from and how it is collected. At least four sources of information are available: primary and secondary information and internal and external sources.

Primary information is firsthand information from an original source and expensive to gather. **Secondary information** is secondhand information and inexpensive to collect. Internal sources involve facts about an organization (e.g., sales data, customer data, financial data, and product data). Internal sources are used in planning and performance measurement. **External sources** are facts about the world outside the organization, such as facts about competitors, markets, demographics, the environment, and the economy. Managers often make decisions without external sources as such sources usually are not considered that important; they are more difficult to obtain and often are neglected, resulting in bad consequences. The auditor's goal should be to combine external sources with internal sources.

Managers should think of problems and opportunities as information needs, as a series of questions that need to be answered. *Information consciousness means to think information when thinking about problems.*

SAMPLING METHODS AND STATISTICAL ANALYSIS

This section presents three major topics: sampling methods, statistical analysis, and statistical methods.

Sampling Methods

Statistical sampling or nonstatistical sampling methods can be used to collect audit evidence and to control risk based on quantified and scientific evidence.

Sampling Theory and Nonstatistical Sampling

The primary reason to use statistical sampling is to allow the auditor to quantify, and therefore control, the risk of making an incorrect decision based on sample evidence. Statistical sampling does not prevent auditors from using professional judgment in conducting reviews. Statistical sampling is merely a tool to help them make wise decisions. Auditors still decide what type of review to make, how and when to use sampling, and how to interpret the results. In applying statistical sampling techniques to audit testing, auditors must make six decisions that involve professional judgment.

1. **Auditors must define the problem.** They must decide what to measure, what type of information will provide sufficient facts for the formation of an opinion, and what testing procedures to use.

Sampling Theory and Nonstatistical Sampling (continued)

2. **They must specify the level of confidence.** This is precision, or the probability that an estimate made from the sample will fall within a stated interval of the true value for the population as a whole. Auditors may think of it as the percentage of times that a correct decision (within the specified precision limits) will result from using an estimate based on a sample.

3. **Auditors must define the population for size and other characteristics.** They decide what type of items will be included and excluded and specify the time period to be covered.

4. **They must determine the areas applicable to sampling.** The auditors' assessment of the internal control system for an area may determine whether statistical sampling is appropriate. A strong internal control system may reduce testing to the minimum necessary for verification and may, therefore, call for a different sampling plan or no statistical sampling at all. Prior experience, as well as information from prior audits, plays a role here. Prior audits may suggest that certain kinds of records are more prone to error and need higher verification rates than other kinds of records. Thus, auditors may have to stratify the population between records likely to have a high error rate and those likely to have a low error rate.

5. **Auditors must decide the maximum error rate that they will consider acceptable, and they must define an error.** Or, if auditors are attempting to estimate the value of some balance sheet amount, they must determine the required precision of the estimate in terms of the materiality of the amount being examined and the overall objective.

Sampling Theory and Nonstatistical Sampling (continued)

6. **They must draw conclusions about the population from the sampling results.** In arriving at these conclusions, auditors must judge the significance of the errors they have discovered.

Because statistical sampling provides more and better information, it permits greater use of professional judgment and enables auditors to more effectively analyze the results of tests. And by reducing the workload, statistical sampling allows more time to use professional judgment.

Basically, there are two approaches to audit sampling: statistical and nonstatistical. The choice is based on costs and benefits. Sampling risk—the risk that the sample is not a representative of the population—is present in both approaches. Exhibit 3.1 summarizes similarities and differences between statistical and nonstatistical sampling approaches.

Sampling Theory and Nonstatistical Sampling (continued)

Statistical sampling approaches	Nonstatistical sampling approaches
Require auditor's judgment	Require auditor's judgment
Basic audit procedures are the same	Basic audit procedures are the same
Permitted as a professional standard	Permitted as a professional standard
Use the laws of probabilities to measure sampling risk associated with the sampling procedures	Cannot measure the sampling risk
Sample selection methods use statistics	Sample selection methods may use statistics, but evaluation of the sample results could be nonstatistical
Additional costs involved due to technical training required	Fewer costs due to minimal training requirements
Sampling risk can be explicitly measured and controlled	Sampling risk cannot be explicitly measured or controlled
Require computer software and hardware for efficient use	Do not require computer facilities
Provide objective conclusions based on sample results	Provide subjective conclusions that are subject to challenge
Compatible with limited number of sample selection methods	Compatible with a wider variety of sample selection methods
Sample is larger and is based on mathematics	Sample is smaller and is based on judgment

Exhibit 3.1: Statistical and nonstatistical approaches

Sampling Plan

When designing a sampling plan, auditors should keep in mind the desirability of obtaining a sample that is as representative, corrective, protective, and preventive as possible. To do so, they should stratify the population on the basis of dollar value and the likelihood that the items contain errors, use some random method to select the sample from each stratum, and weight the results from each stratum to compute overall estimates for the population. It is not possible, however, to optimize all four characteristics in a single sample. Instead, a balance must be struck, depending on which characteristic is most important in view of the audit objective. Also, in certain types of audits, one or more of the characteristics may not require consideration at all.

One of the auditor's objectives is to answer questions about a universe of people or things. This universe is called the "population." This objective can be achieved by looking at a sample of things, if the sample is representative of the population. A representative sample has approximately the same distribution of characteristics as the population from which it was drawn.

Sampling Operations

There are three components in the sampling operations: sample design, sample selection procedures, and estimation procedures. The term "sample design" refers to the plans made for the overall way in which a sample will be related to a population. Selection procedures are the methods used to select units of samples from a population. Estimation procedures are the ways of estimating the characteristics of a population from information acquired about a sample.

Interrelationships exist among these three components.

1. The sample design will affect the estimation procedures to be used, and it may also affect the selection procedures. Conversely, the sample design is often affected by the estimation procedures to be used.
2. Selection procedures can have a major effect on how precision is estimated.
3. The types of estimates to be developed can have a bearing on the selection procedures to be used.

Auditors usually form conclusions through testing, or "sampling," a portion of a collection of items (a population). The method by which they choose a sample and the degree to which the sample is representative of every item in the population determine whether they can form valid conclusions.

Sample Size

The determination of an appropriate sample size is part of sample design. Before selecting the sample size, the auditor should decide on the sampling method to be used, the estimation procedure, the sample precision required, and the confidence level desired. If all other factors in a sampling plan are held constant, changing the measure of tolerable error to a smaller value would cause the sample size to be larger and changing the audit risk from 5% to 3% would cause the sample size to be larger.

Precision

Specifying the precision needed for sample estimates is an important part of sample design. The desired precision is the amount of sampling error that can be tolerated but that will still permit the results to be useful. This is sometimes called "tolerable error" or the "bound on error."

In terms of a stated confidence level, precision is the range into which an estimate of a population characteristic is expected to fall. Factors in the choice of a desired precision include the tolerable level of sampling error, the size of an account balance error considered material, and the objectives of the audit test being conducted. Audit resources available for execution of the sampling plan are not a factor.

An application of precision follows. Based on a random sample, it is estimated that 4%, plus or minus 2%, of a firm's invoices contain errors. The plus or minus 2% is known as the estimate's precision.

Precision (continued)

PRECISION VERSUS SAMPLING RISK

- Precision is under the auditor's full control because he or she specifies it.
- Sampling risk is not under the auditor's full control.
- Precision applies to both attributes sampling and variables sampling.
- Sampling risk is present in both attributes sampling and variables sampling work.

Precision and Confidence

Because precision is a way of expressing the amount of error that can be tolerated, it is related to the accounting concept of materiality. Materiality, or importance, is a relative concept rather than an absolute one. For example, a $100,000 overstatement of the assets for a company whose total assets are only $200,000 would be material while it would be immaterial for a company with total assets of multibillions of dollars.

In addition to specifying the precision of the estimate, auditors must specify the degree of confidence that they want placed in the estimate. This is referred to as confidence level, expressed as a percentage. Confidence level is the complement of the chance that our estimate and its precision will not contain the true but unknown population value. The confidence level should be determined by the importance of the sample results to the overall objectives of the audit.

Two examples illustrate the relationship between confidence level and risk:

1. A confidence level of 90% means that there are 90 chances out of 100 that the sample results will not vary from the true characteristics of the population by more than a specified amount.
2. The confidence level is the complement of the risk that an internal auditor will erroneously conclude adequate compliance with a specific management policy.

Precision versus Accuracy

- "Precision" refers to the maximum amount, stated at a certain confidence level, that we can expect the estimate from a single sample to deviate from the results obtained by applying the same measuring procedures to all the items in the population.
- "Accuracy" refers to the difference between the value of the population from which the sample is selected and the true characteristic that we intend to measure.

Types of Risks

Basically, there are two types of risks: sampling and nonsampling risks. **Sampling risk** is the risk that the conclusions reached based on a sample will differ from those conclusions that would be reached by examining the entire population. Usually, the smaller the sample size, the greater will be the sampling risk.

Nonsampling risk arises even if the entire population is tested and is due to errors in auditor judgment, such as use of inappropriate audit procedures and not recognizing errors during sampling. This risk can be controlled with better audit planning and supervision.

Statistical Sampling and Judgmental Sampling

The use of any statistical sample requires a high degree of professional judgment to determine the confidence level and the reliability desired, and thus what sample criteria to use. It takes judgment to evaluate the effectiveness of internal control procedures in order to test the accuracy and reliability of records as well as to recognize any errors in the items examined.

The auditor must use caution in using a statistical sample, bearing in mind that any exceptions or irregularities noted in performing any auditing procedure must be investigated by appropriate means. This may include a subsequent increase in the sample size. If there are no exceptions, the sample size should not be arbitrarily increased. Statistical sampling helps ensure that audit tests are adequate but not excessive and demonstrates objectivity.

When the choice is made to use statistical sampling, the first step is to devise a sampling plan. A statistical sampling plan includes five major steps.

1. Define the audit objectives.
2. Define the population as clearly as possible, noting any distributional or systematic patterns. This step will establish the population size.
3. Determine the appropriate sampling method and sample selection technique that best fits the characteristics of the population.
4. Determine the precision and reliability desired.
5. Calculate the sample size.

Statistical Sampling

Sample Selection Methods

Selection procedures involve the method of actually picking the sampling units—called "drawing the sample" (see Exhibit 3.2). All types of statistical sampling use random selection procedures. Several selection procedures may be used for a single sample design.

Statistical sample selection methods
- Random sampling
  - Using computer programs
  - Using number tables
- Systematic sampling
- Cluster sampling

Nonstatistical sample selection methods
- Haphazard selection
- Block selection
- Judgment selection

Statistical and nonstatistical selection method → Stratified sampling

Exhibit 3.2: Overview diagram for sample selection methods

Cluster Sampling

Cluster sampling is the selection of groups of sampling units (or clusters) rather than the selection of individual sampling units directly. Examples of clusters are folders in filing cabinet drawers, baskets of produce, counties in a state, and persons in a household. Cluster sampling should be used when a built-in pattern is not expected in the population or data.

Three types of cluster sampling exist—one-stage, two-stage, and three-stage—depending on the size and complexity of population (see Exhibit 3.3).

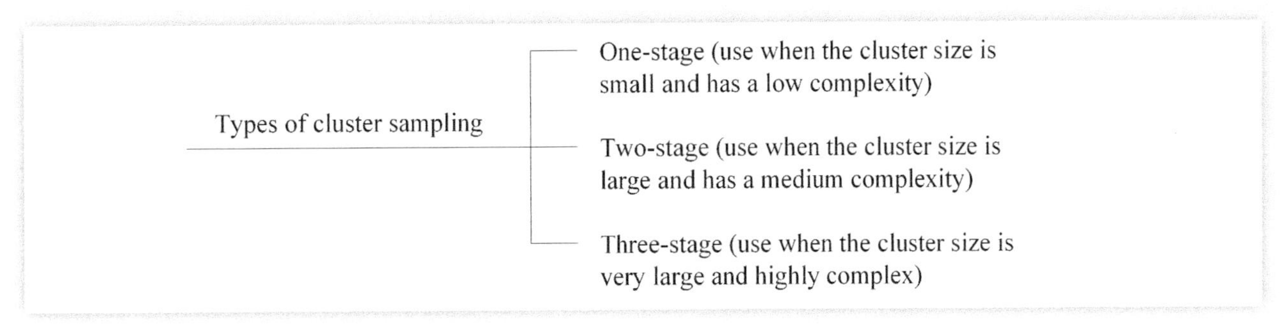

Exhibit 3.3: Types of cluster sampling

Basic Estimation Procedures

Two basic estimation procedures are available: attribute sampling, which is sampling for attributes, and variable sampling, which is sampling for variables. Attributes estimation is used for estimating discrete (e.g., yes or no) characteristics of a population while variables estimation is used for estimating the value of a population (see Exhibit 3.4).

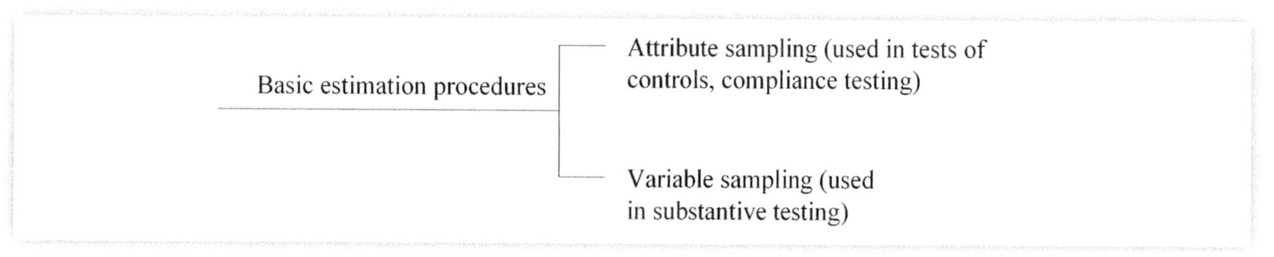

Exhibit 3.4: Basic estimation procedures

When **sampling for attributes**, we want to determine how frequently items having a certain characteristic occur in a population. The characteristic(s) that we are interested in is called the "attribute of the item." Either the item has the characteristic or it does not, although a third, unknown value can be ascribed.

Basic Estimation Procedures (continued)

Some examples of attributes for which we might sample are listed next.

- Travel orders without proper approval
- Health insurance claims that were paid without supporting documentation
- Error rates on travel reimbursement claims exceeding the level set by management
- Determining whether the credit department is requiring a credit check for credit sales when needed
- Determining error rates in cash disbursements

Sampling for variables is used when we are estimating something that can be quantified or measured in dollars, pounds, feet, and so on. This measurement is known as a variable. The measure of variability most useful in variable sampling is the standard deviation. A confidence level of 95% for a variable sampling application can be interpreted as a 95% probability that results of repeated samples will not vary from population characteristics by more than a specified amount.

Some examples of variables are listed next.

- The dollar error in an accounts receivable balance
- A person's weight

Basic Estimation Procedures (continued)

- The value of a population of accounts receivable outstanding
- Reviewing the accuracy of total charges to employee fringe benefit accounts
- Estimating the number of units in a certain class of inventory without counting each one
- Estimating the average account balance of a bank depositor based on a sample

We can use a single sample to develop estimates for both variables and attributes. For example, in examining purchase orders, we can take one sample to estimate both the rate of occurrence and the dollar amount of unadjusted purchases. However, *in general, the sample sizes required for estimating variables are larger than those required for estimating attributes.* Therefore, when we calculate the sample size, we should base it on the precision we want to obtain for the variables estimate, not the attributes estimate.

Attribute Sampling

Sometimes we want to estimate the proportion, percentage, or total number of items in a population that possess some characteristic (attribute) or that fall into some defined classification. When sampling for errors, the auditor is looking for one of only two possible conditions: the presence or absence of an error. The attributes sampling method is used to sort the erroneous accounts from the good accounts.

The sample selection methods can be fixed or sequential. Under a fixed approach, the auditor selects a single sample of a calculated size in one step. Multiple steps are used in a sequential sampling plan where each step is dependent on the audit results of the previous step.

Attribute Sampling (continued)

EXAMPLE OF APPLICATION OF ATTRIBUTE SAMPLING

One example of application of attribute sampling is the percentages of the purchase requisitions that were not approved. Assume that the auditors are reviewing a supply store's efficiency of operations in a manufacturing plant. For this audit, they want to estimate the number of requisitions the store was unable to fill during the past fiscal year because requisitioned items were out of stock and the rate at which the store was unable to fill them. The population consists of all 12,000 requisitions received by the store that year.

We use N to represent the size of the population and n to represent the sample size. In the example, the sample consists of a simple random sample of 100 requisitions. Therefore, N equals 12,000 and n equals 100.

The characteristic of interest is, of course, a requisition that was not filled because the item was out of stock. We will let a represent the number of items in the sample that have the characteristic of interest. In this case, assume a equals 36. We calculate the estimated rate of occurrences, p, as

$$p = a/n = 36/100 = 0.36 = 36\%$$

Given an estimated rate of occurrence of 36% for unfilled requisitions in our population of 12,000, after multiplying the population size times the rate of occurrence, we estimate that the number of unfilled requisitions is 4,320 (i.e., $12{,}000 \times 0.36 = 4{,}320$).

Variable Sampling

Variables are things that can be quantified, or measured, in dollars, pounds, and the like. When sampling for variables, we usually want to estimate the total value for the universe of interest—for example, the total amount of assessed taxes that were not collected.

Calculating the sampling error for variable sampling

Assume that our objective is to estimate the dollar amount of small purchases made by a company during a specific fiscal year, and there were 100 such purchases. To compute the sampling error, or precision, of the estimated total, we first compute the standard deviation of the purchases amounts. The standard deviation is a numerical measure of the dispersion of a group of values about their mean. It is a measure of the average squared deviation from the mean.

The sampling error is calculated by multiplying the standard deviation by a *t*-value corresponding to the stipulated level of confidence and dividing by the square root of the sample size. The formula is:

$$E_y = \frac{ts}{\sqrt{n}}$$

Calculating the sampling error for variable sampling (continued)

Suppose that we have previously decided that the confidence level for the precision of our estimate should be 95%. The *t*-value for 95% is 1.96 or 2. Using this value and $48.71 for *s*, and assuming a simple random sample size of 30, we obtain

$$E_y = \frac{(1.96)(48.71)}{\sqrt{30}} = 17.43$$

Thus, the sampling error of the mean is $17.43. To get the sampling error of the total, we simply multiply the sampling error of the mean by the number of items in the universe. Thus, the sampling error of the total is (100) × (17.43) = $1,743.

Using the 95% confidence level, we state that if all small purchase orders were reviewed, the chances are 19 in 20 that the results of a review would differ from the estimate obtained from the sample by less than the sampling error. The best estimate—the point that is likely to be closest to the true population total—is $18,230. This is obtained by multiplying the arithmetic mean of the sample purchases, 182.3, by the number of small purchases, 100.

Calculating the sample size for variable sampling

Whether we sample for variables or sample for attributes, one advantage of statistical sampling is that it permits us to determine objectively the sample size required to achieve a given degree of precision at a specified confidence level. To make this computation, we need to estimate the standard deviation of the universe, not the sample.

In computing the sample size, we must consider three factors: confidence level, precision, and standard deviation. The auditor specifies two factors—confidence level and precision. The third factor, the standard deviation, is based on the characteristics of the universe.

Suppose we want to reduce the sampling error of the total small purchases in the example given above from $1,743 to $1,400 at the 95% confidence level. The first step is to convert the precision that is wanted (or tolerable error) of the total to the tolerable error of the mean (E). The computation is E = desired precision of estimated total divided by N. In our example, it is $E = 1{,}400 / 100 = 14$. Thus, the tolerable error of the mean is $14. Once we have the tolerable error of the mean, we compute the required sample size by using the formula

$$n = \frac{t^2 s^2}{E^2} = \frac{(1.96)^2 (48.71)^2}{(14)^2} = 46.48 = 46$$

This means that 16 purchase orders, in addition to the first sample of 30, would have to be sampled in order to achieve the required precision. Note that we have used the standard deviation obtained from our first sample as an estimate of the true universe standard deviation. If the true standard deviation were known, we would not be sampling.

Calculating the sample size for variable sampling (continued)

Sometimes it is stated that a larger universe requires a larger sample or that the sample must always be a certain percentage of the universe. This is *not* true. As noted in the formula for calculating sample size, the size of the universe does not enter into the calculations.

ATTRIBUTE SAMPLING VERSUS VARIABLE SAMPLING

- Attribute sampling is sampling for error rates (percentages). Attributes are counted.
- Variable sampling is sampling for amounts (dollars). Variables are measured.
- Attribute sampling is applied in compliance testing (tests of controls).
- Variable sampling is applied in substantive testing.
- Attribute sampling is mostly used by internal auditors.
- Variable sampling is mostly used by external auditors.

Advanced Estimation Procedures

Ratio estimation, difference estimation, and mean-per-unit estimation procedures are different approaches to variables sampling. Selection of an approach depends on the data being audited. Ratio estimation and difference estimation procedures are advanced estimation sampling procedures that yield more efficient (or precise) estimates and give more information than basic estimation procedures, such as attributes sampling and variables sampling (see Exhibit 3.5).

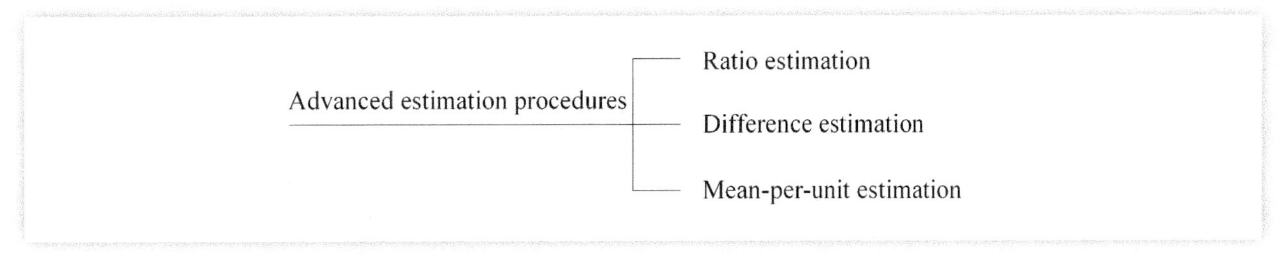

Exhibit 3.5: Advanced estimation procedures

Ratio Estimation Procedure

Sometimes, in a sampling application, the summary statistic we want to estimate is a ratio between two variables, both of which can vary from sampling unit to sampling unit: for example, the ratio of Medicare reimbursements for prescription drugs to total reimbursements. Ratio estimation yields a smaller sampling error because the positive correlation between the auxiliary and primary variables reduces the sampling error.

In other applications, we may want to estimate the total value of an unknown variable that is related to another variable for which we already know the universe total value. For example, we may want to estimate the total meals cost claimed on a department's travel vouchers for a year, when we already know the total amount of travel reimbursement (the population total) for the year and the number of vouchers paid (the population size). We record two variables for each sample travel voucher: The auxiliary (independent) variable describes the amount paid, and the primary (dependent) variable describes the amount of meals claimed. The summary statistic is the ratio in which the total of the primary variables (the meal costs) is the numerator, and the total of the auxiliary variables (the amount paid) is the denominator.

We should also use ratio estimation when we suspect that there is a positive correlation between the two variables, even if we are interested not in the ratio but only in the estimated total of the primary variable. If the correlation is positive and if it is strong enough, the estimate that can be obtained will be more precise than the estimate that can be obtained with simple expansion estimation.

Ratio Estimation Procedure (continued)

SIMPLE ESTIMATION VERSUS ADVANCED ESTIMATION

- In simple expansion estimation, we calculate a sample mean or proportion and multiply it by the population size to obtain the estimated total or the estimated number of occurrences in the population.
- In advanced estimation, we take account of other information that we can obtain from the samples and the population.

The ratio estimate has a slight mathematical bias that can usually be ignored if the sample size is large, say 50 or more. The bias results from the assumption that the line representing the ratio is a straight line passing through the origin. This almost never happens in practice.

Ratio estimation can be used with more complex sample designs, such as stratified samples and single-stage and multistage cluster samples.

Note that with ratio estimation, we obtain two estimated results, ratio and total. For many purposes, the ratio is more meaningful than the total, because it permits us to make useful statements about meeting the audit objective.

Ratio Estimation Procedure (continued)

Examples of Ratio Estimation Procedures

1. A department made 10,000 small purchases totaling $5,100,000 over one year. The auditors, suspecting that purchases could have been made at a lower cost, decided to estimate the savings that would have resulted if suppliers offering lower costs had been used. The confidence level is set at 95%, and a preliminary random sample of 50 cases is taken. The sum of the savings in the sample is $3,600, and the sum of the purchase costs is $24,800.

   The first step is to compute the ratio of savings to the department purchase costs (*R*) by dividing the sum of the savings in the sample ($3,600) by the sum of the department purchase costs in the sample ($24,800).

   $$R = \$3{,}600/\$24{,}800 = 0.14516$$

   The ratio of 0.14516 tells us that 14.5 cents of every dollar could have been saved had purchases cost less.

   The next step is to estimate the total savings (Y) by multiplying the total purchase costs (X) of $5,100,000 by 0.14516, the ratio of savings to costs.

   $$\text{Total savings} = \$5{,}100{,}000 \times 0.14516 = \$740{,}316$$

Examples of Ratio Estimation Procedures (continued)

2. An auditor discovered that discounts for prompt payment were frequently not being taken. About 30% of the suppliers' invoices offered discounts ranging from 2% to 5% of the invoice amount. To estimate the amount lost from not taking these discounts during the past year, the most efficient and effective sampling technique would be ratio estimation.

Difference Estimation

Difference estimation is used when we want to obtain a “corrected” estimate of a previously stated “book” value. For example, suppose we wanted to estimate the “correct” total value of an inventory when we know the value per book and can take a sample from the inventory items and correct the items examined in the sample, if necessary. It is also an attempt to increase precision by obtaining two measurements on a single sampling unit. However, difference estimation will increase precision only if the differences between the primary and auxiliary variables are very small. To use difference estimation, we must know the population total for the auxiliary variable.

Example of Difference Estimation Procedures

Using the same example as used for the ratio estimation, assume that the auditors decided to audit the accuracy of the payments that were made. To save work, they decided to use the same sample of 50 purchases. We need to obtain or calculate three items: the purchase costs, the audited amounts that should have been paid, and the differences between the first two items.

The first step is to calculate the mean difference as the sum of all differences (+$1,048) divided by the sample size, which is equal to + $1,048 / 50 = + 20.96.

The next step is to obtain the estimated total difference as multiplying the mean difference by the population of 10,000. This is equal to 10,000 × 20.96 = + 209,600.

Example of Difference Estimation Procedures (continued)

The next step is to add or subtract the estimated total difference to the population total of $5,100,000. Since the estimated total difference is positive, we should be adding to the population total. This gives $5,100,000 + 209,600 = $5,309,600.

Thus, using the difference method, we can estimate the correct amount that should have been paid at $5,309,600. The actual payments were more than this amount by $5,309,600 – $5,100,000 = $209,600.

RATIO ESTIMATION VERSUS DIFFERENCE ESTIMATION

- One big advantage of ratio and difference estimation procedures is that they adjust the sample results to known population data when we compute totals.
- If the sample mean for the auxiliary variable turns out to be lower than the population mean, the sample results are adjusted upward.
- If the sample mean for the auxiliary variable turns out to be higher than the population mean, the sample results are adjusted downward.
- When the calculations must be done manually, difference estimation has one advantage over ratio estimation: the formulas for computing estimates and sampling errors are simple. Also, because of the simplicity of the formulas, difference estimation can be easily adapted to stratified sampling.

Mean-per-Unit Estimation Procedures

Mean per unit is a sampling plan that can be used to estimate unknown values, such as that of an inventory where book values either do not exist or are unreliable. An important measure for such estimates is the standard error of the mean. Sample size affects the size of the standard error.

In general, the mean-per-unit method is used when the book value of a population is unknown, the population can be stratified, and the variability of the book value is low. This procedure can be performed with a nonstatistical population. Mean-per-unit method, discovery sampling, and attributes sampling methods are based on normal-curve mathematics while dollar-unit-sampling method is not. A major characteristic of normal-curve mathematics is that the sampling distribution of the sample means approaches the normal distribution as the sample size becomes larger and larger.

Example of Mean-per-Unit Estimation Procedures

Mean-per-unit method is appropriate when an auditor for the state highway and safety department needs to estimate the average highway weight of tractor-trailer trucks using the state's highway system.

Discovery Sampling Procedures

Discovery sampling is a type of sampling procedure that has a specified probability of including at least one item that occurs very rarely in the population. It is used when there is a possibility of finding such things as fraud and avoidance of internal controls. In discovery sampling, auditors can specify the probability of including in the sample at least one item with a particular characteristic, if the characteristic occurs at a specified rate in the population. If the sample does not turn up an item with this characteristic, auditors can make a probability statement that the characteristic's rate of occurrence is less than that specified.

Discovery sampling can be regarded as a special case of attribute sampling. However, in its usual applications, it does not yield an estimated rate of occurrence, and usually it is used only if the particular characteristic's rate of occurrence is thought to be very small—that is, close to zero. For example, discovery sampling is usually used in financial audits to guard against an intolerable rate of fraud.

Procedures

The auditor must specify two things: the rate of error, fraud, or abuse that would be intolerable and the probability of finding at least one occurrence in the sample. The sample sizes can be found from the tables (consisting of sample size versus total errors in population size) or calculated using the logarithms.

Procedures (continued)

Then the auditors select a simple random sample of items and examine each item until they find one with an error or until they have examined the entire sample and found no errors. If they find an error, they know that the error rate is at least as great as the specified intolerable rate and can extend the review perhaps to the entire population. If they find no deficiencies, they can conclude that the rate of occurrence of deficiencies is less than that specified as intolerable.

Advantages

An advantage of discovery sampling is that the probability of finding at least one error will increase if the rate of occurrence of deficiencies is greater than the intolerable rate specified by the auditors. Thus, the likelihood of more quickly finding the one error in the sample is increased, and the average sample size that actually has to be examined is smaller.

Example of Discovery Sampling Procedures

An auditor samples cash disbursement records for significant errors of $5 or more. Upon finding one such error, these records are scheduled for a complete review. This conclusion is based on a discovery sample.

Monetary Unit Sampling Procedures

Monetary unit sampling is an efficient method used to determine how many items need to be examined and the reliability of the conclusions drawn from sampling results. The monetary unit sampling procedure is used for substantive audit testing and is based on the assumption that the variable to be measured is highly correlated with some data already known about the cluster, such as the dollar value of transactions. If the assumption is correct, this selection method will yield a smaller sampling error than other methods would.

Selection with Probability Proportional to Size (PPS)

When auditors apply random selection procedures to cluster sampling, the clusters can be selected with PPS or with a related variable that can be used as a measure of size. The cluster sampling method is based on the assumption that the variable to be measured is highly correlated with some data already known about the cluster, such as dollar volume of transactions. If the assumption is correct, the PPS method will yield a smaller sampling error than other methods would.

If clusters were chosen with equal probability, the variation in cluster sizes would increase the computed variation between clusters and thus the overall precision of the estimate. Using two-stage cluster sampling and PPS sampling to select the primary units, the auditor can calculate subsampling rates within the primary units in a way such that the second-stage sample sizes within each primary unit are equal and, at the same time, the sample is self-weighing. Therefore, the sample can be treated as if it were a simple random sample of cluster, which greatly simplifies the calculations.

Statistical Analysis

A system should be put in place to allow the organization to determine systematically the degree to which products and services please customers and to focus on internal process improvement. Data should be collected on features of customer satisfaction such as responsiveness, reliability, accuracy, and ease of access. The measurement systems should also focus on internal processes, especially on processes that generate variation in quality and cycle time. **Cycle time** is the time required from conception to completion of an idea or a process. When customer data indicate a problem, or when the organization wants to raise the level of customer satisfaction, the organization should focus on improving the processes that deliver the product or service.

In order to ensure that processes are continuously improved, data should be collected and analyzed on a continuing basis, with particular attention to variation in processes. The causes of variation are examined to determine whether they result from special circumstances (special causes) or from recurring (common) causes. Different strategies should be adopted to correct each occurrence. The immediate objectives of the analysis and measurement effort are to reduce rework, waste, and cycle time and to improve cost-effectiveness and accuracy. The ultimate objectives are to ensure that the organization understands the extent to which customer satisfaction is being realized and where there are deficiencies and why, and to isolate causes that can be attacked systematically.

Variation

It is true in manufacturing that no two products are ever made exactly alike. Similarly, no two individuals provide the same service in exactly the same way. The term "variation" means deviation from specifications, standards, or targets. The variation concept is a law of nature: No two items are the same. Variation can result in poor quality to the customer and cost to the producer. Variation must be measured and reduced for proper functioning of a process. Before variation can be controlled or stabilized, it must be measured. When the variation is reduced, quality is improved and costs are reduced. Both input and process variation must be reduced in order to reduce the overall variation in a product. These relationships can be shown in the next equation.

Reduced input variation + Reduced process variation = Reduced product variation

Variation is present in every process as a result of a combination of four variables:

1. Operator variation (due to physical and emotional conditions)
2. Equipment variation (due to wear and tear)
3. Materials variation (due to thickness, moisture content, and old and new materials)
4. Environmental variation (due to changes in temperature, light, and humidity)

Variation is either expected or unexpected.

Variation (continued)

Variation affects the proper functioning of a process; this process output deviates from the established target **(off-target)**. From a statistics point of view, the term "off-target" relates to a process average. **Common causes** affect the standard deviation of a process and are caused by factors internal to a process. These causes, which are present in all processes, are called "chance (random) causes." Chance causes are small in magnitude and are difficult to identify. Examples of common random causes include worker availability, number and complexity of orders, job schedules, equipment testing, work center schedules, changes in raw materials, truck schedules, and worker performance.

Special causes affect the standard deviation of a process and are factors external to a process. Special causes, also known as assignable causes, are large in magnitude and are not so difficult to identify. They may or may not be present in a process. Examples of special (assignable) causes include equipment breakdowns, operator changes, new raw materials, new products, new competition, and new customers.

Structural causes affect the standard deviation of a process; they are factors both internal and external to a process. They may or may not be present in a process; they are a blend of common and special causes. Examples of structural causes include sudden sales/production volume increase due to a new product or a new customer, seasonal sales, and sudden increase in profits.

Control Charts

A control chart is a statistical tool that distinguishes between natural (common) and unnatural (special) variations. The control chart method is used to measure variations in quality. The control chart, which is a picture of the process over time, shows whether a process is in a stable state and is used to improve the process quality.

Natural variation is the result of random causes. Management intervention is required to achieve quality improvement or quality system. It has been stated that 80% to 85% of quality problems are due to management or the quality system and that 15% to 20% of problems are due to operators or workers. Supervisors, operators, and technicians can correct the unnatural variation. Control charts can be drawn for variables and attributes.

The control chart method for **variables** is a means of visualizing the variations that occur in the central tendency and dispersion of a set of observations. It measures the quality of a particular characteristic, such as length, time, or temperature.

A variable chart is an excellent technique for achieving quality improvement. True process capability can be achieved only after substantial quality improvement has been made. Once true process capability is obtained, effective specifications can be determined. The sequence of events taking place with the control chart is shown next.

Variable chart → Quality improvement → Process capability → Specifications

The attribute chart refers to those quality characteristics that conform to specifications (specs) or do not conform to specs. It is used where measurements are not possible, such as for color, missing parts, scratches, or damage.

Stable and Unstable Process

When only chance causes of variation are present in a process, the process is considered to be in a state of statistical control (i.e., the process is stable and predictable). When a process is in control (stable), there occurs a natural pattern of variation, and only chance causes of variation are present. Small variations in operator performance, equipment performance, materials, and environmental characteristics are expected and are considered to be part of a stable process. Further improvements in the process can be achieved only by changing the input factors—that is, operator, equipment, materials, and environment. These changes require action by management through quality improvement ideas.

When an assignable cause of variation is present in a process, it is considered to be out of statistical control (i.e., the process is unstable and unpredictable). When an observed measurement falls outside its control limits, the process is said to be out of control (unstable). This means that an assignable cause of variation is present. The unnatural, unstable variation makes it impossible to predict future variation. The assignable causes must be found and corrected before a natural, stable process can continue.

Attribute Control Charts

Two types of attribute control charts exist: the chart for nonconforming units and the chart for nonconformities. A nonconforming unit is a product or service containing at least one nonconformity. A nonconformity is a departure of quality characteristic from its intended level that is not meeting a specification requirement.

The nonconforming unit is based on the binomial distribution. It is shown as proportion (p) chart that is expressed as a fraction or a percentage of nonconforming units in a sample. Another chart is number proportion (np) chart to represent the number of nonconforming units. The fraction nonconforming, p, is usually quite small, say 5% or less. Values greater than 5% require drastic measures other than a control chart. P charts can be used to measure the quantity produced by a work center, by a department, by a production shift, or by an entire plant. They also are used to report the performance of an operator.

Attribute Control Charts (continued)

Example: Calculation for P Chart

Formula:

$$p = np/n$$

where p = proportion of nonconformities in a sample

np = number of nonconforming units in the sample

n = number of units in the sample

During the second shift of production, 400 inspections are made of shipments and 4 nonconforming shipments are found. The second shift produced 10,000 units. What is the fraction of shipments nonconforming?

$$p = np/n = 4/400 = 0.01 = 1\%$$

Since 1% is less than 5% target, shipments conform to specifications or standards. Here, 10,000 units of production is not relevant.

The nonconformity is based on the Poisson distribution. It has two charts: the c chart, which shows the count of nonconformities in an inspected unit, and the u chart, which shows the count of nonconformities per unit. The u chart is similar to the c chart except in scale and size. The scale for a u chart is continuous, but the scale for a c chart is discrete. This makes the u chart more flexible. The subgroup size is 1 for the c chart; the subgroup size varies for the u chart.

Attribute Control Charts (continued)

The most common types of attribute control charts are listed next.

- The p chart is used to control the fraction of units with some characteristic such as the fraction defective. It is based on binomially distributed count.
- The np chart is used to control the number of units with some characteristic, such as the number of defectives per batch. It is based on binomially distributed count.
- The c chart is used to control the number of events, such as defects in some fixed area of opportunity (e.g., single unit). It is an example of an area of opportunity chart and based on Poisson distribution.
- The u chart is used to control the number of events, such as defects in a changeable area of opportunity, (e.g., square yards). It is an example of an area of opportunity chart and is based on Poisson distribution.
- The individual chart is used to control the count when the assumptions for the other attribute charts cannot be met. It is used when attribute data are neither binomial nor Poisson in nature.

Variable Control Charts

To improve the process continuously, variable control charts can be used to overcome the limitations of attribute control charts. Continuous process improvement is the highest level of quality consciousness. Control charts based on variable data reduce unit-to-unit variation, even within specification limits. Variable data consist of measurements such as weight, length, width, height, time, and temperature. Variable data contain more information than attribute data. Variable control charts can decrease the difference between customer needs and process performance.

Two types of variable control charts exist: the X bar chart, which is used to record the variation in the average value of samples (process average), and the R chart, which measures the range or the dispersion (process spread, standard deviation, or variability).

The most common types of variable control charts are listed next.

- The X bar chart is used to control the process average.
- The R chart is used to control the process range.
- The s chart is used to control the process standard deviation.
- The median chart is used as a simple alternative to the combination of an X bar and an R chart.
- The individual chart is used to control subgroups of size 1 drawn from a process; it frequently is used when sampling is expensive or only one observation is available per subgroup (e.g., production per month).

Statistical Methods

Descriptive Statistics

Descriptive statistics (also known as deductive statistics) is concerned about the properties of the observed data and does not assume that the data came from a larger population. Applications of descriptive statistics include developing indices, quartiles, percentiles, ranges, outliers, and coefficient of dispersion and performing content analysis and context analysis. A descriptive statistic is one used to describe a set of cases on which observations were made. It consists of techniques and measures that help managers describe data. Frequency distribution transforms ungrouped data into more meaningful forms.

Inferential Statistics

Inferential statistics (also known as inductive statistics) infers properties about a population, including testing hypotheses, developing estimates, and drawing conclusions. The population is assumed to be larger than the sampled data or observed data.

Time-Series Analysis

Time-series analysis uses past data points to project future data points and has four components:

1. Trends (upward or downward data movement)
2. Cycles (data patterns that occur every several years that are tied into business cycles)
3. Seasonality (data patterns that repeat periodically in weeks and months)
4. Random variation (no data patterns; bumps or blips in the data caused by chance and unusual conditions and hence cannot be predicted)

The scope of time-series models includes the naive (intuitive) approach, moving average, exponential smoothing, and trend projection. The **naive approach** assumes that demand in the next period will be equal to demand in the most recent period. The **moving averages method** uses an average of the most recent periods of data to forecast the next period. The **exponential smoothing method** uses a weighted-moving averages technique in which data points are weighted by an exponential function. The **trend projection method** fits a trendline to a series of historical data points and then projects the line into the future.

Conjoint Analysis

Conjoint analysis is a decompositional model that disaggregates the model's attributes. It is a statistical technique used in marketing and consumer research where customers' preferences for different attributes (such as product offers or advertising impacts) are decomposed to determine customers' inferred utility function and relative value for each attribute. In other words, it breaks down customers' preferences.

Regression Analysis

Regression analysis is a mathematical procedure used to determine and measure the predictive relationship between one variable (dependent variable) and one or more other variables (independent variable). It is a causal forecasting method that can be used to develop forecasts when time-series data are not available. Regression analysis is a statistical technique that can be used to develop a mathematical equation showing how variables are related.

Two types of regression analysis are simple linear regression and multiple regression. In simple linear regression, there are only two variables: one dependent variable and one independent variable. In multiple regression, there are more than two variables: one dependent variable and more than one independent variable.

Linear Regression Analysis

Linear regression analysis, which is an associative model, considers several variables that are related to the quantity being predicted. The linear regression method is more powerful than time-series methods that use only historical values for the forecasted variable. Two types of variables exist: the dependent variable (the forecasted item of interest) and the independent variable (which is related to the dependent variable). The multiple regression method uses more than one independent variable; the linear regression method uses only one independent variable.

Cluster Analysis

Clusters are geographic concentrations of interconnected companies and institutions in a particular field. **Cluster analysis** is a geographical grouping and labeling of individual customers based on their buying behavior, demographics, and lifestyles. It is used to create a classification by using single or multiple dimensions and involves coding things and identifying patterns in data.

Cluster analysis is a statistical technique to identify groups of entities that have similar characteristics that can be applied to data mining and market research areas. For example, cluster analysis can be used:

- In data mining applications to find groups of similar customers from customer order and demographic data.
- By market researchers to divide the population of subjects to interview into mutually exclusive groups (e.g., city blocks and counties) and draw a sample of the groups from the segmented population.
- To geographically group and label individuals based on their buying behavior, demographics, and lifestyles.
- To create a classification of customers by using a single dimension or multiple dimensions.

Correlation Analysis

Correlation analysis predicts the cause-and-effect relationships between two variables whereas regression methods cannot. Two types of correlation measures exist: coefficient of correlation, which is a measure of the strength of the relationship between two variables, and coefficient of determination, which is the square of the coefficient of correlation. The coefficient of determination is the percentage of variation in the dependent variable that is explained by the regression equation. Correlation analysis and factor analysis play an important role in canonical analysis.

Discriminant Analysis

Discriminant analysis is an identification procedure. This technique can be applied to a wide variety of research and predictive problems and interpretation and classification of data. It studies the differences between two or more groups and a set of discriminant variables simultaneously. For example, multiple discriminant analysis is used for constructing credit-scoring indexes when granting a personal credit to an individual customer or to a business customer for granting a trade credit and identifying businesses that might go bankrupt.

Multivariate Analysis

Multivariate analysis is a research technique used to determine how a combination of variables interacts to cause a particular outcome. For example, multivariate analysis can be applied to determine the multiple variables affecting an employee's productivity. Examples of these multiple variables include conscientious personality, high challenging task, and higher satisfaction with job and life. It is called bivariate analysis when an employee's productivity is solely based on morale (i.e., one-to-one causal relationship between two variables such as productivity and morale).

Factor Analysis

Factor analysis is used in the exploratory or confirmatory of "interdependence" among variables. It is a statistical technique that examines the relationships between a single dependent variable and multiple independent variables. For example, it is used to determine which questions on a customer questionnaire are related to a specific question, such as "Would you buy this product again?"

Factor analysis can reveal how different variables change in relation to each other and how they are associated. It is used in the exploratory or confirmatory of "interdependence" among the variables. It is a statistical technique that examines the relationships between a single dependent variable and multiple independent variables. However, factor analysis is sensitive to the presence of outliers, which may introduce spurious variables in the data. It is also sensitive to problems with small sample sizes, especially when the number of variables is small.

Canonical Analysis

Canonical analysis considers possible interrelationships among independent and dependent variables. It extends the basic relationship to an entire set of dependent variables as it discovers and explores factors that are correlated across datasets but uncorrelated within a dataset. Canonical analysis depends on an understanding of factor analysis and correlation analysis.

Link Analysis

Link analysis detects known and unknown relationships and explicit and implicit connections among various data elements in a database consisting of transactional data. It connects relevant data segments with each other, forming categories, clusters, or networks of information. It examines large amounts of data collected from multiple datasets and social media networks for connections, relationships, and associations indicating fraud, waste, and abuse. Link analysis can be applied to employees, vendors, suppliers, contractors, business partners, and customers to discover fraudulent schemes such as improper payments and money laundering.

Causal Analysis

Causal analysis is a method for analyzing the possible causal associations among a set of variables. Two related methods are the causal forecasting method and causal distributions. Causal forecasting methods relate a time-series to other variables that are believed to explain or cause the behavior of the time-series. They link the forecast values of an effect variable to one or more hypothesized causes. Causal distributions are a set of outcomes characterized by situations where a predictor variable has changed from what was expected, causing the forecast variable to deviate from what was expected.

Bayesian Statistics

Bayesian statistics help managers making nonrepeating decisions in a changing or dynamic business environment. Managers make an initial decision based on old or prior information with its associated probabilities, opinions, or beliefs about certain events occurring. Later, they gather new data with the goal of revising prior opinions and beliefs and improving or updating the initial decision. The outcome of this new learning exercise is new information, new probabilities, new opinions, and new beliefs with subsequent new decisions, plans, and actions to result in a new final decision.

Markov Chain Analysis

A Markov process consists of a set of objects and a set of states where objects move from one state to another state, say from a current state to any future state. A Markov process becomes a Markov chain when the number of states is finite. Markov process models and Markov chain models are useful in studying the evolution of certain systems over repeated trials.

Markov process analysis is useful in studying the evolution of certain systems over repeated trials as it shows the probability of moving from a current state to any future state. Markov process analysis does not optimize a system; instead, it describes the future and steady-state behavior of a system. Basically, Markov chain predicts where a state moves next based on where it is now. Bayesian statistics are behind the Markov chain analysis.

Monte Carlo Methods

Monte Carlo methods deploy computational algorithms that rely on repeated random number sampling to obtain numerical results to solve problems involving probabilities and uncertain outcomes. These methods require large amounts of random numbers (i.e., applying the law of large numbers) with unknown parameters to use in resource optimization, resource integration, and computer simulation applications.

A major application of Monte Carlo method is simulation of business games in which business events are repeated many times to obtain the distribution of unknown probabilistic outcomes (i.e., success or fail).

Monte Carlo Methods (continued)

Monte Carlo simulation uses probabilistic distributions, meaning it uses probabilities and time intervals of outcomes. When probabilities are involved, it is called a stochastic model. Moreover, Monte Carlo simulation does not use the traditional, static, deterministic models. Bayesian statistics are behind the Monte Carlo methods.

Data Simulation Models

The primary objective of simulation models is to describe the behavior of a real system. A model is designed and developed and a study is conducted to understand the behavior of the simulation model. The characteristics that are learned from the model are then used to make inferences about the real system. Later, the model is modified (asking what-if questions) to improve the system's performance. The behavior of the model in response to the what-if questions is studied to determine how well the real system will respond to the proposed modifications. Thus, the simulation model will help the decision maker by predicting what can be expected in practice—in the real world. A key requisite is that the logic of the model should be as close to the actual operations as possible. In most cases, a computer is used for simulation models. Computer simulation should not be viewed as an optimization technique but as a way to improve the behavior or performance of the system through adjusting model parameters. Monte Carlo simulation can be used in data simulation models.

Data Simulation Models (continued)

Examples of Data Simulation Models

Data simulation models can be used to:

- Determine risk levels (e.g., success or failure) in a new product development idea
- Select an inventory replenishment level that would balance the profit level and customer service level
- Predict machine breakdowns in a machine shop
- Identify traffic flow patterns in a highway
- Understand a bank's customer waiting lines
- Identify airline ticket overbooking patterns

DATA ANALYSIS AND EVALUATION TECHNIQUES

The scope of data analysis and evaluation techniques includes two major topics: computerized audit tools and techniques and data mining and extraction methods.

Computerized Audit Tools and Techniques

Auditing around the Computer versus Auditing with the Computer

There are two approaches to testing computer-based data: auditing around the computer and auditing with the computer. The appropriate approach or combination of approaches is dependent on the nature of the related system (see Exhibit 3.6).

	Auditing around the Computer	**Auditing with the Computer**
Time involved to do the audit	High	Low
Cost involved to do the audit	Low/Medium	Medium/High
Audit effectiveness	Low/Medium	High
Technical knowledge required of auditor	Low	High

Exhibit 3.6: Auditing around the computer and auditing with the computer

Embedded Audit Modules

Embedded audit data collection modules use one or more specially designed data collection modules embedded in the computer application system to select and record data for subsequent analysis and evaluation. The data collection modules are inserted in the application system or program at points that the auditor determines to be appropriate. The auditor also determines the criteria for selection and recording. Other automated or manual methods may be used to analyze the collected data. This technique is intended to highlight unusual transactions and subject them to audit review and testing. This technique is also known as system control audit review file (SCARF).

Unlike other audit methods, this technique uses "inline" code; that is, the computer application program performs the audit data collection function at the same time it processes the data for normal production purposes. This has two important consequences for the auditor: (1) inline code ensures the availability of a comprehensive or very specialized sample of data as desired by the auditor, since strategically placed modules have access to every data element being processed; and (2) retrofitting this technique to an existing system is costlier than implementing the audit module during system development. Therefore, it is preferable for auditors to specify requirements in this regard while the application system is being designed. Ideally, data collection control points should be inserted in the application program processing logic where errors, irregularities, or security breaches are most likely to occur.

Audit Hooks

Audit hooks are similar to red flags to auditors. They are computer programs used in high-risk systems and are triggered by a condition or event designed by the auditor in conjunction with the information systems staff and the user. The objective is to act before an error, abnormality, or irregularity gets out of hand. Audit hooks are inserted in application programs to function as red flags. For example, bank internal auditors can use an audit hook in a program that processes dormant customer accounts to observe the activity in the account and, if need be, initiate timely action to correct or eliminate any identified irregularities. The difference between the audit hooks technique and the SCARF technique is that an audit hook is used more specifically for sensitive applications.

Extended Records

The extended record technique collects, by means of a special program(s), all the significant data that have affected the processing of an individual transaction. This includes the accumulation of the results of processing into a single record covering the time period that the transaction required to complete its processing. The extended record includes data from all the computer application systems that contributed to the processing of a transaction. Such extended records are compiled into files that provide a conveniently accessible source of transaction data. Auditors can extract the transactions that have such extended records using generalized audit software or utility programs and prepare reports for audit review and analysis.

Extended Records (continued)

With this technique, the auditor no longer needs to review several computer data files to determine how a specific transaction was processed. With extended records, data are consolidated from different accounting periods and from systems interfacing with the application system being reviewed so that a complete transaction audit trail is physically included in one computer record. This facilitates tests of compliance to organization policies and procedures.

Generalized Audit Software

Generalized audit software is an all-purpose audit software (e.g., ACL and IDEA) that should be used to achieve cost-effective audits of computer-based systems where similar audit tasks are required to meet a variety of objectives. Generalized audit software can:

- Provide totals of unusual items.
- Check for duplications, missing information, or range of values.
- Verify calculation totals and analyses produced.
- Examine the existence and consistency of data maintained in files.
- Perform concurrent auditing of data files.
- Select and generate audit confirmations.

Generalized audit software is most effective in verifying the clerical accuracy of an account balance. It is least effective in evaluating the logic of a specific computer program, evaluating the adequacy of internal controls embedded in a computer program, or confirming the existence of internal controls in manual operational procedures.

A limitation to using the audit software is that it can be used only on hardware with compatible operating systems. The audit software does not require significant programming knowledge to be used effectively. It does not require lengthy detailed instructions in order to accomplish specific tasks. It does not require significant modification of the program to be of use. The audit software cannot specify which data elements will be tested and the criteria to be used. The auditor specifies the criteria.

Generalized Audit Software (continued)

Generalized audit software packages can foot, cross-foot, balance, stratify, select a statistical sample, select transactions, total, compare, and perform calculations on diverse data elements contained within various data files.

Advantages of generalized audit software are listed next.

- It is most widely used to analyze and extract data from computer files.
- It allows the auditor to examine more data on computer records in more detail than when using manual records.
- It can be used to automate workpaper preparation.
- It enables auditors to control their own programming and testing work.
- It minimizes audit staff time allocated to audit testing.
- It minimizes the cost of adapting audit program routines to frequent changes in the application program being used due to a parameter-driven approach used in the audit software.

Disadvantages of generalized audit software are listed next.

- It is least likely to be used for inquiry of online data files.
- It cannot flowchart an application program logic.
- It cannot perform a physical count of inventory or cash.
- It cannot perform continuous monitoring and analysis of transactions.
- It can require technical knowledge of information systems.

Spreadsheet Analysis

Auditors perform spreadsheet analysis very extensively with the use of microcomputer-based software packages, such as Spreadsheet Auditor and Spreadsheet Analyst. These software packages are designed to serve as an aid in creating error-free spreadsheets. The software prints out a description of ranges; a map indicating which cells contain formulas, labels, numbers, or macros; and a formula report. A critical point is the accuracy of formulas used in spreadsheet cells and their applicability to business rules.

Automated Workpapers

Automated workpaper software helps auditors to increase efficiency and productivity because it relieves the boredom of writing out by hand. The software automatically refers to audit work program sections and related audit objectives. Any corrections or changes can be done with ease and without losing the continuity.

Program or system flowcharts, tables, or graphs generated by the automated documentation aids provide a correct picture of what is in the computer programs and data files as opposed to relying on incorrect, obsolete, or incomplete documentation maintained on paper.

Source Code Comparison

The best audit tool and technique that an auditor in charge of reviewing program changes can find is a source code compare utility program. Why review and compare source code? Source code is the media through which program changes, whether authorized or unauthorized, can be made. Source code explains the functions, features, and capabilities of a computerized application system. Programmers write a source code in a programming language, such as COBOL. Hence it is most vulnerable to program changes. After the source code is developed, it is placed in a production source code library, which is often protected from unauthorized modifications by the use of program library management software packages.

Simply stated, a source code compare utility program takes two versions of a source code, compares each line of code, and indicates differences and whether the line of code is added, changed, or deleted. This output can be used in a structured walkthrough or for management and auditor reviews. The auditor then locates and analyzes the supporting documentation (system, program, computer operations, and user) prepared to authorize and implement the program changes. Lack of supporting documentation is a weakness in controls, which is an indication of potential risk and exposure. The auditor needs to inform management to strengthen internal controls over software maintenance activities.

Object Code Comparison

As mentioned, programmers write source code in a programming language, such as COBOL. Later the source code is translated into machine-readable language, object code, for proper execution of the program. Compiler software supplied by vendors performs the translation of source code into object code. Load/executable code, which comes after the object code is link edited, is then placed in a production library and used for the processing of live data for an application system.

The source code compare utility software package, described in the previous section, may not be sufficient to ensure that programs are changed properly and effectively. An additional approach is needed to ensure that the object code being executed in production mode is in agreement with the authorized source code.

The auditor can use object code compare utility software packages to compare two versions of a program's object code to report any differences.

File Comparison Utility Program

File compare is performed by a utility program supplied by a software vendor (e.g., IBM's IEBCOMPR). The purpose of the tool is to identify differences in data field names and values in two files of data at a static point in time. For example, in a manufacturing environment, an "on-hand inventory balance" data field appearing in two different files can be compared with the use of a file compare utility program to determine if the values are the same. If not, an abnormal situation exists that may require analysis and correction if the two values are supposed to be the same.

File Comparison Utility Program (continued)

Another example is to compare file control totals in accounts receivable or payable subsidiary ledger files to file control totals maintained in the general ledger file. Accounting logic requires that these two file control totals be the same. If not, an abnormal situation exists. Also, this tool can be used to compare job control language file contents at two points in time to detect any changes. The auditor needs to be imaginative to use this powerful tool in software maintenance and development activities.

Test Data Method

The test data method verifies computer-processing accuracy of application programs by executing these programs using manually prepared sets of test cases, test data, and expected results of processing. Actual processing results are compared with the expected results. If the two results are identical, then the auditor may infer that the program logic is consistent with the documentation.

This method provides auditors with a procedure for review, testing, and evaluation of computer program logic. However, because of continual program changes, preparing and maintaining test data manually is very difficult and time-consuming. In addition, the test data method is not an appropriate technique for verification of the accuracy and completeness of production data or master files.

Base Case System Evaluation

Base case system evaluation (BCSE) is a technique that applies a standardized body of data (input, parameters, and output) to the testing of computer application programs. User staff, with auditor participation, establishes this body of data (the base case) as the criterion for correct functioning of the computer application system. This testing process is widely used as a technique for validation of production systems.

Some organizations use the base case approach to test computer programs during their development, demonstrate the successful operation of the system prior to implementation, and verify its continuing and accurate processing during its production life. As a result, this approach requires and represents a total commitment by data processing and user department management to the principles and disciplines of BCSE.

Integrated Test Facility

Integrated test facility (ITF) is a technique to review application program logic and functions to provide the auditor with evidence on operating procedures (computer and/or manual) and error-handling conditions. The auditor's test data for a fictitious entity (i.e., a branch, department, division, or subsidiary) are used to compare ITF processing results to precalculated and expected test results. Here the auditor's test data are processed with normal production data. The auditor must ensure that the ITF results for the fictitious entity are removed from the regular production data files either at the end of testing process or later, in order to eliminate its impact on the organization's financial and operating transactions and records. ITF can be used in batch and online application systems.

Parallel Simulation

Parallel simulation is the use of one or more special computer programs to process "live" data files and simulate normal computer application processing. As opposed to the test data method and the ITF, which process test data through "live" programs, the parallel simulation method processes "live" data through test programs. Generalized audit software can be used to create a test model or simulation of relatively simple application systems or a portion of more complex application systems.

Parallel simulation programs include only the application logic, calculations, and controls that are relevant to specific audit objectives. As a result, simulation programs are usually much less complex than their application program counterparts. Often large segments of major applications that consist of several computer programs can be simulated for audit purposes with a single parallel simulation program. Parallel simulation permits the auditors to independently verify complex and critical application program controls and procedures. Parallel simulation is also used to test computer programs and complex processing logic, such as interest calculations, during system development projects.

Snapshot

Both auditors and IT staff periodically encounter difficulty in reconstructing the computer decision-making process. The cause is a failure to keep together all the data elements involved in that process. Snapshot is a technique that, in effect, takes a picture of the parts of computer memory that contain the data elements involved in a computerized decision-making process at the time the decision is made.

Input transactions are tagged and written to an audit log file with date, time, and indication of the point in the program at which the snapshot occurred. The results of the snapshot are printed in a report for review and analysis.

The snapshot audit technique offers the ability of listing all the data that were involved in a specific decision-making process. The technique requires that the necessary logic is preprogrammed in the system. A mechanism, usually a special code in the transaction record, is added for triggering, logging, and printing of the data in question for analysis.

The snapshot audit technique may help auditors answer questions as to why computer application systems produce questionable results. It provides information to explain why the computer made a particular decision.

Used in conjunction with other audit techniques (e.g., ITF or tracing), this technique aids in the determination of what results would occur if a certain type of input entered the application system. The snapshot technique can also be an invaluable aid to systems and programming staff in debugging the application system because it can provide "pictures" of the computer memory. Ideally, the snapshot technique should be designed as part of the original application system development process. The auditor participates in the system development process by defining requirements and reviewing system design specifications and system test results.

Tracing

In an IT environment, it is not possible to follow the path of a transaction through its processing cycle solely by following the paperwork flow, since the computer accomplishes many of the functions performed by employees and no hard-copy documents are produced. A new type of audit evidence (electronic) is introduced.

Tracing is an audit technique that provides the auditor with the ability to perform an electronic walkthrough of a computer application system. The audit objective of tracing is to verify compliance with policies and procedures by substantiating, through an examination of the path a transaction followed through a program, how that transaction was processed. Tracing can be used to detect omissions.

Tracing shows what instructions have been executed in a computer program and in which sequence they have been executed. Since the instructions in a computer program represent the steps in processing, the processes that have been executed can be determined from the results of the tracing audit technique. Once an auditor knows what instructions in a program have been executed, he or she can perform an analysis to determine if the processing conformed to the organization's policies and procedures.

Mapping

Mapping is a technique used to assess the extent of system testing and to identify specific program logic that has not been tested. Mapping is performed by software measurement tools that analyze a computer program during execution and indicate which program statements have been executed. The software measurement tool can also determine the amount of central processing unit time consumed by each program segment.

Mapping (continued)

The original intent of the mapping concept was to help computer programmers ensure the quality of their programs. Auditors can use the same software measurement tools, however, to look for unexecuted program statements. This analysis can provide auditors with insight into the efficiency of program operation and can reveal unauthorized program segments or statements included, if any exist.

Control Flowcharting

A graphic technique, or flowchart, for simplifying the identification and interrelationships of controls can be a great help in evaluating the adequacy of those controls and in assessing the impact of system changes on the overall control profile.

Flowcharts facilitate the explanation of controls to system analysts, auditors, or people unfamiliar with specific functions of the system. They also aid in ascertaining that controls are operating as originally intended or planned.

The control flowcharting technique provides the documentation necessary to explain the system of control. Often an organization's information about controls is fragmented, which makes obtaining a clear picture of the controls operating within the organization difficult. The availability of an overall picture of controls, using several levels of flowcharts, facilitates understanding.

Control Reprocessing

Control reprocessing is a technique to identify lost or incomplete records during an update cycle. An update cycle of importance is reprocessed to compare against the original update to determine whether the results are the same between the two updates, original and reprocessed. If the results are not the same, analysis is conducted to identify the sources causing the difference.

Audit Test Lab

An effective audit function develops and maintains an Audit Test Model or Audit Test Lab for repeated use in several audits as a template to gain economies-of-scale benefits. This model contains audit test scripts, test beds, test data, test cases, and test results for use in various audit test scenarios. This model saves time, energy, and frustration from not having to repeat or start all over again for each audit (i.e., benefits). One-time audits, routine audits, ad-hoc audits, special audits, continuous audits, and agile audits are the best candidates for the application of this audit test model.

Audit Test Lab (continued)

WHICH COMPUTER-ASSISTED AUDIT TECHNIQUE METHOD USES WHAT?

- The test data method uses test data with production programs.
- The parallel simulation method uses production data with test programs.
- The ITF method uses test data with production programs.
- The embedded audit data collection, generalized audit software, snapshot, audit hooks, tracing, mapping, extended records, and transaction selection methods all use production data with production programs.

Conventional and Concurrent Audit Techniques

In a conventional audit using a computer-assisted audit technique (CAAT) on an after-the-fact-basis, auditors evaluate the controls at periodic intervals. Using concurrent audit techniques, controls are evaluated on a continuing basis. Audit evidence is collected in a timely manner.

Exhibit 3.7 presents a comparison between conventional and concurrent audit techniques.

Conventional audit techniques	Concurrent audit techniques
Examples: generalized audit software, test data method, transaction selection, extended records, tracing, mapping, utility programs	Examples: ITF, SCARF, simulation, snapshots, audit hooks
Most appropriate for computerized batch, simple, and normal application systems	Most appropriate for computerized online, complex, and sensitive application systems
Require less data processing technical knowledge on the part of the auditor	Require more data processing technical knowledge on the part of the auditor
Mostly use test data instead of production data	Mostly use production data instead of test data
Not part of user production application systems	Part of production application systems
Auditor has more control over test data	Auditor has less control over test data
Auditor initiates CAAT program execution to test plans and schedules	Application system initiates CAAT program execution according to specified event, transaction, date, time, and other criteria

Exhibit 3.7: Conventional and concurrent audit techniques

Data Mining and Extraction Methods

Data Mining Defined

Data mining is the application of database technologies and advanced data analytics to uncover hidden patterns, trends, correlations, outliers, anomalies, and subtle relationships in data and to infer rules that allow for the prediction of future results and outcomes. Data mining analyzes data for relationships that have not previously been discovered and other insights not suggested by a priori hypotheses or explicit assumptions. For example, these insights might apply to retail market trend in terms of customer buying preferences and customer shopping behaviors.

Today, mining can be performed on many types of data, including those in structured, textual, web, or multimedia forms. Simply stated, mining can be performed on structured data, unstructured data, and semistructured data (e.g., XML and HTML). Data mining overlaps with a wide range of analytical activities, including data profiling, databases, data warehouses, data marts, virtual databases, online analytical processing (OLAP), structured query language (SQL), statistical analyses, data modeling, and predictive data analytics.

Both private sector and public sector organizations are increasingly using data mining applications for a number of purposes.

Data Mining in the Private Sector

Private sector organizations are using data mining applications to explore new business opportunities with the sole goal of growing their business. A list of major and minor purposes follows.

- Improving service or performance in increasing sales, revenues, and profits (major purpose)
- Detecting fraud, waste, and abuse (major purpose)
- Analyzing intelligence and detecting terrorist activities (minor purpose)
- Analyzing scientific and research information (major purpose)
- Detecting criminal activities and patterns (major purpose)
- Improving employee, customer, and vendor safety (minor purpose)

Broadly speaking, private sector applications of data mining include customer relationship management, market research, retail, supply chain, medical analysis and diagnostics, financial analysis, and fraud detection.

Data Mining in the Public Sector

Public sector organizations are using data mining applications for a variety of purposes ranging from improving service or performance to analyzing and detecting terrorist patterns and activities. A list of major and minor purposes follows.

- Improving service or performance levels to citizens (major purpose)
- Detecting fraud, waste, and abuse such as improper payments (major purpose)
- Analyzing scientific and research information for new drugs and new medical treatments (major purpose)
- Managing human resources for promotions, pay scales, pay grades, contractor security clearances, and employee background checks (major purpose)
- Detecting criminal activities or patterns such as identity theft cases (major purpose)
- Analyzing intelligence and detecting terrorist activities using the Internet source (minor purpose)

Broadly speaking, public sector applications of data mining focus on detecting financial fraud and abuse in procurement and credit card programs and analyzing intelligence and detecting terrorist activities.

Privacy Concerns over Data Mining

Privacy concerns about mined or analyzed personal data are listed next.

- The quality and accuracy of the mined data
- The use of the data for other than the original purpose for which the data were collected without the consent of the individual
- The protection of the data against unauthorized access, modification, or disclosure
- The right of individuals to know about the collection of personal information, how to access that information, and how to request a correction of inaccurate information

Technologies in Data Mining

Eight technologies deployed in data mining—databases, virtual databases, data warehouses, data marts, online analytical processing (OLAP), structured query language (SQL), artificial intelligence (AI), and machine language (ML)—and miscellaneous tools and techniques are described next. Dashboards can be used to display the output results from these tools and techniques.

Databases

A database contains facts and figures on various types of information such as sales, costs, and personnel. These files are collectively called the firm's database. A database is a collection of related data about an organization, intended for sharing of this data by multiple users. A database management system (DBMS) is comprised of software, hardware, and procedures. The DBMS acts as a software controller enabling different application systems to access large numbers of distinct data records stored on direct access storage devices (e.g., disks).

The DBMS should be compatible with the operating system environment and handle complex data structures. Unauthorized access to data elements is a major concern in a database system due to concentration of data. The DBMS helps in providing user interface with the application system through increased accessibility and flexibility by means of data views (i.e., data windows).

A data model describes relationships between the data elements and is used as a tool to represent the conceptual organization of data. A relationship within a data model can be one to one (e.g., between patient and bed in a hospital environment—at any given time, one bed is assigned to one patient), one to many (e.g., between hospital room and patients—one hospital room accommodates more than one patient), and many to many (e.g., between patient and surgeon—one surgeon may attend to many patients and a patient may be attended by more than one surgeon).

The primary purpose of any data model is to provide a formal means of representing information and a formal means of manipulating the representation. A good data model can help describe and model the application effectively. A DBMS uses one or more data models such as relational, hierarchical, network, object, or distributed.

Virtual Databases

A virtual database is created when data from multiple database sources is integrated to provide a total perspective on a specific topic. It is virtual in that such database does not exist physically but is created on demand. For example, an auditor comparing performance of a multiplant organization can use virtual database technology to view key operating and financial ratios of each plant side by side.

Data Warehouses

The purpose of a data warehouse is information retrieval and data analysis. It stores precomputed, historical, descriptive, and numerical data. It is the process of extracting and transferring operational data into informational data and loading it into a central data store, or warehouse. Once the data is loaded, users can access the warehouse through query and analysis tools. The data warehouse can be housed on a computer different from the production computer.

A data warehouse is a storage facility where data from heterogeneous databases are brought together so that users can make queries against the warehouse instead of against several databases. The warehouse is like a big database. Redundant and inconsistent data are removed from the databases, and subsets of data are selected from the databases prior to placing them in a data warehouse. Usually a data warehouse contains summary, correlated, or otherwise massaged data.

Data Warehouses (continued)

Issues of data integrity and security are as applicable to warehouses as they are to databases. An issue is: What happens to the warehouse when the individual databases are updated?

Data modeling is an essential task for building a data warehouse along with access methods, index strategies, and query language. For example, if the data model is relational, then an SQL-based language is used. If the data model is object-oriented, an object-based language may be appropriate.

Metadata management is another critical technology for data warehousing. Metadata includes mapping between the data sources (databases) and the warehouse. Another issue is whether the warehouse can be centralized or distributed.

Data Marts

A data mart is a subset of a data warehouse (i.e., a mini-data warehouse). A data mart brings the data from transaction processing systems to functional departments (i.e., finance, manufacturing, and human resources), business units, or divisions. Data marts are scaled-down data warehouses, where targeted business information is placed into the hands of more decision makers.

Online Analytical Processing

OLAP programs are available to store and deliver data warehouse information from multidimensional databases. OLAP allows users to explore corporate data from a number of different perspectives, such as product, geography, time, and salesperson.

OLAP servers and desktop tools support high-speed analysis of data involving complex relationships, such as combinations of a company's products, regions, channels of distribution, reporting units, and time periods. Access to data in multidimensional databases can be very quick because they store the data in structures optimized for speed, and they avoid using SQL and index processing techniques. In other words, multidimensional databases have greater retrieval speed and longer update times.

Consumer goods companies (e.g., retail) use OLAP to analyze the millions of consumer purchase records and transactions captured by electronic scanners at checkout stands. This data is used to spot trends in purchases and to relate sales volume to store promotions (coupons) and store conditions (displays). The data in OLAP is generally aggregated, giving information such as total or average sales in dollars or units. Users can examine the OLAP's hierarchical data in the time dimension, such as sales by year, by quarter, by month, by week, or by day.

Structured Query Language

The primary components of an SQL database are schemas, tables, and views, parser, optimizer, executor, access rights checker, and access rights grantor or revoker. A schema describes the structure of related tables and views. Tables hold the actual data in the database; they consist of rows and columns. Each row is a set of columns; each column is a single data element. Views are derived tables and may be composed of a subset of a table or the result of table operations (e.g., a join of different tables). A parser is a program that breaks input into smaller chunks so that a program can act on the information.

SQL is a standard query language for relational DBMS that is also used to query and update the data managed by the DBMS. The SQL standard, which is used by most commercial DBMSs, includes specific requirements for enforcing discretionary access controls.

Artificial Intelligence and Machine Learning Technology

Artificial intelligence (AI) is the simulation of human intelligence processing by machines and computer software. These processes contain learning rules, logical reasoning, and self-correction methods. For example, AI uses natural language processing technology so it will process a retail shopper's questions and requests and provide answers. Other applications can be found in expert systems and speech recognition systems.

Machine learning (ML) is a type of AI that provides computers with the ability to learn without being explicitly programmed. ML focuses on the development of computer programs that can change their behavior when exposed to new data. Computers can handle new situations through analysis, self-training, observation, and experience, all with minimal supervision and involvement by people. ML is a part of predictive analytics and is related to cognitive computing.

Examples

- Macy's is testing AI technology to improve sales. Customers can ask the Macy's mobile tool designed with the AI technology to receive answers related to the visited store, such as where a particular brand is located or what is in stock. Normally, customers would ask a sales associate about these questions face to face.
- Retailers are using the AI technology so customers can receive answers to their questions on the retailer's websites, not face to face.
- Transportation and package delivery companies can use AI-based chatbots so internal employees and external customers can track delivery of customer packages.

Miscellaneous Tools and Techniques

Miscellaneous tools and techniques include neural networks and text-mining. Neural networks learn by training and can be used in reviewing credit card transactions to detect anomalies and fraudulent activities. Text-mining tools are used to scan unstructured documents, such as emails, web pages, and audio/video files, and to scan structured data found in databases or data warehouses.

Technologies used in data mining are summarized in the next list.

- A database contains raw data.
- A data warehouse contains massaged or cleaned-up data.
- End users query many points with heterogeneous databases.
- End users query only a single point with homogeneous data warehouses.
- A data warehouse provides summary data for the entire business.
- A data mart provides detailed data for a specific function of a business.
- Data mining is an end user tool to select information from a data warehouse.
- Data mining is an auditing tool to detect fraud, intrusion incidents, and security problems in a data warehouse.

Applications in Data Mining

Data mining is the process of asking (posing) a series of questions (queries) against a database or data warehouse containing large amounts of data to extract some meaningful, relevant, and useful information to perform management analysis. Data warehouses and data marts do not attempt to extract information from the data they contain. A data mining tool is needed to do this.

Data mining applications are best suited to data-intense organizations with millions of customers' data collected in their databases or data warehouses. Examples of such organizations include retailers, market research firms, governmental agencies, online order takers, casinos, travel agencies, vacation cruise line firms, hotels, rental car companies, and airline companies. There is no end to data mining applications; their use is limited only by the imagination of the person requesting the data analysis work.

Data mining applications software is available from numerous vendors. This off-the-shelf software is easier to use and less expensive than custom-built software.

Data mining is data analysis, data fishing, data snooping, and data drilling in order to get to the bottom of the vast amounts of data (big data) collected by organizations during their business operations. Data analytics is another name for data mining.

Management uses various quantitative techniques, such as regression analysis, factor analysis, cluster analysis, sampling, and other statistical methods, to analyze data, to find relationships between data elements, and to draw meaningful conclusions that can be incorporated into its decision-making process. The ultimate goal is to improve business operations and increase profits.

Applications in Data Mining (continued)

Data mining can be applied to databases as well as to data warehouses. A warehouse structures the data in such a way as to facilitate query processing. Data mining is a set of automated tools that convert the data in the warehouse into some useful information. Data mining selects and reports information deemed significant from a data warehouse or database.

Before data mining software tools are applied, data needs to be cleaned or normalized (the target data, raw datasets) to remove missing data, erroneous data, or inappropriate data. Here, data mining tools can discover data relationships and data clusters, where the latter is a grouping of similar data items. Data mining also uncovers patterns and trends in data.

The data cleansing and data normalizations actions are performed in a preprocessing step, shown next.

Preprocessing	→	**Data mining**	→	**Postprocessing**
Raw data		Software tools		Insights and decisions
Data cleansing		Data analytics		Results and reports
Data normalization				

There are several types of data mining applications, including data classifications, data sequencing, data dependencies, and deviation analysis. Data records can be classified or grouped into clusters or classes so that patterns in the data can be found. Data sequencing can be determined from the data. Data dependencies, such as relationships or associations between the data items, can be detected. Deviation analysis can be performed on data. Fuzzy logic, neural networks, and set theory are some techniques used in data mining tools.

Applications in Data Mining (continued)

Data mining techniques can also be used for intrusion detection, fraud detection, and auditing the databases. Data mining tools can be used to detect abnormal patterns in data, which can provide clues to fraud. A security problem can be created when a user poses queries and infers sensitive hypotheses. That is, the inference problem occurs via the data mining tool. A data mining tool can be applied to see if sensitive information can be deduced from unclassified information legitimately obtained. If so, then there is an inference problem. An inference controller can be built to detect the motives of the users and prevent the inference problem from occurring. The inference controller can be placed between the data mining tool and the database. Since data mining tools are computationally intensive, parallel processing computers are used to carry out the data mining activities.

Harrah's Casino and Hotel in Las Vegas, an entertainment company, is a big user of data mining applications. Interested customers (guests) are given an electronic card before playing. These cards collect data on guests' gambling actions in terms of what games they play, how much time they spend on each type of game, what games they lose or win, how many times they visit the casino in a year, how many days they stay in the hotel for each visit, whether they come alone or with family, and their personal income. For example, if a Harrah's guest's personal income is very high, the system recommends that the guest play high-stakes games with very attractive incentives and rewards. Different incentive and reward programs are available for guests with normal personal income. This outcome is a win-win situation in that the casino makes additional profit on the guest and the guest enjoys extra perks (royal treatment) that he or she would not have received otherwise.

Applications in Data Mining (continued)

Other examples of application of data mining are listed next.

- Market segmentation, where the common characteristics of customers who buy the same products are identified
- Customer defection, where customers who are likely to leave the company are predicted
- Fraud detection, where transactions that are most likely to be fraudulent are identified
- Direct marketing, where prospects who are targets for mailing are identified
- Market basket analysis, where products or services that are commonly purchased together are identified
- Trend analysis, where the difference between a typical customer this month versus last month is revealed

AUDIT ANALYTICS

Several topics are discussed in this section, including cycle times and business velocities; bottleneck management; benchmarking; business process reviews; production process flows; process mapping techniques; value analysis; and analytical review techniques. The focus of most of these topics is to identify duplicate, overlapping, and unnecessary business tasks and activities that waste resources and to remove any roadblocks, bottlenecks, and delays in business processes to make them more effective and efficient.

Cycle Times

Cycle time is the maximum time that a product or service is allowed to spend at a workstation, machine, or office desk. In a manufacturing company, the scope of process analysis starts from raw materials and ends up with finished goods shipping to customers. It includes all the transformation (processing) stages, inspection steps, and transportation stages. Similarly, in a service company, the scope of process analysis starts, for example, with claims application and ends up with making payment to the claimant. The goal of process analysis is to facilitate change for improvement. Doing this requires looking not only at the individual processes where problems exist but also at the upstream and downstream processes that are related to the process in question. Process improvements can be made by rearranging equipment layout, plant layout, inspection points, and testing stages with the help of motion, material, time, and material handling studies. In this effort, both product processes and service processes should be examined for waste, delays, and improvement.

Cycle Times (continued)

Business processes, whether manufacturing or service, go through cycles from initiation to completion of defined tasks and activities. Each process has a beginning point and an ending point, and consumes resources (e.g., time, money, people talent, materials, machinery, and energy) to accomplish the defined tasks and activities. The goal is to consume as few of these resources as possible and complete these tasks and activities as efficiently and effectively as possible. Industrial engineers, also called "efficiency experts," can help in establishing and measuring the cycle times. Cycle time measures focus on the time dimension, expressed as hours or days.

Out of all the resources mentioned, time is a limited and critical resource because lost time cannot be regained. Organizations that can beat the time clock are clear winners in the highly competitive global business environment. The goal is to become the best in the best-in-class group using shorter cycle times. The shorter the cycle time, the better it is, because more work can be accomplished in less time. Cycle times measure the elapsed time between two or more successive events, the time taken to reach from Point A to Point B and back, or the time taken to complete a task from beginning to end.

If the cycle times are found to be unacceptable (i.e., too long), management should do the following to make them acceptable (i.e., shorter):

- Streamline the upstream and downstream work processes through work-study, process-flow, flowcharting, and process-mapping analyses.
- Simplify the work processes by eliminating or decreasing non-value-added activities, deleting duplicate tasks, and removing unnecessary hand-offs.

Cycle Times (continued)

- Standardize the work processes by issuing new policies, procedures, and tools for organization-wide use.
- Institutionalize standardized work processes across the entire organization in phases (i.e., a phased rollout).

The sequence of steps needed to reduce the cycle time in the value chain is:

Streamline → Simplify → Standardize → Institutionalize

Business Velocities

A relationship exists between velocities and cycle times. **Velocity** refers to speed and rate of turnover of something tangible, such as inventory and money currency. As mentioned, cycle time is the time taken to complete a task from beginning to end. "Time" is the common element between velocity and cycle time. Let us look at the velocity concept in two business settings: manufacturing industries and service industries.

Business Velocities for Manufacturing Industries

Sales Velocity → Inventory Velocity → Production Velocity → Finance velocity, Human capital velocity, Systems velocity

Business Velocities for Service Industries

Sales Velocity → Service Velocity → Finance velocity, Human capital velocity, Systems velocity

Business Velocities (continued)

For manufacturing industries, as sales are increasing (sales velocity), inventory is depleted quickly (inventory velocity), when it should be filled with increased production (production velocity). Money needs to be invested to support the increased production in terms of buying raw materials, parts, and components and paying for the workforce (finance velocity). More employees may need to be hired to meet the increased production levels (human capital velocity). All these velocities in aggregate may require developing new systems or modifying existing systems, whether manual or automated (systems velocity). The same logic applies to pure service industries except that they have no inventories to sell.

When sales velocity is increasing (i.e., more sales), production velocity should also be increasing (i.e., more production) in synchronization with each other. However, longer cycle times for specific internal tasks and operations within the production department can delay the required quantities of goods, thus preventing the organization from meeting the sales velocity demand. This delay requires optimizing the cycle times for all internal tasks and operations within production departments prior to handling the production velocity. Cycle times should not become a bottleneck to achieving any type of velocity.

In summary, velocities and cycle times are solidly linked in that shorter cycle times increase any type of business velocity, which in turn can increase revenues, decrease costs, and increase profits. For example, sales velocity in part cannot be increased if time-to-market cycle time for introducing new products is taking longer.

Bottleneck Management

A **bottleneck** is a constraint in a facility, function, department, or resource whose capacity is less than the demand placed on it. For example, a bottleneck machine or work center exists where jobs are processed at a slower rate than they are demanded. Another example is where the demand for a company's product exceeds the company's ability to produce the product.

Bottleneck influences both product profitability and product price. The contribution margin per bottleneck hour or the value of each bottleneck hour should be analyzed. This measure is more meaningful than the normal contribution margin per unit. The contribution margin per hour of bottleneck can be used to adjust the product price to better reflect the value of the product's use of a bottleneck's constraint. Products that use a large number of bottleneck hours per unit require more contribution margin than products that use few bottleneck hours per unit.

Theory of constraints (TOC) is a manufacturing strategy that attempts to remove the influence of bottlenecks on a process. According to Dr. Eliyahu M. Goldratt, TOC consists of three separate but interrelated areas: logistics, performance measurement, and logical thinking. Logistics include drum-buffer-rope scheduling, buffer management, and VAT analysis (all of which are described next). Performance measurement includes throughput, inventory and operating expense, and the five focusing steps. Logical thinking process tools are important in identifying the root problems (current reality tree), identifying and expanding win-win solutions (evaporating cloud and future reality tree), and developing implementation plans (prerequisite tree and transition tree).

Bottleneck Management (continued)

Drum-buffer-rope scheduling is the generalized process used to manage resources to maximize throughput. The **drum** is the rate or pace of production set by the system's constraint. The **buffers** establish the protection against uncertainty so that the system can maximize throughput. The **rope** is a communication process from the constraint to the gating operation that checks or limits material released into the system to support the constraint.

Buffer management is a process in which all expediting in a factory shop is driven by what is scheduled to be in the buffers (constraint, shipping, and assembly buffers). By expediting this material into the buffers, the system helps avoid idleness at the constraint and missed customer due dates. In addition, the causes of items missing from the buffer are identified, and the frequency of occurrence is used to prioritize improvement activities.

VAT analysis is a procedure for determining the general flow of parts and products from raw materials to finished products (the logical product structure). A "V" logical product structure starts with one or few raw materials, and the product expands into a number of different products as it flows through divergent points in its routings. The shape of an "A" logical product structure is dominated by converging points. Many raw materials are fabricated and assembled into a few finished products. A "T" logical product structure consists of numerous similar finished products assembled from common assemblies, subassemblies, and parts. Once the general parts flow is determined, the system control points (gating operations, convergent points, divergent points, constraints, and shipping points) can be identified and managed.

Bottleneck Management (continued)

The **five focusing steps** is a process to continuously improve organizational profit by evaluating the production system and the marketing mix to determine how to make the most profit using the system constraint. The steps consist of:

1. Identifying the constraint to the system
2. Deciding how to exploit the constraint to the system
3. Subordinating all nonconstraints to the system
4. Elevating all constraints to the system level
5. Returning to step 1 if the constraint is broken in any previous step while not allowing inertia to set in

Benchmarking

Benchmarking is the selection of best practices implemented by other organizations. **Best practices** are the best ways to perform a business process. Organizational change and improvement are the major elements of benchmarking. Benchmarks are the result of a study of organizational processes and performance through internal comparisons (i.e., between and among a company's business units and divisions) and external comparisons (i.e., between two or more organizations). A list of best practices at the first level of basic processes that define a company's operations is presented next.

- Understanding markets and customers
- Designing products and services
- Marketing and selling those products and services
- Producing what customers need and want
- Delivering products and services
- Providing service to customers

Supporting these basic processes, management and support processes maximize the value with the use of human resources, information technology, and financial/physical resources.

Benchmarking (continued)

The best way to practice benchmarking is to

- Analyze business processes (inventory major business processes, conduct documentary research, and attend conferences to understand new developments).
- Plan the benchmark study (define scope, request site visits, and develop a methodology for capturing the new data).
- Conduct the benchmark study (analyze best practices and identify performance gaps).
- Implement the benchmark results (incorporate best practices into business processes and reevaluate the business processes).

Two types of benchmarking exist: business process benchmarking and computer system benchmarking. Business process benchmarking deals with business process improvement and business process reengineering to reduce costs and to improve quality and customer service. Computer system benchmarking focuses on computer hardware/software acquisition, computer system design, computer capacity planning, and system performance. Each has its own place and time.

Benchmarking (continued)

In general, business benchmarking is an external focus on internal activities, functions, or operations in order to achieve continuous improvement. The objective is to understand existing processes and activities and then to identify an external point of reference, or standards, by which that activity can be measured or judged. A benchmark can be established at any level of the organization in any functional area, whether manufacturing or service industries. The ultimate goal is to attain a competitive edge by being better than the best.

Value creation is the heart of organizational activity, whether in a for-profit or nonprofit entity. Benchmarking provides the metrics by which to understand and judge the value provided by the organization and its resources. Benchmarking focuses on continuous improvements and value creation for stakeholders (i.e., owners, customers, employees, and suppliers), utilizing the best practices to focus improvement efforts.

Benchmarking targets the critical success factors for a specific organization. It considers the mission of an organization, its resources, products, markets, management skills, and others. It requires an identification of customer(s), whether internal or external to the organization. Benchmarking is an early warning system of impending problems and is not a onetime measurement. It can focus on improving organization structures, analyzing managerial roles, improving production processes, and developing strategic issues. Benchmarking can be done by using published materials, insights gained at trade association meetings, and conversations with industry experts, customers, suppliers, academics, and others.

Business Process Reviews

Two types of business process reviews can occur: business process reengineering and business process improvement.

Business Process Reengineering

In an effort to increase revenues and market growth, organizations are conducting business process reviews. The idea behind business process reviews, whether for a production process or a service process, is to streamline operations and to eliminate waste. The result is increased efficiencies, which can lead to greater effectiveness. A proven technique is business process reengineering (BPR), which requires big thinking and making major, radical changes in the business processes. Work flow analysis is a part of BPR.

BPR is one approach for redesigning the way work is done to support the organization's mission and reduce costs. BPR starts with a high-level assessment of the organization's mission, strategic goals, and customer needs. Basic questions are asked, such as: Does our mission need to be redefined? Are our strategic goals aligned with our mission? Who are our customers? An organization may find that it is operating on questionable assumptions, particularly in terms of the wants and needs of its customers. Only after the organization rethinks **what** it should be doing does it go on to decide **how** best to do it.

Within the framework of this basic assessment of mission and goals, reengineering focuses on the organization's business processes: the steps and procedures that govern how resources are used to create products

Business Process Reengineering (continued)

and services that meet the needs of particular customers or markets. As a structured ordering of work steps across time and place, a business process can be decomposed into specific activities, measured, modeled, and improved. It can also be completely redesigned or eliminated altogether. Reengineering identifies, analyzes, and redesigns an organization's core business processes with the aim of achieving dramatic improvements in critical performance measures, such as cost, quality, service, and speed.

Reengineering recognizes that an organization's business processes are usually fragmented into subprocesses and tasks that are carried out by several specialized functional areas within the organization. Often no one is responsible for the overall performance of the entire process. Reengineering maintains that optimizing the performance of subprocesses can result in some benefits but cannot yield dramatic improvements if the process itself is fundamentally inefficient and outmoded. For that reason, reengineering focuses on redesigning the process as a whole in order to achieve the greatest possible benefits to the organization and its customers. This drive for realizing dramatic improvements by fundamentally rethinking how the organization's work should be done distinguishes reengineering from business process improvement efforts that focus on functional or incremental improvement.

Reengineering is not a panacea. There are occasions when functional or incremental improvements are the method of choice, as when a process is basically sound or when the organization is not prepared to undergo dramatic change. When there is a need to achieve order-of-magnitude improvements, reengineering is the method of choice.

Business Process Improvement

Business process improvement (BPI) should be a continuous, not discrete, process, and it tends to be more of an incremental change that may affect only a single task or segment of the organization. The concept of fundamental or radical change is the basis of the major difference between BPR and BPI. Quite often BPI initiatives limit their focus to a single existing organizational unit. This in itself breaks one of the tenets of BPR, which is that BPR must focus on redesigning a fundamental *business* process, not existing departments or organizational units. While BPR seeks to define what the processes should be, BPI focuses more on how to improve an existing process or service.

Through BPI, organizations can achieve significant incremental improvements in service delivery and other business factors (e.g., increase in employees' productivity). The expected outcomes of BPI are not as dramatic as those associated with BPR initiatives, but the process is also not as traumatic as in achieving the radical changes seen with BPR. In many cases, incremental changes may be achieved in situations lacking the support necessary for more radical changes.

Production Process Flows

Three operational process flow measures include flow time, inventory, and throughput. They are interrelated in that defining targets on any two of them defines a target for the third.

Inventory = Throughput × Flow time

The basic managerial levers for process improvement are:

Decrease in flow time

Increase in throughput

Decrease in inventory and waiting time

Control process variability

Managing process flows and costs

Levers for Managing the Flow Time

Levers for managing flow time include decreasing the work content of a critical path by shortening the length of every critical path in these ways:

Reduce the Work Content of an Activity on the Critical Path

- Eliminate non-value-adding aspects of the activity (i.e., work smarter).
- Increase the speed at which the activity is done (i.e., work faster) by acquiring faster equipment and/or by increasing incentives to work faster.
- Reduce the number of repeat activities (i.e., do it right the first time).

Work in Parallel

- Move work from a critical path to a noncritical path (i.e., perform work in parallel rather than in sequence).
- Move work from a critical path to the "outer loop" (i.e., either preprocessing or postprocessing).

Modify the Product Mix

- Change the product mix to produce products with smaller work content with respect to the specified activity.

Levers for Managing (Increasing) Process Throughput

Levers for managing (increasing) throughput of a process are listed next.

Decrease Resource Idleness

- Synchronize flows within the process to reduce starvation and set appropriate size of buffers to reduce blockage.

Increase Net Availability of Resources to Increase Effective Capacity

- Improve maintenance policies.
- Perform preventive maintenance outside periods of scheduled availability.
- Institute effective problem-solving measures that reduce frequency and duration of breakdowns.
- Institute motivational programs and incentives to reduce employee absenteeism and increase employee morale.

Reduce Setup Waste

- Reduce the frequency of setups and reduce the time required for a single setup.

Levers for Managing (Increasing) Process Throughput (continued)

Increase Theoretical Capacity

- Decrease unit load on the bottleneck resource pool (e.g., work faster, work smarter, do it right the first time, change production mix, subcontract or outsource, and invest in flexible resources).
- Increase the load batch of resources in the bottleneck resource pool (i.e., increase the scale of resource).
- Increase the number of units in the bottleneck resource pool (i.e., increase scale of process).
- Increase the scheduled availability of the bottleneck resource pool (i.e., work longer).
- Modify the production mix.

Levers for Reducing Inventory and Waiting Time

Reduce Cycle Inventory (i.e., reduce batch size)

- Reducing setup or order cost per batch or by reducing forward buying.

Reduce Safety Inventory

- Reduce demand variability through improved forecasting.
- Reduce replenishment lead time and its variability.
- Pool safety inventory for multiple locations or products through either physical or virtual centralization of specialization or some combination thereof.
- Exploit product substitution.
- Use common components.
- Postpone product differentiation closer to the point of demand.

Manage Safety Capacity

- Increase safety capacity.
- Decrease variability in arrivals and service patterns.
- Pool available safety capacity.

Levers for Reducing Inventory and Waiting Time (continued)

Synchronize Flows

- Manage capacity to synchronize with demand.
- Manage demand to synchronize with available capacity.
- Synchronize flows within the process.

Manage Customers' Psychological Perceptions

- Reduce the cost of waiting on line by managing customers' perceptions.

Levers for Controlling Process Variability

Measure, Prioritize, and Analyze Variability

- Check key performance measures over time.

Utilize feedback Control to Limit Abnormal Variability

- Sett control limits of acceptable variability in key performance measures.
- Monitor actual performance and correct any abnormal variability.

Decrease Normal Process Variability

- Design for processing (i.e., simplify, standardize, and mistake-proof).

Immunize Product Performance

- Utilize robust design to minimize process variability.

Levers for Managing Process Flows and Costs

Manage Flows in a Plant

- Process structure with cellular layout.
- Information and material flow using demand pull system.

Levers for Managing Process Flows and Costs (continued)

- Level production with batch size reduction.
- Quality at source with defect prevention and decentralized control.
- Supplier management with partnerships and incentives.
- Supply consistency through maintenance of safety capacity.
- Employee involvement and empowerment.

Manage Flows in a Supply Chain

- Reduce information and material flow times using technology and efficient logistics.
- Reduce fixed costs of ordering and quantity discounts.
- Share information on customer demand and product availability.
- Coordinate forecasts between affected parties.
- Stabilize prices.

Improve Processes

- Utilize continuous improvement and reengineering.
- Utilize increased visibility; incentives; PDCA cycle; and benchmarking.

Process Mapping Techniques

Process mapping techniques include process maps (i.e., relationship, cross-functional, and flowchart), pivot tables, contingency tables, RACI diagrams, spaghetti maps, and workflow analysis.

Process Maps

Three tools exist to map a process, activity, or function to understand it and to improve it. These tools include relationship maps, cross-functional process maps, and flowcharts.

Relationship maps show the customer-supplier relationships or linkages that exist between parts of an organization. These maps show the big-picture view that portrays how the major functions of the business interact with each other. They can also be used to show any individual function.

Cross-functional process maps show how an organization's major work processes cut across several functions. These maps show the sequence of steps that make up the work process as well as the inputs and outputs associated with each process step.

Flowcharts are good to illustrate work processes since they help define, document, and analyze processes at the detailed level, especially about the individual performing the work or to develop the work procedures step by step. Flowcharts are most valuable in providing a summary outline and overall description of the process of transactions.

Process Maps (continued)

Process maps can be used in a variety of ways, such as to:

- Orient new employees
- Organize work
- Clarify employee roles and contributions
- Identify improvement opportunities
- Reduce cycle time
- Measure performance

For example, cross-functional process maps and flowcharts can be used to reduce costs, reduce defects, conduct benchmarks, and reengineer a process. Similarly, relationship maps, cross-functional process maps, and flowcharts can be used to design performance measurement systems and to measure customer satisfaction.

Pivot Tables

A **pivot table** (or chart) is a second, revised table in rows and columns containing reformatted data using the raw data from the first, original table in rows and columns.

First Table ⟶ Original Table

Second Table ⟶ Pivot Table

The basic data values are the same between the original tale and the pivot table. However, the pivot table contains sorted, rearranged, and summarized data, providing better insights.

For example, a retail marketing manager can create a pivot table showing which salesperson has the highest sales dollars in a given month or quarter from the original sales data tables.

Contingency Table

A **contingency table** is a type of table presented in a matrix format displaying frequency distribution and showing their probabilities. Contingency tables (cross-tabulations) are used in business intelligence, market research, and customer surveys where interrelations and interactions between two or more variables can be studied to obtain greater insights of data. Due to their statistical focus, contingency tables show a measure of association between variables. For example, a table can be put together showing how male and female customers prefer to purchase Product A and Product B from a retailer.

Responsibility Assignment Matrix or RACI Diagram

The responsibility assignment matrix, or RACI diagram, deals with four items; "R" means responsible, "A" means accountable, "C" means consulted, and "I" means informed. Typically, a task is associated with one or more roles using the RACI diagram. Simply stated, the RACI diagram connects people to their assigned jobs, duties, tasks, activities, or projects so they can complete them.

Spaghetti Plot

A spaghetti plot (map, chart, or diagram) is a workflow system to visualize data flows through a system where flows appear as noodles. These plots are used in several places, such as to: track product routing and material movement through a factory; reduce inefficiencies in an office, factory, or warehouse workflow system; and show the effects of medical drugs on test patients during a new drug trial. The results of the spaghetti plot can be useful in streamlining or simplifying workflow to save resources such as time, money, materials, and energy,

Workflow Analysis

Workflow analysis looks at the overall flow of work to find ways of improving this flow. It can reveal value-added and non-value-added activities (e.g., waste and delays) and identify interdependence among departments. The outcome would be eliminating the non-value-added activities and waste and improving efficiency and effectiveness. Assembling tasks, whether subassembly or final assembly, and process time are value-added activities of a manufactured product while other activities are non-value-added activities. Examples of non-value-added activities from a customer's viewpoint include inspection time, move time, reporting time, governmental compliance time, storage time, wait time, and queue time.

Workflow systems would make organizations undergo huge managerial and cultural changes. These changes in turn help employees apply business rules, enable process reengineering, provide parallel processing of documents, eliminate information float or overload, and ensure that established policies and procedures are followed. Workflow software allows business processes to be redesigned and streamlined and automatically routes work from employee to employee. Cycle times and business velocities can be helpful during workflow analysis in streamlining manufacturing or service operations.

Workflow analysis is based on interdependent functions, departments, and processes. **Interdependence** means the extent to which departments depend on each other for resources or materials to accomplish their tasks. Low interdependence means that departments can do their work independent of each of other and have little need for interaction, consultation, or exchange of materials. High interdependence means departments must constantly exchange resources and materials.

Workflow Analysis (continued)

Three types of interdependence influence organization structure: pooled, sequential, and reciprocal. Pooled interdependence is the lowest form of interdependence among departments. Work does not flow between units. Each department is part of the organization and contributes to the common good of the organization but works independently. When interdependence is of serial form, with parts or documents produced in one department becoming inputs to another department, then it is called sequential interdependence. Here departments exchange resources and depend on others to perform well. The management requirements for sequential interdependence are more demanding than for pooled interdependence. These requirements include coordination, communication, integrators, and task forces. The highest level of interdependence is reciprocal interdependence, which exists when the output of operation A is the input to operation B, and the output of operation B is the input back again to operation A. The outputs of departments influence those departments in reciprocal fashion. Management requirements for the complex reciprocal interdependence include greater planning, coordination, communication, permanent teams, and frequent adjustments in the work and its associated plans.

Value Analysis

Topics such as value maximization, value chain, value-added concept, value analysis, value engineering, value index, value-stream mapping, and cost improvements through business process reengineering are covered in this section.

Value analysis is the organized study of an item's function as it relates to value and cost. The **value of an item** is defined as the function of the item divided by the cost of the item. The goal of value analysis is to make improvements in a product while the product is being produced and after deciding that a new product is a success.

There will be valued-added and non-value-added tasks in any function due to tasks that were neither changed nor challenged. The goal is to identify those tasks or activities that are not adding value to a function, product, or process. Value-engineering techniques can be implemented to identify non-value-added activities and streamline the business processes in order to improve their efficiency and effectiveness.

Assembling tasks, whether subassembly or final assembly, and process times are value-added activities of a manufactured product while other activities are non-value-added activities. Examples of non-value-added activities from a customer's viewpoint include inspection time, move time, reporting time, governmental compliance time, storage time, wait time, and queue time.

Value Analysis (continued)

VALUE-ADDED AND NON-VALUE-ADDED ACTIVITIES

Enhance or increase value-added activities, such as production pure process time; ingredients mix time; part fabricating time; part plating, soldering, and painting time; part sub-assembly time; part final assembly time; customer order processing time; customer order ship time; internal/external customer access points to manufacturing systems; manufacturing management decision points and control points).

Eliminate or decrease non-value-added activities, such as material storage, handling, and movement steps; inspection steps; rework steps; waiting time; product recall time; product warranty time; and delays at interdepartmental and interdivisional boundaries and at intradepartmental workstations).

Handling these activities requires having the right resources available at the right place and at the right time so that delays and waste in manufacturing operations are decreased.

Value Maximization

In general, productive employees, efficient design of business processes, and effective use of tools and techniques combined with forward-looking management can create a sustainable and synergistic value for an organization's products and services. Institutionalizing value maximization principles and practices will eventually turn normal organizations into world-class organizations.

Creating a new value or adding value to an existing one is the major purpose of business corporations. For example, the total value of a manufacturing corporation is the summation of individual values of each product manufactured. Similarly, the total value of a service corporation is the summation of individual values of each service provided. Specifically,

Value of an individual product = Product price – Cost of all inputs to make that product – Cost of capital invested to make that product

Value of an individual service = Service price – Cost of all inputs to provide that service – Cost of capital invested to provide that service

One way to increase the value of a product or service is by decreasing the cost of all inputs and decreasing the cost of capital invested while keeping the price of a product or service constant.

Other ways of increasing the value of a firm include breaking the value-cost trade-off with a Blue Ocean strategy and investing in human capital and technology capital for innovating new products and services with sustainable value.

Value Chain

The value chain of a manufacturing company includes all activities and departments from idea creation to idea commercialization. This includes suppliers, producers, retailers, and research and development (R&D) to post-sale customer service. Discontinuing a product or department does not take away any value to a customer unless it was providing the value before.

The value chain is improved when delays, defects, waste, and inventories are eliminated in business processes. The goal of value chain is to make such processes lean, flexible, stable, and predictable. Doing this requires elimination of sources of inefficiency, rigidity, and variability, and use of information technology to integrate business subprocesses.

Value-Added Concept

Several partners in the value chain can add value to a product or service. Assume that there are two suppliers, one producer, and one retailer in the value chain. Also, assume that there is no need for the cost of capital invested. The next equations explain how these partners can all add value to a product.

Value added by Supplier 1 = Supplier 1 price – Supplier 1 cost

Value added by Supplier 2 = Supplier 2 price – Supplier 2 cost – Supplier 1 price

Value added by producer = Producer price – Producer cost – Supplier 2 price

Value added by retailer = Retailer price – Retailer cost – Producer price

Total value-added to a product is the summation of value-added by all partners involved in the value chain. The value of a firm is the summation of all value-added for all products that a firm produces. The same logic applies to services.

Value Engineering

The goal of value engineering is to improve a new product's design and specifications before a product reaches the production stage. It focuses on cost reduction and cost-avoidance techniques to improve product value and meet customer requirements in an optimal way. It reduces the complexity of a product with robust design. Management wants to determine how to provide product functions at the lowest cost without reduction in required performance. Value engineering principles can help achieve product functions and cost goals.

VALUE ENGINEERING VERSUS VALUE ANALYSIS

Value engineering focuses on preproduction design work to improve a product's value.

Value analysis focuses on the production stage to make it better and economical, thus improving a product's value.

Value Index

The value index is a ratio of relative importance of a component to a customer. Both numerator and denominator are expressed as percentages. Components with a value index of less than 1 are candidates for value engineering in terms of reducing costs. Components with a value index of more than 1 are candidates for value enhancement, since they need more investment to improve features important to customers.

Components with a value index of less than 1 are candidates for value engineering in terms of cost reduction. This means the components' costs are higher relative to their importance to customers. Components with a value index of more than 1 are candidates for value enhancement, since they need more investment to improve features important to customers. This means that these components' relative importance to customers is more than their cost.

Value-Stream Mapping

The goal of value-stream mapping is to understand the complexities of process design and redesign stages. It focuses on where value is added or not added to a product, starting from the suppliers and manufacturers (producers) and ending with customers. It looks at the production process as well as the management decisions and information systems that support the production process.

Cost Improvements through Business Process Reengineering

Production engineers and quality engineers, in conjunction with the accounting and manufacturing departments, implement target costing methods through value engineering, activity-based costing methods, business process reengineering principles, and just-in-time inventory methods to address legacy costs. They redesign some product components while eliminating others. Management wants to determine the return on assets (ROA) invested in the cost improvement process. The next formulas can be used in this situation.

New return on sales (ROS) = New net income / New sales

New asset turnover (AT) = New sales / New assets

New ROA = New net income / New assets (Check: ROA = ROS × AT)

Although target price is determined by the market forces of supply and demand variables, management can control target cost through BPR principles and value engineering techniques. The interrelationships between target price, target cost, and target profit are:

Target price = Target cost + Target profit

Analytical Review Techniques

Analytical review techniques include basic, traditional, and advanced analytical review techniques.

Basic Analytical Techniques

Basic analytical techniques include ratio estimation, variance analysis, and reasonableness tests.

Ratio Estimation

Four types of measures are used to analyze a company's financial statements and its financial position:

1. Common-size analysis
2. Trend analysis
3. Comparative ratios
4. Single ratios

Common-size analysis expresses items in percentages, which can be compared with similar items of other firms or with those of the same firm over time. For example, common-size balance sheet line items (both assets and liabilities) are expressed as a percentage of total assets (e.g., receivables as *x*% of total assets). Similarly, common-size income statement line items are expressed as a percentage of total sales (e.g., cost of goods sold as *x*% of total sales).

Variations of common-size analysis include vertical analysis and horizontal analysis. **Vertical analysis** expresses all items on a financial statement as a percentage of some base figure, such as total assets or total sales. Comparing these relationships between competing organizations helps to isolate strengths and areas

Ratio Estimation (continued)

of concern. In **horizontal analysis,** the financial statements for two years are shown together with additional columns showing dollar differences and percentage changes. Thus, the direction, absolute amount, and relative amount of change in account balances can be calculated. Trends that are difficult to isolate by examining the financial statements of individual years or comparisons with competitors can be identified.

Trend analysis shows trends in ratios, which gives insight into whether the financial situation of a firm is improving, declining, or stable. This analysis graphs ratios over time, and the graphs can be compared with a firm's own performance as well as that of its industry.

Comparative ratios show key financial ratios, such as current ratio and net sales to inventory, by industry, such as beverages and bakery products. These ratios represent average financial ratios for all firms within an industry category. Many organizations supply ratio data, and each one designs ratios for its own purpose, such as small firms or large firms. Also, the focus of these ratios is different, such as creditors' viewpoint or investors' viewpoint. Another characteristic of the ratio data-supplying organization is that each has its own definitions of the ratios and their components. Due to these differences, examiners must be cautious when interpreting these ratios.

Another type of comparative analysis is comparing the financial statements for the current year with those of the most recent year. By comparing summaries of financial statements for the last five to 10 years, one can identify trends in operations, capital structure, and the composition of assets. This comparative analysis provides insight into the normal or expected account balance or ratio, information about the direction of changes in ratios and account balances, and insight into the variability or fluctuation in an organization's assets or operations.

TREND ANALYSIS VERSUS COMPARATIVE RATIO ANALYSIS

- In trend analysis, trends are shown over time between the firm and its industry.
- In comparative ratio analysis, a single point (one-to-one) comparison is shown between the firm and its industry.
- In both analyses, the industry's ratio is an average ratio, while the firm's ratio is not.

Certain accounts or items in an organization's financial statements have logical relationships with each other. If the dollar amounts of these related accounts or items are expressed in fraction form, then they are called **ratios**. These ratios are grouped into five categories:

1. Liquidity ratios
2. Asset management ratios
3. Debt management ratios
4. Profitability ratios
5. Market value ratios

Ratio Estimation (continued)

Exhibit 3.8 presents individual ratios for each ratio category.

Ratio category	Individual ratios
Liquidity (1)	Current, quick, or acid test
Asset management (2)	Inventory turnover, days sales outstanding, fixed assets turnover, total assets turnover
Debt management (3)	Debt to total assets, time-interest-earned, fixed charge coverage, cash flow coverage
Profitability (4) = (1) + (2) + (3)	Profit margin on sales, basic earning power, return on total assets, return on common equity, earnings per share, payout
Market value (5) = (1) + (2) + (3) + (4)	Price/earnings, book value per share, market/book

Exhibit 3.8: Ratio categories with examples

Variance Analysis

Budgets and standards are used to plan an operation and measure its progress. **Variance** is the difference between budget or standard and actual. For example, if actual spending is greater than the budget, it results in a negative variance. If actual spending is less than the budget, it results in a positive variance. Managers need to analyze both positive and negative variances for reasonableness because people play psychological games with budgets, such as inflating the budget for personal gain.

Reasonableness Tests

The reasonableness test procedure involves the use of selected operating data, associated financial data, and external data to predict an account balance. Reasonableness tests can be used to determine whether input data, updated data, calculated data, or output data are reasonable. Ascending or descending checks for numeric and alphabetic data can be performed. Tolerance tests measuring dollar or percentage deviation can be designed.

Reasonableness tests of the expense accounts are common. For example, auditors or analysts may estimate a value for utilities expense based on average temperature and hours of operation, and they may estimate payroll expense from operating data on the number of employees, the average pay rates, and the number of days of applicable operations.

Reasonableness Tests (continued)

The reasonableness test can be particularly effective because it links the financial data directly to relevant operating data. When variations in operations are the principal cause for variations in the related accounts (especially the expense accounts), reasonableness tests provide a relatively precise means of detecting errors and frauds affecting these accounts. That is, when a fraud is committed, it is likely that the reported financial and operating facts will not agree. The perpetrator will find it difficult to disguise both the financial data and the related operating data.

For example, a reasonableness test of payroll expense can be an effective means of detecting fraud, if there are phony employees or excess time is charged, because personnel records also must be manipulated fraudulently in the same pattern to prevent detection. Because reasonableness tests effectively model the relationships between the financial data and the operating transactions that are the basis for the recorded financial data, these methods are potentially the most effective of the analytical procedures.

Examples of generic reasonableness tests are listed next.

- Airline passenger departure flight time is not reasonable with arrival flight time for the same day.
- Customer order quantity is not reasonable with historical order.
- Prices on purchase orders are not reasonable with the prices on purchase invoices or purchase requisitions.
- Stock-status dollar values are not reasonable with general-ledger amounts.
- Shipment values are not reasonable with billed amounts.

Traditional Analytical Review Techniques

As a part of fieldwork, the internal auditor should perform analytical reviews to understand the relationships between various data. The focus is on determining the reasonableness of data. Techniques such as regression analysis, simple ratio analysis, and trend analysis can be used to provide insights into the financial and operational data. The outcome of the review is to provide a red flag to the auditor so that he or she can adjust the audit scope and the audit procedures accordingly. For example, analytical reviews can be used to indicate the possible existence of fraud.

The key is not to view the data and its relations individually but to integrate that information with other related data to provide greater insights into the dynamics of the data. Some examples of application of analytical reviews are presented next.

- Inventory turnover rates are compared with established industry standards to assess the performance of a business unit or division.
- Regular analytical review of operating divisions would include analysis of sales, cash flow, and profit statistics. Specifically, use of accelerated depreciation methods and sale of capital assets to obtain larger performance bonuses should be looked at in detail.
- The most persuasive means of assessing production quality control is to evaluate the number and reasons for sales adjustments and to perform trend analysis.

Traditional Analytical Review Techniques (continued)

- Change analysis and trend analysis of buyer or vendor activity are analytical techniques to detect irregularities in purchasing. For example, purchases from two new vendors increased dramatically after a new buyer was hired. Based on sales volume, it can be concluded that the buyer was obtaining kickbacks from the two new vendors.
- Analytical procedures in which current financial statements are compared with budgets or previous statements are primarily intended to determine overall reasonableness of statement contents.
- An unexpected decrease in total asset turnover ratio could indicate that fictitious inventory has been recorded.
- Accounts payable schedule verification may include the use of analytical evidence. An example is comparing the balance on the schedule with the balances of prior years.
- Workers' compensation claims can be analyzed for injuries by type of personal computer equipment and extent of use of computers by individual employees.
- Analysis of loan default ratios by a loan officer in a bank should provide good trend analysis of that officer's loan activities and intentions.

Traditional Analytical Review Techniques (continued)

- Analytical procedures revealed an extraordinary increase in account balances in maintenance supplies during the past year. These data need to be analyzed further before reaching conclusions. The increase could be a common indicator of fraud.
- A decrease in the accounts receivable turnover rate indicates a more liberal credit policy; an increase in the accounts receivable turnover rate indicates a conservative (tight) credit policy.
- During an operational audit, an auditor compares the inventory turnover rate of a subsidiary with established industry standards to assess the performance of the subsidiary and to indicate where additional audit work may be needed.
- A regression analysis technique is used to find a correlation between the operating conditions and age of water meters for a municipality.
- An aging analysis is prepared to evaluate the adequacy of the company's allowance for doubtful accounts.
- A comparison of cost data with current market quotations would be a reliable test of the valuation of marketable equity securities.

Advanced Analytical Review Techniques

A list of advanced analytical review techniques that internal auditors can use during their audit work is presented next.

- Statistical analyses, such as regression analysis, factor analysis, cluster analysis, link analysis, and correlation analysis, can be used to detect fraudulent transactions.
- Data analytics and data mining software tools can be used to assess the overall control environment after identifying systemic breakdowns or failures in internal control systems.
- Data analytics and data mining software tools can be used to assess data integrity and security controls over databases, data warehouses, and data marts.
- Big-data analytics can be used during audit planning and engagement work with specific methods, such as predictive analytics, descriptive analytics, and prescriptive analytics.
- Text-mining tools can be used to detect fraudulent activities in structured and unstructured data files by searching for key words.
- Artificial intelligence and machine learning technologies can be used to provide answers to customer questions and to track delivery of customer packages.
- Neural networks that learn by training can be used or reused in reviewing credit card transactions to detect anomalies and fraudulent activities.

AUDIT AND LEGAL EVIDENCE

The scope of audit and legal evidence includes two major topics: types of audit evidence and types of legal evidence.

Types of Audit Evidence

Audit evidence is information that provides a factual basis for audit opinions. It is the information documented by the auditors and obtained through observing conditions, interviewing people, examining records, and testing documents.

Physical evidence is obtained by direct inspection or observation of people, property, or events. Such evidence may be documented in the form of memoranda summarizing the matters inspected or observed, photographs, charts, maps, or actual samples. An auditor's observation of the functioning of an internal control system produces physical evidence.

Examples of physical evidence include: taking a photograph of the auditees' workplace, such as improperly stored materials or unsafe conditions; observing conditions; test counting a batch of inventory; and testing the existence of an asset.

Documentary evidence consists of created information, such as letters, contracts, accounting records, invoices, and management information on performance.

Examples of documentary evidence include: a page of the general ledger containing irregularities placed there by perpetrator of a fraud; and determining whether erroneous billings occurred when the auditor for a

Types of Audit Evidence (continued)

construction contractor finds material costs increasing as a percentage of billings and suspects that materials billed to the company are being delivered to another contractor. A contract is the most appropriate evidence for the auditor to obtain and review when evaluating the propriety of a payment to a consultant.

Testimonial evidence is obtained from others through statements received in response to inquiries or through interviews or responses to questionnaires. Testimonial evidence needs to be evaluated from the standpoint of whether the individual may be biased or have only partial knowledge about the area. Testimonial evidence obtained under conditions where persons may speak freely is more credible than testimonial evidence obtained under compromising conditions (e.g., where persons may be intimidated).

Examples of testimonial evidence include: a written, signed statement from an interviewee in response to a question asked by an auditor during an interview; a written statement by or a letter from an auditee in response to a specific inquiry made by an auditor; and a letter from the company's attorney in response to inquiries about possible litigation.

Analytical evidence includes computations, comparisons, reasoning, and separation of information into components.

Examples of analytical evidence include: evaluating the reasonableness of the quantity of scrap material resulting from a certain production process compared to industry standards, evaluating the reasonableness of account balances; and concluding that there was an adequate separation of duties in the counting and recording of cash receipts.

Standards of Audit Evidence

All audit evidence should meet the three standards of sufficiency, competence, and relevance. Evidence is sufficient if it is based on facts. Competent evidence is reliable evidence. The term "relevance" refers to the relationship of the information to its use. When audit evidence does not meet these three standards, additional (corroborative) evidence is required before expressing an audit opinion.

Appropriateness of Audit Evidence

The phrase "appropriateness of audit evidence" refers to persuasiveness (sufficiency), relevance, and competence (reliability).

Evidence is **sufficient** if there is enough of it to support the auditors' findings. In determining the sufficiency of evidence, it may be helpful to ask: Is there enough evidence to persuade a reasonable person of the validity of the findings? An essential factor in evaluating the sufficiency of evidence is that it must be convincing enough for a prudent person to reach the same decision.

Therefore, *sufficiency deals with the persuasiveness of the evidence.* When appropriate, statistical methods may be used to establish sufficiency. When sampling methods are used, the concept of sufficiency of evidence means that the samples selected provide reasonable assurance that they are representative of the sampled population. Interviewing the auditee is not enough to provide sufficient evidence.

Appropriateness of Audit Evidence (continued)

Evidence used to support a finding is **relevant** if it has a logical, sensible relationship to that finding. Relevant evidence is consistent with the audit objectives and supports audit findings and recommendations. Evidence is **competent** to the extent that it is consistent with fact (i.e., it is valid). "Competent" evidence is satisfied by an original signed document, but copies do not provide competent evidence. *Evidence that is both available and reliable is competent. Competent information is reliable and the best available through the use of appropriate audit functions.*

The next presumptions are useful in judging the competence of evidence. However, these presumptions are not to be considered sufficient in themselves to determine competence.

- Evidence obtained from a credible independent source is more competent than that secured from the audited organization. An external source of evidence should impact audit conclusions most.
- Evidence developed under an effective system of management controls is more competent than that obtained where such control is weak or nonexistent.
- Evidence obtained through the auditor's direct physical examination, observation, computation, and inspection is more competent than evidence obtained indirectly. An example of external and internal evidence is when an auditor reviews the count sheets, inventory printouts, and memos from the last inventory during determination of causes of inventory shortages shown by the physical inventories.

Appropriateness of Audit Evidence (continued)

Examples of competent evidence are listed next.

- An audit objective of an accounts receivable function is to determine if prescribed standard procedures are followed when credit is granted. An audit procedure providing the most competent evidence would be selecting a statistical sample of credit applications and testing them for conformance with prescribed procedures.
- The most "reliable" (competent) evidence of determining a company's legal title to inventories is paid vendor invoices.
- A contract dispute has arisen between a company and a major supplier. To resolve the dispute, the most competent evidence would be the original contract.
- A positive confirmation of an account receivable that proves that it actually exists is competent evidence.
- In deciding whether recorded sales are valid, the most "competent" evidence would be obtained by looking at the shipping document, the independent bill of lading, and the invoice for the merchandise.

Auditors should, when they deem it useful, obtain from officials of the audited entity written representations concerning the competence of the evidence they obtain. Written representations ordinarily confirm oral representations given to the auditor, indicate and document the continuing appropriateness of such representations, and reduce the possibility of misunderstandings concerning the matters that are the subject of the representations.

An example of relevant evidence is aging of accounts receivables, which provides relevant evidence regarding the validity of receivables and thus the allowance account.

Information Sources for Audit Evidence

The auditor's approach to determining the sufficiency, relevance, and competence of evidence depends on the source of the information that constitutes the evidence. Information sources include original data gathered by auditors and existing data gathered by either the auditee or a third party. Data from any of these sources may be obtained from computer-based systems.

Types of Legal Evidence

Both legal evidence and audit evidence have common objectives of providing proof and fostering an honest belief about the truth or falsity of any proposition at issue. The focus of audit evidence differs somewhat from that of legal evidence. Legal evidence relies heavily on oral testimony. Audit evidence relies more on documentary evidence. Legal evidence permits certain presumptions. Audit evidence is not bound by any presumptions. This requires auditors to question all evidence until they themselves are satisfied with its truth or falsity.

Best evidence is often referred to as primary evidence, and it is the evidence that is the most natural and reliable. It is confined to documentary evidence and applies to proof of the content in writing. Oral evidence may not be used to dispute a written instrument such as a contract or a deed; however, oral evidence can be used to explain the meaning of the instrument where such an instrument is capable of more than one interpretation.

Secondary evidence is inferior to primary evidence and cannot be given the same reliance. Examples include a copy of a writing or oral evidence of its contents. A copy of writing is permissible when the original is lost, destroyed, or controlled by a public entity.

Types of Legal Evidence (continued)

Direct evidence proves a fact without having to use presumptions or inference to establish that proof. The testimony of a witness to a fact is direct evidence. The most likely source of evidence indicating employee theft of inventory would be a warehouse employee's verbal charge of theft.

Circumstantial evidence proves an intermediate fact(s) from which one can infer the existence of some primary fact that is significant to the issue under consideration. It provides a logical inference that it exists.

Conclusive evidence is incontrovertible evidence, irrespective of its nature. It is so strong that it overbears all other evidence. It cannot be contradicted and needs no corroboration.

Corroborative evidence is additional evidence of a different character concerning the same point. It is evidence supplementary to that already given and tends to strengthen or confirm it.

Opinion evidence is based on the opinion rule, which holds that witnesses must ordinarily testify to fact only—to what they actually saw or heard. Opinions may be biased, self-serving, or uninformed. However, experts are permitted to offer an opinion based on the facts.

Hearsay evidence is based on the hearsay rule, which renders objectionable any statements made by someone, other than a witness, to prove the truth of the matter stated. Hearsay evidence is any oral or written evidence brought into court and offered as proof of things said out of court.

Business documents (e.g., sales slips, purchase orders) made during regular business routines are admissible. Photographs represent hearsay evidence but are considered admissible if properly authenticated by witnesses who are familiar with the subject.

AUDIT WORKPAPERS

This section describes the purpose of audit workpapers, explains how to develop and review them, and shows how to automate the workpapers for efficiency.

Purpose of Audit Workpapers

Workpapers document the audit work performed, observations and analysis made, and support for the audit conclusions and audit results. Workpapers should contain sufficient information regarding the audit scope, audit objectives, and audit program modifications and waiver of any audit issuers not included in the final audit report. Workpapers also should document the specific sampling methodology, including minimum sample sizes, and the rationale for such methodology. They should contain information that reflects all phases of the audit process, including planning, fieldwork, reporting, and audit issues tracking and follow-up. On an ongoing basis, a comprehensive supervisory review should be performed on all audit work, including any outsourced or third-party internal audit procedures.

Workpapers serve three purposes: They provide the principal support for the auditors' report, aid the auditors in conducting and supervising the audit, and allow others to review the audit's quality.

Develop and Review Audit Workpapers

Workpapers document the basis for findings, conclusions, and auditors' recommendations, and should contain sufficient information to enable an experienced auditor previously not connected with the audit to ascertain from them what work the auditors performed to support the findings, conclusions, or recommendations. This is the ultimate objective of the audit workpapers. The workpapers not only document the auditors' work but also allow for the review of audit quality. Workpapers are the link between fieldwork and the audit report. The requirements to prepare workpapers may be satisfied with documentation maintained on disks and flash drives.

Audit organizations should establish policies and procedures to ensure the safe custody and retention of workpapers for a time sufficient to satisfy legal and administrative requirements. These policies should also cover the need to make the workpapers available for others to review audit quality. These quality reviewers need a written explanation of the basis for the auditor's significant judgments. Arrangements need to be made to ensure that the director of internal audit will make workpapers available to others after approval.

Workpapers should contain:

- The objective, scope, and methodology, including any sampling criteria used, and results of the audit.
- Evidence of the work performed to support findings, judgments, and conclusions.
- Evidence of supervisory reviews of the work conducted.

Develop and Review Audit Workpapers (continued)

Workpapers can be prepared electronically. The contents of the workpapers will be the same whether they are paper or electronic. However, the electronic media requires additional considerations due to technological factors. These considerations include generating backup copies of workpapers, security and control procedures to access workpapers, and data file retention procedures.

A workpaper can include flowcharts, findings cross-referenced to supporting documentation, and tickmarks explained in footnotes. The question of whether a workpaper is complete or not is determined by whether the audit objective has been met and supported. Workpapers should describe objectives, procedures, facts, conclusions, and recommendations. Workpaper summaries can be used to promote efficient workpaper review by supervisors. Workpaper control is best described by restricting access to only those who have a legitimate need to know.

Automated Workpapers

Automated workpaper software helps auditors to increase efficiency and productivity because it relieves the boredom of writing out by hand. The software automatically references to audit work program sections and related audit objectives. Any corrections or changes can be done with ease and without losing the continuity.

Other documentation aids can also help the internal auditor during the fieldwork. One of the ways that an auditor can make sure that the intentions of program/system changes have indeed been achieved is through the use of automated documentation aids. If used properly, these documentation aids can provide flowcharts, tables, or graphs of the program or the system that can be compared at two different points in time (i.e., before and after the program change). Any differences indicate changes to the program logic, data file contents, and Job Control Language (JCL) procedures. The auditor then locates and analyzes the supporting documentation prepared to authorize and implement the changes.

Automated Workpapers (continued)

Program or system flowcharts, tables, or graphs generated by the automated documentation aids provide a correct picture of what is in the computer programs and data files as opposed to relying on incorrect, obsolete, or incomplete documentation maintained on paper. Some of the features of automated documentation aids are listed next.

- Automated flowchart software packages, which read the source code for a computer program and convert it into an easy-to-read flowchart
- Computer data file translation software packages, which read the data file descriptions in the computer program and convert them into a convenient and readable format (tabular and graphic)
- Job Control Language software packages, which depict the job control flow as a graph or table showing the sequence of jobs or steps executed and indicating their procedure names and numbers

ENGAGEMENT SUPERVISION

Engagement supervision addresses two topics: audit scheduling and audit supervision.

Audit Scheduling

An audit schedule is an essential part of planning internal auditing department activities. Since audit resources, in terms of available time and the number of auditors, are limited, the audit manager needs to balance the needs of the audit plan and the availability of resources. It is prudent to hire auditors with different skill and experience levels so that all required skills are available among the audit staff even though each auditor may not have all the required skills.

It is the audit manager's responsibility to match the available audit resources to the audit requirements. If the required resources are not available, the audit manager should try to acquire them from either internal or external sources.

The audit manager will notice that there are constraints on the conduct of the audit that may affect the completion of the audits as planned. Some examples of such constraints are staff unavailability due to illness or termination; auditee not ready for the audit due to some business considerations such as mergers, demergers, and other extraordinary events; and time constraints, such as accounting month closing work, quarter-end work, or year-end work. The audit manager needs to consider all these constraints with alternative plans in place.

Audit Scheduling (continued)

When it comes to assigning the audit staff to particular audit responsibilities, the two approaches most often taken are the team concept and the pool concept. Under the team concept, individuals are given responsibility only for certain segments of the organization. Under the pool concept, individuals are made available for assignment to any audit. What works best is determined by the needs of individual organizations, but both approaches have their advantages and drawbacks.

The team approach offers the opportunity for the individual staff members to become proficient in given areas quickly. Experienced audit staff members are more likely to work in specialized team-type areas. The pool approach allows individual staff members to gain broad experience in many areas of the organization. What usually works in practice is a blending of the two approaches, with new staff auditors being available under the pool concept and more experienced auditors developing supervisory skills as well as expertise in more specialized areas.

During the planning of the audit, the audit manager needs to break down the audit project into small and manageable tasks, which can be assigned to audit staff to facilitate monitoring the audit results and progress. Project management tools and techniques, such as program evaluation and review techniques, critical path methods, and periodic progress reports, might help the audit manager to plan and control major and complex audit projects.

Audit Supervision

The most effective way to ensure the quality and expedite the progress of an audit assignment is by exercising proper supervision from the start of the planning process to the completion of audit work and reporting. Supervision adds seasoned judgment to the work performed by less experienced staff and provides necessary on-the-job training for them.

Assigning and using staff is important to satisfying audit objectives. Since skills and knowledge vary among auditors, work assignments must be commensurate with skills and abilities.

Supervisors should satisfy themselves that staff members clearly understand their assigned tasks before starting the work. Staff should be informed not only of what work they are to do and how they are to proceed but also why the work is to be conducted and what it is expected to accomplish. With experienced staff, the supervisors' role may be more general. They may outline the scope of the work and leave details to assistants. With a less experienced staff, a supervisor may have to specify not only how to gather data but also techniques for analyzing them.

Effective supervision ensures that audit assignments are properly planned and produce a high-quality and consistent product. A competent supervisor can help in preparing audit plans, developing and controlling budgets and schedules, improving auditor and auditee relationships, ensuring the preparation of consistent and quality workpapers, and reviewing audit reports.

Audit Supervision (continued)

Supervision is a continuing process, beginning with audit planning and ending with the conclusion of audit assignments and distribution of the final audit report. Supervisors should attend the initial and final meetings with the auditee, when possible. Supervisors should approve both the initial audit work program and any revisions to the audit work program. Nonconformance to the approved audit work program should be recorded in the workpapers, giving adequate reasons. Supervisors should review the workpapers and monitor and control audit budgets and schedules through observation and periodic progress and time reports. When supervisors review the audit report, they should refer to the workpapers to ensure that all evidence and findings are adequately supported and that the deficiency audit findings are objective, fair, significant, and factual.

Domain 4: Communicating Results and Monitoring Progress (20%)

This domain focuses on a few key theoretical topics. It develops audit reports using criteria for quality reporting and key elements required in the audit reports and performs audit closing procedures, such as audit exit meeting, and communicates the audit results to audit clients. It also monitors the audit engagement outcomes with management action plans to implement audit recommendations, assesses residual risk, and communicates risk acceptance. It follows up with the management on the status of implementation of audit recommendations, including their completion, escalation, resolution, and final disposition.

COMMUNICATION QUALITY AND ELEMENTS

Topics such as audit reporting, including audit report purpose, audit report timeliness, audit report contents, report presentation, report distribution, oral reports, and summary reports are presented in this section. Quality attributes of audit communication ensure that the communication is accurate, objective, clear, concise, constructive, complete, and timely. Essential elements of quality communication include describing objectives, scope, conclusions, recommendations, and action plans.

Audit Report Purpose

Written audit reports serve multiple purposes. They communicate the results of the audit work to auditees and others, make the results less susceptible to misunderstanding, and facilitate follow-up reviews to determine whether appropriate corrective actions have been taken.

Audit Report Timeliness

To be of maximum use, the audit report must be timely. A carefully prepared report may be of little value to decision makers if it arrives too late. Therefore, the audit organization should plan for the prompt issuance of the audit report and conduct the audit with this goal in mind.

During the audit, the auditors should consider interim reporting of significant matters to appropriate auditees. Such communication, which may be oral or written, is not a substitute for a final written report, but it does alert auditees to matters needing immediate attention and permits them to correct the problems before the final report is completed.

Summary reports highlighting audit results may be appropriate for levels of management above the auditee. They may be issued separately from or in conjunction with the final report.

Audit Report Timeliness (continued)

Advantages and Disadvantages of Interim Reports

Advantages

- Final report-writing time can be minimized.
- Communication of critical information requiring immediate attention is facilitated.
- Informal and verbal communication can take place.

Disadvantages

- A formal, written interim report may negate the need for a final report in certain circumstances.
- Interim reports put more demand on auditors to make sure the evidence is solid and complete.
- Summary reports highlighting audit results may be appropriate for higher levels of management (e.g., the board members and senior management) above the audit clients (e.g., functional management and operational management). They may be issued separately from or in conjunction with the final report.

Audit Report Contents

The contents of the audit report should include: objectives, scope, and methodology; audit findings, conclusions, and recommendations; compliance with standards, regulations, and laws; management (auditee's) responses; and noteworthy accomplishments (see Exhibit 4.1).

Components of Report Contents

- Objectives, scope, and methodology
- Audit findings, conclusions and recommendations
- Compliance with standards, regulations, and laws
- Auditee's (management) responses
- Auditee's noteworthy accomplishments

Exhibit 4.1: Components of report contents

Objectives, Scope, and Methodology

Readers need knowledge of the objectives of the audit, as well as the audit scope and methodology for achieving the objectives, to understand the purpose of the audit, judge the merits of the audit work and what is reported, and understand any significant limitations.

Objectives, Scope, and Methodology (continued)

The statement of objectives being reported on should explain why the audit was made and state what the report is to accomplish. Articulating what the report is to accomplish normally involves identifying the audit subject and the aspect of performance examined. Because what is reported depends on the objectives, the statement should also communicate what finding elements are discussed and whether conclusions and recommendations are given.

The statement of objectives tells the reader the boundaries of the audit. To preclude misunderstanding in cases where the objectives are particularly limited and broader objectives can be inferred, it may be necessary to clearly define the audit boundaries by stating objectives that were *not* pursued.

The statement of scope should describe the depth and coverage of the audit work conducted to accomplish the audit's objectives. As applicable, it should explain the relationship between the universe and what was audited, identify organizations and geographic locations at which audit work was conducted and the period covered, cite the kinds and sources of evidence used and the techniques used to verify it, and explain any quality or other problems with the evidence. Significant constraints imposed on the audit approach by data limitations or scope impairments must be disclosed.

The statement on methodology should clearly explain the evidence-gathering and analysis techniques used to accomplish the audit's objectives. The explanation should identify any assumptions. It should describe any comparative techniques applied and measures and criteria used to assess performance in conducting the audit. If sampling is involved, the statement should describe the sample design and state why it was chosen.

Objectives, Scope, and Methodology (continued)

Every effort should be made to avoid any misunderstanding on the part of the reader concerning the work that was and was not done to achieve the audit objectives, particularly when the work was limited because of constraints on time or resources.

Determining the Significance of Audit Findings

Audit findings and recommendations have a direct link in that recommendations should address or correct the findings. The benefit from audit work is not in the recommendations made but in their effective implementation. Important measures of audit organization's effectiveness are the type of issues it tackles and the changes or improvements it is able to effect.

Audit findings need to be significant to be of any use to the audited organization. This is because correcting a deficient audit finding requires resources. The significance of audit findings can be assessed from two aspects: the nature of the finding itself and the quality of the recommendations.

With respect to the nature of the findings themselves, both quantitative and qualitative aspects of findings should be considered when determining their significance. Examples of quantitative aspects include revenues increased, costs decreased, and number of defects reduced. Examples of qualitative aspects include customer satisfaction increased, employee morale improved, and the achievement of compliance to laws and regulations.

Objectives, Scope, and Methodology (continued)

With respect to quality, recommendations should be action-oriented and effective. To achieve the desired action, action-oriented recommendations must be

- Properly directed
- Hard-hitting
- Specific
- Convincing
- Significant

To be effective, recommendations must identify a course of action that will correct identified problems or cause significant improvements. Effective recommendations

- Deal with underlying causes
- Are feasible
- Are cost-effective
- Consider alternatives

The significance of a recommendation depends on the subject matter and the specific situation. Frequently, significance can be assessed in terms of dollars. For example, assume that implementation of an audit recommendation would correct inadequate internal controls in an area where very significant amounts of money are subject to theft or manipulation. The inadequate controls are readily recognizable as a significant deficiency. A recommendation to strengthen the internal controls in an area of such significance and susceptibility would be key and worthy of special emphasis.

However, dollars are only one measure of significance, not necessarily the most important one. For example, the need to ensure implementation of recommendations to provide safe operations of a manufacturing or nuclear plant can hardly be overemphasized. Implementing such recommendations could prevent the loss of life, substantial bodily injury, or environmental contamination.

There is a vast difference between recommendations dealing with conditions that are imminently life threatening and those that are just significant enough to be reportable.

The significance of a finding and a recommendation should be known to the auditor and communicated to the auditee early during an assignment. The fact that a recommendation is considered to be a key one should not come as a surprise to the auditee being audited. It should have been made apparent during early discussions with the auditee and certainly at the exit conference.

Emphasis on key recommendations should be continued as the findings and recommendations are reported. Key recommendations should be identified and highlighted in reports in a context that makes their significance apparent. Executive summaries and transmittal memorandums can be used to further establish and emphasize the significance of key recommendations.

Audit Findings, Conclusions, and Recommendations

The report should include a full discussion of the significant audit findings and, where applicable, auditors' conclusions.

The report should present the significant findings developed in response to each audit objective. Any audit finding not included in the audit report because of insignificance should be separately communicated to management, preferably in writing. The audit report should reference findings communicated in a management letter.

All communications should be documented in the workpapers. Sufficient, competent, and relevant information about findings should be included to promote adequate understanding of the matters reported and to provide convincing but fair presentations in proper perspective. Appropriate background information that readers need to understand the findings should also be included.

Desirable Attributes of a Deficiency Audit Finding

Audit findings have often been regarded as containing the elements of criteria, condition, and effect, plus cause when problems are found. However, the elements needed for a finding depend entirely on the objectives of the audit. This means the elements "cause" and "effect" may be optional for a compliance audit, but they are musts for an operational audit. Thus, a finding or set of findings is complete to the extent that the audit objectives are satisfied and the report clearly relates those objectives to the finding's elements.

A deficiency audit finding should have four elements or attributes—criteria, condition, cause, and effect with a recommendation as optional.

Criteria. Criteria are the standards used to determine whether an operation, function, or program meets or exceeds expectations. Criteria provide a context for understanding the results of the audit. Where possible, the audit plan, should state the criteria to be used. In selecting criteria, auditors have a responsibility to use only criteria that are reasonable, attainable, and relevant to the matters being audited. Some examples of different types of criteria are

- Targets or goals set by management or prescribed by law or regulation
- Technically developed standards or norms

- Expert opinions
- Prior years' performance
- Performance of similar entities
- Expected direction of change in outcomes

When the criteria are vague, the auditors should seek interpretation. If interpretation is not available, auditors should strive to agree on the appropriateness of these measures with the interested parties or, if applicable, indicate that they were unable to report on performance because of the lack of definite criteria. It represents "what should be" at the time of the audit.

Condition. Condition is a situation that exists. It has been observed and documented during the audit. It represents "what is" at the time of the audit.

Cause. Cause has two meanings, which depend on the audit objectives. When auditors' objective is to explain why the poor (or good) performance observed in the audit happened, the reasons for the observed performance are referred to as "cause." Identifying the cause of problems is necessary before making constructive recommendations for correction. Because problems can result from a number of plausible factors, auditors need to clearly demonstrate and explain with evidence and reasoning the link between the problems and the factor(s) they identified as the cause. When auditors' objectives include estimating the impact of a program on changes in physical, social, or economic conditions, they seek evidence of the extent to which the program itself is the "cause" of those changes.

Effect. Like cause, effect also has two meanings, which depend on the audit objectives. When auditors' objectives include identifying the actual or potential consequences of a condition that varies (either positively or negatively) from the criteria identified in the audit, "effect" is a measure of those consequences. Auditors often use effect in this sense to demonstrate the need for corrective action in response to identified problems. When auditors' objectives include estimating the effectiveness of an operation or a program in causing changes in physical, social, or economic conditions, "effect" is a measure of the impact achieved by the operation or program. Here effect is the extent to which positive or negative changes in actual physical, social, or economic conditions can be identified and attributed to program or operations.

Recommendations. Recommendations state what an audit organization believes should be done to accomplish beneficial results. They do not direct what must be done but seek to convince others (e.g., the auditee) of what needs to be done.

Recommendations should be action-oriented, convincing, well supported, and effective. When appropriately implemented, they should get the desired beneficial results.

Audit Findings, Conclusions, and Recommendations (continued)

When called for by the audit objectives, the audit report should contain conclusions. Conclusions are logical inferences about the function or operation based on auditors' findings. Conclusions should be specified and not left to be inferred by readers. The report should not be written on the basis that a bare recital of facts makes the conclusions inescapable. The strength of auditors' conclusions depends on the persuasiveness of the evidence supporting the findings.

The audit report should contain recommendations when the potential for significant improvement in operations and performance is substantiated by the reported findings. Recommendations to effect compliance with laws and regulations and improve management controls should also be made when significant instances of noncompliance are noted or significant weaknesses in controls are found. The audit report should also disclose the status of known uncorrected significant findings and recommendations from prior audits that affect the objectives and findings of the current audit.

Reports containing constructive recommendations can encourage improvements in the conduct of audited activities. Recommendations are most constructive when they are directed at resolving the cause of identified problems, are action-oriented and specific, and are addressed to parties that have the authority to act, and are feasible and, to the extent practical, cost-effective.

Compliance with Standards, Regulations, and Laws

The **statement of conformity** refers to the applicable standards that the auditors should have followed during the audit. The statement need not be qualified when standards that were not applicable were not followed. When applicable standards were not followed, the auditors should modify the statement to disclose in the scope section of their report the required standard that was not followed, why, and the known effect not following the standard had on the results of the audit.

The auditors' report should include all instances of noncompliance that auditors determine are significant. All instances of fraud or other illegal acts that could result in the entity, or manager or employee of the entity, being subject to criminal prosecution should also be reported.

In reporting significant instances of noncompliance identified in response to the audit objectives, the auditors should place their findings in proper perspective. To give the reader a basis for judging the prevalence and consequences of noncompliance, the instances of noncompliance should be related to the universe or the number of cases examined and quantified in terms of dollar value, if appropriate.

Management Responses

One of the most effective ways to ensure that a report is fair, complete, and objective is to obtain advance review and comments by responsible auditee (management) and others, as may be appropriate. Including the views of the auditee produces a report that shows not only what was found and what the auditors think about it but also what the responsible persons think about it and what they plan to do about it.

Management Responses (continued)

In general, auditors should request that the responsible auditees' views on significant findings, conclusions, and recommendations adversely affecting the audited entity be submitted in writing. When written comments are not obtained, oral comments should be requested.

Advance comments should be objectively evaluated and recognized, as appropriate, in the report. A promise or plan for corrective action should be noted but should not be accepted as justification for dropping a significant finding or a related recommendation.

When the comments oppose the report's findings, conclusions, or recommendations and are not, in the auditors' opinion, valid, auditors may choose to state their reasons for rejecting them. Conversely, auditors should modify their report if they find the comments valid.

Noteworthy Accomplishments

Significant management accomplishments identified during the audit that were within the scope of the audit should be included in the audit report, along with deficiencies. Such information is necessary to fairly present the situation the auditors found and to provide appropriate balance to the report. In addition, inclusion of such accomplishments may lead to improved performance by other department heads or managers who read the report.

Report Presentation

The audit report should be complete, accurate, objective, convincing, and as clear and concise as the subject permits.

Complete

Being complete requires that the report contain all information needed to satisfy the audit objectives, promote an adequate and correct understanding of the matters reported, and meet the applicable report content requirements. It also means including appropriate background information.

Giving readers an adequate and correct understanding means providing perspective on the extent and significance of reported findings, such as frequency of occurrence relative to the number of cases or transactions tested and the relationship of the findings to the entity's operations.

Except as necessary to make convincing presentations, detailed supporting data need not be included. In most cases, a single example of a deficiency is not sufficient to support a broad conclusion or a related recommendation. All that it supports is that there was a deviation, an error, or a control weakness.

Accurate

Accuracy requires that the evidence presented be true and that findings be correctly portrayed. The need for accuracy is based on the need to assure readers that what it reported is credible and reliable. One inaccuracy in a report can cast doubt on the validity of an entire report and can divert attention from its substance. Also, inaccurate reports can damage the credibility of the issuing audit organization and reduce the effectiveness of reports it issues.

The report should include only information, findings, and conclusions that are supported by competent and relevant evidence in the auditors' workpapers. That evidence should demonstrate the correctness and reasonableness of the matters reported. The term "correct portrayal" means describing accurately the audit scope and methodology and presenting findings and conclusions in a manner consistent with the scope of audit work.

Objective

Objectivity requires that the presentation of the entire report be balanced in content and tone. A report's credibility is significantly enhanced when it presents evidence in an unbiased manner so that readers can be persuaded by the facts.

The audit report should be fair and not be misleading and should place the audit results in proper perspective. This means presenting the audit results impartially and guarding against the tendency to exaggerate or overemphasize deficient performance. In describing shortcomings in performance, auditors should present the explanation of responsible auditees, including the consideration of any unusual difficulties or circumstances they faced.

The tone of reports should encourage favorable reaction to findings and recommendations. Titles, captions, and the text of reports should be stated constructively. Although findings should be presented clearly and forthrightly, auditors should keep in mind that one of their objectives is to persuade and that this can best be done by avoiding language that generates defensiveness and opposition. Although criticism of past performance is often necessary, the report should emphasize needed improvements.

Convincing

Being convincing requires that the audit results are responsive to the audit objectives, the findings are presented persuasively, and the conclusions and recommendations follow logically from the facts presented. The information presented should be sufficient to convince the report readers of the validity of the findings, the reasonableness of the conclusions, and the desirability of implementing the recommendations. Reports designed in this way can help focus the attention of management on the matters that warrant attention and can help stimulate correction.

Clear

Clarity requires that the report be easy to read and understand. Reports should be written in language as clear and simple as the subject permits. Use of straightforward, nontechnical language is essential to simplicity of presentation. If technical terms and unfamiliar abbreviations and acronyms are used, they should be clearly defined. Acronyms should be used sparingly.

Both logical organization of material and accuracy and precision in stating facts and in drawing conclusions are essential to clarity and understanding. Effective use of titles and captions and topic sentences make the report easier to read and understand. Visual aids (i.e., pictures, charts, graphs, and diagrams) should be used when appropriate to clarify and summarize complex material.

Concise

Being concise requires that the report be no longer than necessary to convey the message. Too much detail detracts from a report, may even conceal the real message, and may confuse or discourage readers. Also, needless repetition should be avoided. Although room exists for considerable judgment in determining the content of reports, those that are complete but still concise are likely to receive greater attention.

Report Distribution

The final report should be distributed to auditees directly interested in the audit work results and those responsible for acting on the findings and recommendations. Higher-level members in the organization may receive only a summary report. Reports may also be distributed to other interested or affected parties, such as external auditors and the board of directors.

Certain information may not be appropriate for disclosure to all report recipients because it is privileged, proprietary, or related to improper or illegal acts. Such information, however, may be disclosed in a separate report. If the conditions being reported involve senior management, report distribution should be to the board of the organization.

Oral Reports

In some circumstances, it might be appropriate for auditors to issue oral reports. If they issue an oral report, auditors should keep a written record of what they communicated and the basis for not issuing a written report. An oral report may be most appropriate when emergency action is needed. Before issuing an oral report, auditors should determine that both of these conditions exist:

1. An oral report would effectively meet decision makers' needs for information about the results of the audit.
2. It is unlikely that parties other than those who would receive the oral report would have a significant interest in the results of the audit.

Summary Reports

Summary written audit reports are generally intended for high-level management and/or the audit committee. However, a detailed audit report dealing with payroll department with significant control weaknesses, for example, should be most useful to the payroll department manager.

AUDIT REPORTING PROCESS

Audit fieldwork begins with an entrance conference and ends with an exit conference with audit client management or engagement client. Between these two conferences, most of the audit work is done, such as developing an audit program, conducting the actual audit work, collecting audit evidence, developing workpapers, writing the draft audit report, obtaining the audit client management's response to the audit report's findings and recommendations, writing the final audit report, and receiving audit client management's action plans about the treatment of such audit findings and recommendations, as shown next.

Entrance Conference ⟶ Fieldwork ⟶ Exit Conference ⟶ Draft Audit Report ⟶ Final

Purpose of Audit Reports

Internal audit reports have several purposes when informing the board, senior management, and audit committee of an organization and include:

- Whether an organization's business function, department, division, or activity adheres to policies, procedures, and applicable laws or regulations
- Whether operating processes, internal control systems, and risk management activities are effective
- What corrective action the organization's management has taken or must take for new audit issues or outstanding audit issues

The audit report should also address potential and emerging concerns. The auditor should communicate findings and recommendations to appropriate parties and distribute audit reports as soon as practical after completing the related audit work. Audit workpapers should adequately document and support the audit reports.

Types of Audit Reports

Generally, there are two types of audit reporting: individual audit reports and executive summary reports, which are the outputs of the audit work. The summary reports are issued to the board or audit committee.

Individual audit reports should be structured to fit the needs of the internal audit function and the audit areas being audited. These reports contain:

1. Audit scope and objectives
2. Detailed audit results
3. Recommendations with benefits
4. Audit client management's commitment to correct material weakness presented as audit findings

Audit reports present a concise summary of key results and conclusions, including an overall assigned audit rating and identification of root causes of material weaknesses. Generally, individual audit reports should discuss established audit criteria, existing problems, root causes and impacts for significant problems, and recommendations for correcting the reported problems.

Types of Audit Reports (continued)

Executive summary reports are more concise briefings of individual audit reports. These reports contain several different items, such as:

1. Status of meeting annual audit plans and schedules
2. Activity reports for audits completed, in-process, deferred, or canceled
3. Audit staffing and training reports
4. Summaries of audits
5. Risk assessments, evaluations, or summaries
6. Results of regulatory audits
7. Tracking reports for outstanding audit and control issues (open audit issues)

Report Development Process

After completing an audit fieldwork, the internal auditor usually meets with the manager of the audit department to discuss the draft audit report, correct any inaccurate information, and possibly reach agreement on audit client management's commitments and actions. A final audit report is then distributed to the affected audit client management, senior management, and the audit committee within an appropriate time frame after the completion of fieldwork. Compliance with issuance time frames should be monitored and reported to the audit committee.

Internal audit management should ensure that audit client management considers the level and significance (magnitude) of risk when assigning resources to address and remediate initial audit findings and open audit issues. Internal audit management should document the audit client management's action plans either within the audit report or separately.

A structured approach to develop and distribute the audit reports is shown next.

Draft Report → Review → Final Report → Approve → Distribute

RESIDUAL RISK AND RISK ACCEPTANCE

This section defines a residual risk, explains the nature of the residual risk, quantifies residual risk, and further explains it in the form of mathematical equations. It also shows a relationship between risk appetite, de-risking, and residual risk.

Residual Risk Defined

Residual risk is leftover exposure to risk (remainder risk) that is uncontrolled, unmitigated, unmanaged, and unaddressed by audit client management. Residual risk is the risk remaining after management takes action to reduce the impact and likelihood of an adverse event, including control activities in responding to a risk. Residual risk is current risk with existing control systems. Residual risk is calculated as potential risks minus covered risks, resulting in uncovered risk. Residual risk is net risk where it is the portion of inherent risk that remains open after management has accepted the residual risk and after it executed and implemented its risk responses.

Audit cycles are usually driven by the risk scores of the business activities or areas in the audit risk assessment. The audit risk assessment process identifies both an inherent risk score and a residual risk score to each auditable entity. The residual risk score is most commonly used in assigning the audit cycle, taking into account mitigating

Residual Risk Defined (continued)

controls. Because of this complexity in residual risk exposure, it must be measured and monitored by the internal audit management. If risk management is defined as identifying, assessing, and mitigating risks, then the residual risk is defined as measuring and monitoring risks, as shown:

Risk management = Identifying risks + Assessing risks + Mitigating risks

Residual risk = Measuring risks + Monitoring risks

Explanation of Residual Risk

Audit-related residual risk is different from the general definition of residual risk. Audit-related residual risk occurs when audit clients reject auditors' recommendations and when audit clients accept recommendations but do not fully implement them. Practically speaking, even the recommendations that were fully accepted and fully implemented could have a residual risk if auditors' recommendations did not achieve the intended goal of reducing all the known risks because errors, obstacles, or resource constraints occurred during implementation.

The general definition of residual risk refers to the remainder risk—for example, even after an individual purchases an insurance policy (e.g., auto, home, or life), that the individual is still responsible for paying the deductible amount because the policy does not cover all expenses. Here, the deductible amount is the residual

Explanation of Residual Risk (continued)

risk for an individual. Using the insurance case, which is a risk transfer example, residual risk is present even in situations of risk avoidance, risk reduction, and risk acceptance.

It is a fact that original risks and residual risks are inherent in life and business; they cannot be eliminated completely or entirely regardless of costs incurred. The real question to internal auditors is how much residual risk is too much or too little. Internal auditors and audit clients could vary widely in this respect in that an audit client may be willing to accept more residual risks than the internal auditors and the organization as a whole are willing to accept.

Quantification of Residual Risk

Even if audit client management wants to accept all the residual risks, regardless of their size and impact, internal auditors have a professional duty to highlight the impact of excessive residual risks by showing management quantified examples of potential negative outcomes. Audit client management understands the negative consequences of the residual risk better in terms of dollars and cents than in terms of abstract description, although audit clients can question or challenge that monetary quantification.

Residual Risk Equations

Because residual risk is a difficult concept to comprehend, the best way to understand it better is through simple equations:

Residual risks = Total risks – Mitigated risks = Unmitigated risks = Ignored risks

Residual risks = Unmitigated risks = Unmanaged risks = Exposed risks

Residual risks = Accepted risks = Retained risks = Avoided risks

Residual risks = Potential risks – Covered risks = Uncovered risks

Residual risks = Total risks – Addressed risks = Unaddressed risks

Residual risks = Uncovered risks = Unaddressed risks = Unresolved risks

Residual risks = Total risks – Discovered risks = Undiscovered risks

Residual risks = Total risks – Transferred risks or Shared risks

Residual risks = Potential risks – Countermeasures (controls) applied = Uncontrolled risks

Residual risks = Known risks = Identified risks = Uncommitted risks

Residual risks = Lack of management's commitment to reduce risks = Uncommitted risks

Residual risks = Lost business opportunities when residual risks are ignored

Residual risks = Risks after some risks are treated = Untreated risks

Risk Appetite versus Residual Risk

There is an inverse or indirect relationship between risk appetite and residual risk. **Risk appetite** is defined as the amount of risk that an organization is willing to *accept*. The **residual risk** is defined as the amount of risk that an organization is willing to *reject*. Hence, a reverse relationship exists; that is, risk appetite is high when the residual risk is low and vice versa.

Residual risk = (1 – Risk appetite)

Because the risk-based internal audit plan is based on the risk appetite, the audit plan considers the residual risk during the development of the audit plan because the residual risk comes after the original audit plan was developed, audit work was completed, audit recommendations were made, and audit clients decided to reject the auditors' recommendations.

De-Risking versus Residual Risk

De-risking has an inverse (indirect and opposite) relationship with the residual risk in that while de-risking efforts reduce the overall risk, residual risk decisions result in adding risk to the overall risk.

De-Risking versus Residual Risk (continued)

De-risking means risk lessening, risk downsizing, or risk modifying. It can also include reducing a current risk or a future risk with various methods such as:

- Risk transferring (e.g., hold-harmless agreements, incorporation, business partnerships, insurance, self-insurance, reinsurance, coinsurance, risk securitization (captive insurance), hedging, new contracts, and re-contracting).
- Risk management program (i.e., a mature risk framework with management support), risk mitigation efforts (i.e., controls and resources), and an approach to balance risks and returns.
- Risk sharing, risk diversifying, risk spreading with third-parties, risk-shifting (e.g., between stockholders and bondholders and vice versa), including surety bonds, performance bonds, and blanket bonds.
- Incorporation methods (e.g., a public corporation is less risky than a private corporation; a regular corporation is less risky than a proprietorship or partnership; and a limited liability corporation is less risky than a regular corporation). A proprietorship poses the highest risk because the sole owner is responsible for all losses and gains.

Residual risk is the risk remaining after management's actions to reduce the impact and likelihood of an adverse event, including control activities in responding to a risk. Residual risk is current risk; it is also called unmanaged risk, leftover risk, or net risk after existing controls are applied. Residual risk is the portion of inherent risk that remains open after management executes its risk responses.

MONITORING AUDIT PROGRESS

This section discusses topics such as management actions on audit outcomes, tracking of open audit issues, and establishing escalation procedures. All are part of audit monitoring and follow-up and resolution of senior management's acceptance of risks.

Management Actions on Audit Outcomes

Audit monitoring and follow-up can be sophisticated or simple depending on a number of factors, including the size and complexity of the audit organization. Regardless of the type chosen, each audit should include: a firm basis for monitoring and follow-up actions, active status monitoring, and a determination of the results of actions taken on recommendations.

Audit client responses to the audit report are reviewed to assess their adequacy and the timeliness and appropriateness of proposed corrective actions. Auditee responses and their corrective actions are monitored to ensure their timely completion. Effective follow-up is essential to get the full benefits of audit work. If monitoring and follow-up disclose that action on major recommendations is not progressing, additional steps should be promptly considered. Follow-up should be elevated to progressively higher levels of management of the organization to obtain prompt action. Continued attention is required until expected results are achieved. At this point, audit recommendations are closed.

Management Actions on Audit Outcomes (continued)

Reasons for closing audit recommendations include only one of these:

- The recommendation was effectively implemented.
- An alternative action was taken that achieved the intended results.
- Circumstances have so changed that the recommendation is no longer valid.
- The recommendation was not implemented despite the use of all feasible strategies.

When a recommendation is closed for the last reason, a judgment is made on whether the objectives are significant enough to be pursued at a later date in another assignment.

It is a business fact that audit clients do not accept all findings and recommendations made by auditors for various reasons. Examples of reasons could be that these findings are trivial; nitpicking; have no real value to the audit client; waste resources such as time, money, and effort; and the auditor who performed the audit work is incompetent with no proper training and relevant experience. The more delays in accepting and implementing an auditor's findings and recommendations by the audit clients, the larger the size of the open audit issues. This is one of the reasons for the audit function to establish escalation procedures where open audit issues are moved up the organization's management hierarchy from functional management to senior management to the audit committee of the board for timely resolution. The audit function's goal is to reduce the number of open audit issues as fast as they can and move on.

Tracking of Open Audit Issues

Audit monitoring includes a method to **track and monitor** open-audit issues and to follow up on such issues. The timely remediation of open audit issues is an essential component of an organization's risk reduction or risk mitigation efforts. This is because open audit recommendations are risky, meaning an identified and existing risk is not addressed. Internal audit management, functional managers, and senior management should discuss and agree to an appropriate resolution date, based on the level of work and effort necessary to complete remediation processes.

When an audit client owning an open audit issue indicates that her work to close an issue is completed, the internal audit function should perform validation work prior to closing the issue. The level of validation necessary may vary based on the issue's risk level (i.e., high, medium, or low). For higher-risk issues, internal audit should perform and document substantive testing to validate that the issue has been resolved. Issues should be tested over an appropriate period of time to ensure the sustainability of the remediation.

Establishing Escalation Procedures

An internal audit function is effective when it establishes **escalation procedures** for resolving any differences of opinion between audit staff/management and organization management (audit clients) concerning reported audit findings and recommendations. Audit clients can reject, dispute, or even challenge the audit findings and recommendations. The escalation procedures take these disputes to the audit committee for resolution. Under these conditions, the audit function should develop an aging analysis of recommendations that are still open, outstanding, not accepted, or not implemented by the audit clients (i.e., open audit issues with delays). The aging analysis can indicate how old these open recommendations are (e.g., 90, 180, 270, 360 days old or longer with no resolution or implementation).

From a big-picture perspective, audit reports and their disposition take two distinct routes, as shown next:

Audit Reports → Issuance → Acceptance → Disposition

Audit Reports → Issuance → Rejection → Escalation and Resolution → Disposition

Appendix

RISKS TO INTERNAL AUDIT ACTIVITY

Like other functions, the internal audit function is a risk-prone activity, as there is no function in an organization that is risk-resistant. Risks to internal audit activities fall into three broad categories: audit failure risks, false assurance risks, and reputation risks.

Audit Failure Risks

In addition to control breakdowns and fraud occurrences, the internal audit activity itself could be a contributing factor to audit failures. Problems could involve auditors:

- Showing negligence in performing their professional work.
- Not following professional standards.
- Not identifying high-risk auditable areas during the planning of individual audits.

Audit Failure Risks (continued)

- Not paying attention to fraud alerts and red flags.
- Not doing the right audits at the right time.
- Wasting resources on doing the wrong audits at the wrong time.
- Not delivering a quality audit product.

Specific causes leading to audit failure risks include these failures:

- Failure to design effective internal audit procedures to test the "real" risks and the right controls.
- Failure to evaluate both the design adequacy and the control effectiveness as part of internal audit procedures.
- Failure of adequate internal audit supervision.
- Failure to exercise professional skepticism and judgment.
- Failure to undertake extended internal audit procedures related to negative findings or control deficiencies.
- Failure to communicate fraud suspicions to the right people at the right time.
- Failure to assign competent auditors to perform complex audit engagements.

Audit Failure Risks (continued)

Remedies to address the audit failure risks include:

- Periodic reviews of the audit universe and audit plan.
- An effective audit planning process and audit design of the system of internal controls.
- Escalation procedures within the internal audit activity indicating when and what types of issues to escalate to which level of audit management's hierarchy.
- Ensuring that high-risk audit engagements are staffed with auditors possessing a combination of right experience, knowledge, skills, competencies, or talents (i.e., right mix of audit resources with a blend of hard skills and soft skills).
- Ensuring that lead auditors have strong project management skills to complete an audit engagement on time and within budget.
- Implementing an effective QAIP conducting internal assessments and external assessments.

False Assurance Risks

False assurance is a level of confidence or assurance based on perceptions or assumptions, not on facts. False assurance risks result when auditors are unknowingly overselling themselves or underperforming and making empty promises to audit clients who take those promises very seriously and who hold auditors accountable for what they promised. Simply put, false assurances result from what was said, when it was said, and how it was said. Examples of empty promises or false assurances that could raise **expectation gaps** include phrases like "We will take care of it," "We will help you, don't worry about it," or "I will talk to my audit management and let me see what I can do for you."

Specific causes leading to false assurance risks include:

- Not keeping the proper mental distance between auditors and audit clients.
- Not monitoring an auditor's independence and objectivity issues.
- Not clearly defining and documenting the auditor's roles and responsibilities (role gap) when business units request the audit staff's help in implementing a new computer system project in accounting department or analyzing customer service department's problems with product warranty and guarantee claims (loaned audit resources).

False Assurance Risks (continued)

- Not communicating scope inclusions (what is covered, in scope) and scope exclusions (what is not covered, out of scope) in the audit's work when conducting risk assessments, developing internal audit plans, and performing internal audit engagements (expectation gap). Auditors need to realize that they may have a role gap and expectation gap in the minds of audit clients.

  Auditors' role gap = Audit clients' perceived role of auditors – Auditors' actual role

  Auditors' expectation gap = Audit clients' expected deliverables – Auditors' actual deliverables

  Loaned audit resources can create false assurance risks, in part due to expectation gaps.

  Remedies to address the false assurance risks include:

- Communicating frequently and clearly to all the affected parties about the auditors' role, their professional mission and mandate, and adherence to the professional *Standards*.
- Communicating scope inclusions and exclusions in every audit engagement project.
- Documenting "project risk" information at the beginning of a project describing the types and sources of risks a project is facing, including its risk immunity levels (risk resistant or risk prone) and risk sensitivity levels (sensitive or insensitive).
- Installing a "project acceptance" process at the beginning of a project where auditors document their specific roles and project outcomes and deliverables, the types of project risks being handled, the types of audit talent and competencies required or available, and the independence of auditors.

Reputation Risks

Reputation risks primarily deal with positive or negative impressions or images of auditors in the eyes of audit clients. Positive image can take many years to earn, whereas it takes very little time to earn a negative image; it can be gained through one high-profile and high-impact adverse event. Both audit failure risks and false assurance risks in combination can result in reputation risks, as they are interconnected.

Reputation risks = Audit failure risks + False assurance risks

For example, when auditors are assigned to a business function to assist its day-to-day work due to that function's staff shortages or to participate in a special project of considerable duration (say three to six months), these auditor-loaned resources can create false assurance situations and reputation risks. This is because non-auditors think that auditors are highly experienced and highly knowledgeable people carrying a strong "brand" name for perfection and excellence and that they never make mistakes. When something goes wrong in an auditor-assisted work, auditors are the first ones to be blamed for problems because auditors are outsiders and because they are assumed to do a perfect work and that they know, or should know, everything. Examples of loaned audit resources can be found in the accounting, finance, treasury, corporate tax, insurance, and loss prevention departments.

Reputation Risks (continued)

Specific causes leading to reputation risks include:

- Using auditors as loaned resources to other business functions, whether short term or long term.
- Auditors' behavior and performance as loaned resources in other business functions and the associated impressions and images left on the minds of employees and managers of that business function.
- The auditors' inability to understand, protect, and maintain their own strong audit "brand" name (goodwill), leading to credibility issues (**credibility gaps**). There is a clear connection between the reputation gap, role gap, expectation gap, and credibility gap, as shown:

  Reputation gap = Role gap + Expectation gap + Credibility gap

Remedies to address the reputation risks are listed next.

- Training all internal auditors about the scope and nature of false assurances, reputation risks, and brand-name protections.
- Educating auditors in that each auditor is a source for creating or for eliminating audit failures, false assurances, and reputation risks.

Reputation Risks (continued)

- Conducting a self-audit of the internal audit department by outsiders, similar to what internal auditors do at an internal audit-client location.
- Maintaining an audit incident log describing all the audit failures, false assurances, and reputation issues and not revealing the auditors' names and locations.
- Posting, publicizing, and notifying every internal auditor about the lessons learned from recent observations and experiences regarding audit failures, false assurances, and reputation risks.
- Installing a suggestion box system within the internal audit department for improving or removing audit failures, false assurances, and reputation risks.
- Selecting internal auditors for job rotational assignments in nonaudit functions (job rotations) based on a careful blend of hard skills and soft skills they possess and those that can protect internal audit's brand reputation. Note that it requires the CAE to be open-minded (transparent), forward-thinking, and proactive in nature for maintaining an audit incident log, similar to a security incident log maintained in the IT function. The security incident log documents all the data security breaches and cyberattacks that occurred on data files and websites respectively.

THE IIA'S THREE-LINES-OF-DEFENSE MODEL

Similar to information systems security requiring multiple layers of defense (i.e., security controls using defense-in-depth and defense-in-breadth concepts) to protect technology assets (e.g., computers, networks, and mobile devices), organizations need three lines of defense (three layers of defense) to protect and preserve human assets (e.g., employees, customers, suppliers, vendors, visitors, and contractors), tangible assets (e.g., buildings, inventory, plant, and equipment), intangible assets (e.g., copyrights, trademarks, service marks, and patents), financial assets (e.g., cash, stocks, and bonds), and information assets (e.g., data, plans, policies, procedures, and practices). The scope of the three-lines-of-defense model applies to risk management and control activities and processes. The nature of this model includes vigilant employees observing people and things for unusual and strange behavior, manual control procedures, automated control procedures, and daily work rules and practices.

The idea behind the three-lines-of-defense model is that:

- If the first line of defense does not work for some reason, then the second line of defense comes into play to protect and preserve the assets.
- If the first line and second line of defense do not work for some reason, the third line of defense (last line of defense) should work in protecting and preserving the assets.

The concept behind the three-lines-of-defense model is that two hands are stronger than one hand and that multiple lines of defense provide a much stronger support and protection than a single line of defense. This model can be installed at two levels: organization level and internal audit level.

Organization-Level: Three Lines of Defense

Examples of organization-level three lines of defense follow:

First line of defense:	Operational and functional management working in manufacturing, marketing, merchandising, procurement, information technology, human resources, accounting, loss prevention, finance, and operations departments. This first defense is a form of initial exercise of controls through management controls and internal control measures. This defense is provided by risk owners and managers who own, manage, and oversee risks. These risk owners implement corrective actions to address process weaknesses and control deficiencies.
Second line of defense:	Employees working in compliance function, health and safety department, customer service department, technical support group, environmental management, IT security analysts, physical security guards, legal staff, risk analysts, financial control analysts, product quality inspectors, internal quality assurance providers, and external quality assurance providers. This second defense is a form of intermediary exercise of controls and provides risk control and compliance.
Third line of defense:	Internal auditors, physical security guards, fraud specialists, public relations officers, insurance claims adjusters, and corporate gatekeepers (e.g., accountants, auditors, and attorneys). This third defense is a form of final exercise of controls and provides risk assurance.

Organization-Level: Three Lines of Defense (continued)

Fourth line of defense:	Although not officially and explicitly defined, external auditors and regulatory auditors can be treated and recognized as providing fourth-line-of-defense services. These outside auditors can be asked to provide a separate and comprehensive review of an organization's risk management framework and practices (e.g., ERM), to assess the adequacy of the three lines of defense, and to report their review results to senior management, the board, and shareholders.

Both the second and third lines of defense provide oversight and/or assurance services over risk management. The key difference between the second and third lines is the concepts of independence and objectivity of internal auditors. (Source: Internal Audit and the Second Line of Defense, IPPF's Supplemental Guidance, Practice Guide, IIA, January 2016, www.theiia.org.)

Responsibilities may become blurred across internal audit function and second-line-of-defense functions when internal auditors were asked to assume second-line-of-defense activities due to their special skills and talents. Examples of these assumed activities include new regulatory requirements (e.g., assistance in training and implementation of Sarbanes-Oxley Act of 2002 (SOX 2002), change in business (e.g., entry into new markets, new products, and new line of business), resource constraints (internal auditors are requested to fill the staffing and management gap), and efficiency in performing compliance and risk management functions better than the others.

Organization-Level: Three Lines of Defense (continued)

Where safeguards to maintain internal audit's independence and objectivity are not possible, the responsibility for performing the second-line-of-defense activities should be reassigned to an internal nonaudit function or outsourced externally to a third-party provider. Moreover, the second-line-of-defense activities performed by internal audit should be referenced in the audit's charter document and/or included in the board update report issued at least annually by the internal audit department.

Internal auditors should avoid activities that compromise their independence and objectivity, including:

- Setting the risk-appetite levels
- Owning, managing, and overseeing risks
- Assuming responsibilities for accounting, business development, and other first-line-of-defense functions
- Making risk-response decisions on the organization's management behalf
- Implementing or assuming accountability for risk management or governance processes
- Providing assurance on second-line-of-defense activities performed by internal auditors

Audit-Level: Three Lines of Defense

Similar to the three lines of defense found at an organization level, internal audit activity has three lines of defense or three layers of defense within its own department or function, as follows:

First line of defense	Staff auditor who is assigned to an audit engagement (engagement auditor), who developed the audit program, who prepared audit workpapers, and who drafted the initial audit reports can act as the first line of defense. Signoff letters received from the engagement auditor after completing the audit work support and strengthen the audit work.
Second line of defense	In-charge auditor or lead auditor who reviewed the audit program, workpapers, and audit reports to confirm adherence to the audit plan, objectives, and scope can act as the second line of defense. Signoffs received from the in-charge auditor or lead auditor support and strengthen the audit work completed.
Third line of defense	Audit supervisor or manager who reviewed the audit plan, audit program, workpapers, and audit reports to confirm adherence to the IIA's Standards, including the audit quality assurance standards, can act as the third line of defense. Signoffs received from the audit supervisor or manager support and strengthen the audit work completed. Note that the audit supervisors and managers should act as the last line of defense (last resort) because there is no one after them to protect and defend the audit work.

AUDIT METRICS AND KEY PERFORMANCE INDICATORS

Internal audit activity is a function requiring a measurement of its performance similar to other functions in an organization. Audit metrics and KPIs are self-checks for internal auditors to measure and manage progress of their own performance levels. Audit metrics and KPIs can be organized, structured, and monitored in terms of management KPIs, operational KPIs, strategic KPIs, professional KPIs, financial KPIs, and board-level KPIs.

Management KPIs

- Time to complete an audit engagement in hours or days (time to audit in hours or days).
- Average time to complete an audit engagement in hours or days (average time to audit in hours or days).
- Elapsed time between the audit fieldwork completion and audit report issuance. Longer time periods require improvements.
- Average time to issue audit reports in days or weeks. This measures how much time was taken to issue an audit report after an audit engagement was completed.
- Time since the last audit (in years). This actual time should be compared with the planned audit cycle time, and proper actions should be taken.
- Elapsed time between the audits (in years). This actual time should be compared with the planned audit cycle time, and proper actions should be taken.

Management KPIs (continued)

- Time to take corrective actions by audit client management regarding audit recommendations. Longer time periods require audit monitoring and follow-up.
- The longest time an auditor's job is open for months, quarters, and years.
- The shortest time an auditor's job is open for months, quarters, and years.

Operational KPIs

- Percentage of the annual audit plan completed. Higher percentages indicate successful audits while lower percentages indicate unsuccessful audits, where the latter results in residual risks.
- Percentage of actual risks addressed, assured, or covered to the total number of risks discovered or uncovered. The difference results in an assurance gap.
- Percentage of audit reports issued as scheduled or planned. This shows that the audit activity can deliver its reports on time and that it is disciplined in doing so.
- Percentage of follow-up audits conducted as scheduled or planned. This indicates auditors' lack of seriousness and shows that auditors are there just to make recommendations and that they are not serious about whether they help the organization that they work for. It is a sign of disservice to the organization.
- Percentage of recommendations implemented resulting from internal assessments and external assessments regarding the internal audit activity's QAIP program.

Strategic KPIs

- Percentage of audit recommendations accepted by audit clients at a point in time. This indicates the usefulness (benefit) of audit recommendations to audit clients.
- Percentage of audit recommendations rejected by audit clients at a point in time. This indicates the nonuse of (no benefit) of audit recommendations to audit clients.
- Percentage of audit recommendations implemented after they are accepted by audit clients at a point in time. This indicates that audit recommendations are practical and useful.
- Percentage of unimplementable audit recommendations after they were accepted by audit clients at a point in time. This indicates that audit recommendations are theoretical in nature with no practical benefits.
- Percentage of significant audit recommendations (vital few of 20/80 rule) to the total number of audit recommendations made in a year. This indicates that internal auditors are clearly adding and enhancing value to their organization.
- Percentage of insignificant audit recommendations (trivial many of 20/80 rule) to the total number of audit recommendations made in a year. This indicates that internal auditors are not at all adding value to their organization.

Professional KPIs

- Percentage of auditors certified in internal auditing with the CIA designation.
- Percentage of auditors with audit-related multiple certifications.
- Average number of professional certifications held by auditors.
- Average number of continuing professional development hours earned in a year by auditors.
- Average number of auditors' work experience in years in internal auditing.
- Percentage of technology auditors to nontechnology auditors.
- Average turnover of audit staff in a year.

Financial KPIs

- Percentage of audits completed over the budget.
- Percentage of audits completed under the budget.
- Variance analysis between budgeted hours and actual hours.

Board KPIs

- Percentage of independent directors to total board members. The goal should be a higher percentage in the industry.
- Percentage of a company's executives on the board to total board members. The goal should be a smaller percentage in the industry.
- Percentage of shadow directors to total board members. The goal should be a zero percentage because shadow directors (e.g., outsiders such as lobbyists, activists, friends, family members, consultants, and majority shareholders) can exercise greater pressure on and influence over the board.
- Percentage of nonexecutive directors to risk management committee members. The goal should be a higher percentage because executive directors, such as chief executive, chief financial, and chief risk officers, can exercise greater influence on the risk committee, which is not good for the company.
- Percentage of independent directors to audit committee members. The goal should be a higher percentage because the audit committee oversees the entire financial reporting process and coordinates between internal auditors and external auditors, which is a major responsibility. The audit committee should not oversee the risk management and regulatory compliance functions as they are the responsibility of senior management (executives).

Board KPIs (continued)

- Percentage of female directors to total board members. The goal should be a comparable percentage in the industry and nation's data.
- Percentage of directors with little or no compensation or remuneration paid. The goal should be a zero percentage because it follows the simple principle of no money, no work. Two outcomes are possible here: say on pay and no pay, no say. Without a comparable compensation and remuneration, directors are hired just for their names only to act as a rubber stamp for the CEO; they simply become routine box-checkers in their work, and they have no strong voice (or no teeth) in the board's matters and decisions.
- Percentage of board-level qualitative metrics to the total number of board-level metrics. Total metrics include both qualitative and quantitative metrics, which should be given equal importance. Examples of quantitative metrics include: (1) sales, revenues, profits, market share, company stock prices year over year; and (2) earnings per share and returns on investment, assets, equity, and capital. Examples of qualitative metrics include: low employee morale; negative comments posted on social media by unhappy customers; and cyber-, supply chain, product recall, public relations, and customer dissatisfaction risks.

CHARACTERISTICS OF EFFECTIVE AUDITORS AND AUDIT FUNCTION

In general, effectiveness means achieving the stated mission, vision, goals, objectives, plans, programs, or activities in the most economical manner after considering their costs and benefits. In this section, we present characteristics that define internal auditors as effective and the internal audit function as effective; they are not the same.

Characteristics of Effective Auditors

A list of characteristics that can define internal auditors as effective is presented next. Note that the list is not all-inclusive. Effective auditors can make an audit function effective due to their professionalism and competency levels.

Effective auditors possess competencies and skills in these areas:

- Business acumen
- Critical thinking
- Communications
- Basic legal and ethical principles

Characteristics of Effective Auditors (continued)

- Audit and legal evidence
- Forensics and investigations
- Analytical and functional knowledge
- Assurance services and consulting services
- Risk management and insurance
- Sampling and statistics
- Information technology in systems development and systems security
- Big-data analytics and data mining
- Industry knowledge

  Effective auditors acquire the core knowledge of the business or industry they work in. This means possessing:

- Business acumen when working for business organizations.
- Core knowledge about how a government operates when working for governmental agencies.

Characteristics of Effective Auditors (continued)

- Core knowledge about academic world (e.g., schools, colleges, and universities) when working in educational institutions.
- Core knowledge about how hospitals and medical research institutions operate when working in healthcare industry.
- Core knowledge about how nongovernmental organizations (NGOs) operate when working for NGOs.

It is very difficult for auditors to understand, operate, and contribute when they do not have the required core knowledge of their work.

- Effective auditors adhere to professional standards and possess the required core business knowledge combined with the right mix of business skills (hard skills and soft skills) to implement such professional standards. Up-skilling auditors is the major focus here (i.e., unskilled auditors must be up-skilled, reskilled, and cross-skilled).
- Effective auditors play several roles, such as:
    - Trusted advisors
    - Control assessors

Characteristics of Effective Auditors (continued)

    - Control evaluators
    - Cyberadvisors
    - Internal business consultants/partners to the board of directors (board) and senior management (company executives and officers)
- During their work in providing assurance and consulting services, effective auditors can link:
    - Audit strategy to business strategy.
    - Audit objectives to business objectives.
    - Audit risks to business risks.
    - Audit value to business value.
- Effective internal auditors can work with external auditors in coordinating and communicating during standard assurance services (e.g., financial audit) and special services, such as during governance, risk, and control reviews.
- Effective auditors pay equal attention to financial reporting (revenues, costs, and profits) and nonfinancial reporting (e.g., operations, marketing, legal, ethical, and social improvements and issues).

Characteristics of Effective Auditors (continued)

- Effective auditors are independent in appearance and action and are objective in mind and in reporting their work results.
- Effective auditors can use data analytics techniques and data mining software tools to assess data integrity and security controls over databases, data warehouses, and data marts.
- Effective auditors can use statistical analyses, such as regression analysis, factor analysis, cluster analysis, link analysis, and correlation analysis, to detect fraudulent transactions.
- Effective auditors can use data analytics and data mining software tools to assess the overall control environment after identifying systemic breakdowns in controls.
- Effective auditors can use big-data analytics as a part of their analytical reviews conducted during audit planning and engagement work.
- Effective auditors apply critical thinking skills and possess judgment rules when collecting and analyzing audit evidence and when reaching audit conclusions and recommendations. They know the differences between:
    - Strong evidence and weak evidence.
    - False evidence and true evidence.

Characteristics of Effective Auditors (continued)

- Good conclusions and bad conclusions.
- Big recommendations (vital few) and small recommendations (trivial many).
- Value-creating opportunities and value-destroying events.

An auditor's recommendations must be big in scope, size, and significance.

- Effective auditors are good in identifying or differentiating between value-creating and value-destroying plans, programs, policies, procedures, and practices. This can save an organization from undertaking value-destroying plans. The same thing applies to value-adding tasks and activities and non-value-adding tasks and activities.
- The chief audit executive (CAE) wears several hats, such as supervisor, manager, leader, change agent, coach, mentor, delegator, motivator, inspirer, agile performer, and above all futurist.
- Internal auditors are effective when they treat audit clients and outside auditors with respect, dignity, and humility during their interactions in audit work and nonaudit work.

In summary, effective auditors are value creators, value enhancers, change agents, team players, agile performers who are resourceful and competent, and business partners with other members of the organization while they also maintain their independence and objectivity standards.

Characteristics of Effective Audit Function

A list of characteristics that can define an internal audit function as effective is presented next. Note that the list is not all-inclusive.

- An audit function is effective only when its auditors are effective. This means auditors must be effective first.
- An effective audit function follows and encourages auditors to adhere to professional standards when conducting audit work. Any deviations from standards are explained or permissions for exceptions are obtained.
- An effective audit function:
    - Performs continuous planning of audit work.
    - Schedules audit resources for audit engagements.
    - Supervises or manages audit engagements.
    - Conducts auditors' performance appraisals.
    - Provides continuing education programs to auditors.
    - Conducts succession planning moves for senior audit management.
    - Coaches audit supervisors, senior auditors, and staff auditors about career plans and paths.

Characteristics of Effective Audit Function (continued)

- Effective audit planning focuses on:
  - Traditional assurance services (e.g., reviewing policies, procedures, and systems for compliance).
  - Consulting services (e.g., consulting auditors offer advice and insight in reviewing business processes and practices to improve their performance, productivity, and progress).
  - Value-for-money (VFM) audits (e.g., focusing on the three *E*s—economy, efficiency, and effectiveness—to ensure maximum utilization of resources and to prevent and detect fraud, abuse, and waste of resources).
  - Agile audits (e.g., small-size, short-time, target-based, and focus-based reviews with quick results on critical issues).

    VFM audits require auditors to wear an industrial engineer's hat focusing on the 4*M*s: men, machines, money, and materials. Industrial engineers are often called efficiency experts. Expertise drives the three *E*s.
- An internal audit function is effective when it develops yearly audit plans with a major focus on target-based (agile), strategy-based, and risk-based audits in addition to cycle-based, operational-based, compliance-based, performance-based, and schedule-based audits (repeat/routine audits).

Characteristics of Effective Audit Function (continued)

- An effective audit function manages audit resources through budgeting, reporting, monitoring, and feedback.
- An effective audit function supports and strengthens the core business functions, such as operations, marketing, and finance through its audit work, analysis, findings, conclusions, and recommendations for improvements. It provides outside-in views and perspectives to a business function with fresh mind and new outlook as if it manages that function.
- An effective audit function acquires the required audit talent through a combination of in-sourcing, co-sourcing, and outsourcing methods as needed to complete an audit engagement. For example, some technical and complex skills (e.g., information technology, engineering, actuarial science, and statistical knowledge) are not needed in every auditor as long as the audit team as a whole possesses such skills. Audit talent is needed in cybersecurity (e.g., data breaches and ransomware attacks), emerging technologies (e.g., bitcoins), artificial intelligence (machine learning), robotics, business analytics with big data, business intelligence, and data mining).
- An effective audit function is an internal business partner with other functions of a business in terms of:
    - Focusing on value-creating tasks and separating non-value-added activities from value-adding activities.
    - Focusing on risk identification and risk mitigation efforts.

Characteristics of Effective Audit Function (continued)

- Implementing best practices or metapractices in governance, risk management, and control.
- Recommending implementation of cost-effective and time-sensitive continuous controls (automated and manual).

- An effective audit function obtains a 360-degree feedback from audit clients or audit stakeholders, such as internal customers (e.g., audit committee members and senior and functional managers) and external customers (e.g., external auditors, bank examiners, and regulatory auditors). Kano principles can be applied to this feedback process using three rating scales, such as satisfied, neutral, and dissatisfied for measuring the effectiveness of internal audit. Each rating must give reasons and explanations. In a way, the Kano principles validate what the audit stakeholders value the most.
- The internal audit function is effective when outside auditors (e.g., external auditors, bank examiners, and regulatory auditors) and inside nonauditors (e.g., risk officer, compliance officer, quality auditor, environmental auditor, and control assessor) rely on the work performed by the internal auditors. This reliance can be achieved through coordination and cooperation efforts between these parties and due to the effect of economies of scope and size here. Reliance leads to assurance, as shown next.

  Low reliance = Low assurance

  High reliance = High assurance

Characteristics of Effective Audit Function (continued)

- An effective and efficient internal audit function establishes a quality assurance and improvement program to add value, improve an audit organization's internal operations, and gain credibility in the eyes of third parties and outsiders.
- The audit function is effective when it is performing value-adding audits, not doing nitpicking audits, not focusing on fault-blaming audits, and not conducting error-seeking audits. This requires conducting audits outside of typical accounting and financial areas, such as:
  - Sales and marketing
  - Human resources
  - Capital planning and budgeting projects
  - Business process improvement projects
  - Production and supply-chain operations
  - New product/service development projects
  - New systems development projects
  - New contract development projects, including outsourcing contracts
  - Mergers, acquisitions, and divestitures projects

Characteristics of Effective Audit Function (continued)

- The CAE in partnership with legal counsel and the ethics, compliance, and risk officers must conduct a governance audit to ensure that the board:
  - Addresses long-term strategy with goals and objectives.
  - Reviews the compensation and benefit programs to the chief executive officer (CEO) and other officers and executives.
  - Focuses on the board's reputation.
  - Looks into succession planning for key officers and executives.
  - Identifies separation-of-duties problems between the CEO and the board chair.
  - Focuses on the board's composition (i.e., inside, outside, and shadow directors).
  - Recognizes conflict-of-interest situations (i.e., abuse of insider information and management scandals).
  - Reviews risk management, control, and compliance matters.

Characteristics of Effective Audit Function (continued)

Reputation management deals with risks and exposures facing the board resulting from the board's own practices, philosophies, operating styles, litigations, and public statements. It deals with the board's overall image in the eyes of senior management of the company, stakeholders of the company, affected regulators and bankers; and the public at large (e.g., strong board or weak board, ethical board or unethical board, effective board or ineffective board, or good reputation or bad reputation).

- Prior to making the decision to outsource the internal audit function, the audit committee and the CAE of the outsourcing organization should conduct cost-benefit, reputation risk, and T-account analyses (i.e., listing the pros on one side of T and the cons on the other side of T).
- The entire internal audit function will be effective when its internal policies, procedures, practices, processes, and operations are streamlined, simplified, and standardized to provide quick responses and faster results to management with agility to increase performance and productivity and to show progress.
- Effective audit function develops and maintains an audit test model or audit test lab for repeated use as a template to gain the benefits of economies of scale. This model contains audit test scripts, test beds, test data, test cases, and test results for use in various audit test scenarios. This model saves time, energy, and frustration from not having to repeat or start all over again for each audit (i.e., benefits). One-time audits, routine audits, ad hoc audits, special audits, continuous audits, and agile audits are the best candidates for the application of this audit test model.

Characteristics of Effective Audit Function (continued)

- An effective audit function develops and maintains an audit dashboard tool (i.e., audit reporting tool) to show various items of interest to management, including audit progress reports, actual versus budgeted spending, and actual audit plan completion versus estimated audit plan completion.
- An internal audit function is effective when it establishes escalation procedures for resolving any differences of opinion between audit staff/management and organization management (audit clients) concerning reported audit findings and recommendations.
- An internal audit function is effective when it establishes a tracking system to track and monitor all open-audit issues accompanied with aging analysis showing the number of days the audit issues are open and are not addressed or implemented.

In summary, an effective audit function always looks for continuous improvement regarding its scorecard or metrics reporting to the board and senior management (i.e., audit clients and audit stakeholders).

SARBANES-OXLEY ACT OF 2002

The SOX Act contains provisions affecting the corporate governance, auditing, and financial reporting of public companies, including provisions intended to deter and punish corporate accounting fraud and corruption. The SOX Act generally applies to those public companies required to file reports with the Securities and Exchange Commission (SEC) under the Securities Act of 1933 and the Securities Exchange Act of 1934 and registered accounting firms. Visit www.pcaobus.org or www.aicpa.org for SOX.

Specifically, the SOX Act required publicly traded companies to establish a system of internal controls over financial reporting, similar to the Foreign Corrupt Practices Act of 1997 (FCPA) and the Federal Deposit Insurance Corporation Act of 1991 (FDIC). Under the SOX Act, a company management has to establish, assess, and report on the issuer's system of internal controls over financial reporting, and auditors must report on the effectiveness of that system of internal controls. Studies show that better internal controls result in better financial reporting and more investor confidence in financial reports. The SOX Act contains 11 titles and several sections within each title. This appendix contains only the titles and sections that are of interest to internal auditors.

Title I—Public Company Accounting Oversight Board

Section 101: Public Company Accounting Oversight Board Establishment and Administrative Provisions

Establishes the Public Company Accounting Oversight Board (PCAOB) to oversee the audit of public companies that are subject to the securities laws.

Section 102: Registration with the PCAOB

Requires accounting firms that prepare or issue audit reports to public companies to register with the PCAOB.

Section 103: Auditing, Quality Control, and Independence Standards and Rules

Requires the PCAOB, by rule, to establish auditing and other professional standards to be used by registered public accounting firms in the preparation and issuance of audit reports.

Section 104: Inspections of Registered Public Accounting Firms

Requires the PCAOB to annually inspect registered public accounting firms with more than 100 issuer audit clients and to triennially inspect registered public accounting firms with 100 or fewer issuer audit clients.

Section 105: Investigations and Disciplinary Proceedings

Requires the PCAOB to establish fair procedures for investigating and disciplining registered public accounting firms and associated persons and authorizes the PCAOB to investigate and discipline such firms and persons.

Title II—Auditor Independence

Section 201: Services Outside the Scope of Practice of Auditors

Registered accounting firms cannot provide certain nonaudit services to a public company if the firm also serves as the auditor of the financial statements for the public company. Examples of prohibited nonaudit services include bookkeeping, appraisal or valuation services, internal audit outsourcing services, and management functions. Specifically, the act prohibits a public company from outsourcing its internal audit to its external auditor since doing so would lead to a potential conflict-of-interest situation for the external auditor.

Title III—Corporate Responsibility

Section 301: Public Company Audit Committees

Listed company audit committees are responsible for the appointment, compensation, and oversight of the registered accounting firm, including the resolution of disagreement between the registered accounting firm and company management regarding financial reporting. Moreover, this section establishes certain oversight, independence, and funding requirements for the audit committee. The SEC issued rules to issuers that prohibit any national securities exchange or national securities association from listing the securities of an issuer that fails to comply with these audit committee requirements.

Section 302: Corporate Responsibility for Financial Reports

For each annual and quarterly report filed with the SEC under the SEC's Exchange Act, the CEO and CFO must certify that they have reviewed the report; that, based on their knowledge, the report does not contain untrue statements or omissions of material facts resulting in a misleading report; and that, based on their knowledge, the financial information in the report is fairly presented.

Section 303: Improper Influence on Conduct of Audits

This section requires the SEC to issue rules prohibiting officers and directors, and persons acting under their direction, from fraudulently influencing, coercing, manipulating, or misleading the issuer's independent auditor for purposes of rendering the issuer's financial statements materially misleading.

Section 304: Forfeiture of Certain Bonuses and Profits

The issuer's CEO and CFO have to reimburse the issuer for any bonus or compensation and profits received from sale of securities during the 12-month period following the filing of a financial document that required an issuer to prepare an accounting restatement due to misconduct or material noncompliance. Here the compensation can be either incentive based or equity based. This reimbursement is called a clawback provision. Where material noncompliance has occurred with the SEC's securities laws, it forces the CEO and CFO to forgo compensation stemming from financial restatements made because of wrongdoing. First, a captive insurance policy, if available, can cover the wrongdoing claim. Later it can extend to compensation, bonuses, and incentives to pay for the remainder of the wrongdoing claim. This wrongdoing can create a personal reputation risk to the CEO and CFO.

Section 306: Insider Trading during Pension Fund Blackout Periods

- The SEC prohibits the directors, officers, and executives of a company from purchasing, selling, or transferring any equity security of their company during a pension plan "blackout period" for that security, which is three consecutive business days. These prohibitions apply only if the securities acquired or disposed of by the director, officer, or executive were acquired in connection with his or her service or employment with the issued company. The following transactions are exempted from the statutory trading prohibitions:
  - Acquisitions or dispositions of equity securities involving a bona fide gift or a transfer by will or the laws of descent and distribution
  - Acquisitions or dispositions of equity securities in connection with a merger, acquisition, divestiture, or similar transaction occurring by operation of law
  - Increases or decreases in equity securities holdings resulting from a stock split, stock dividend, or pro rata rights distribution

  The blackout period is the period in which the company refrains from repurchasing its own shares because of insider trading concerns.

Section 308: Fair Funds for Investors

The civil penalties can be added to the disgorgement fund for the benefit of the victims of a security law violation. A disgorgement sanction requires the return of illegal profits.

Title IV—Enhanced Financial Disclosures

Section 401: Disclosures in Periodic Reports

The SEC issues rules that prohibit issuers from including misleading pro forma financial information in their filings with the SEC or in any public release. The SEC requires that issuers should not have to reconcile any pro forma financial information with the issuer's final financial statements prepared in accordance with generally accepted accounting principles (GAAP). This means that professional care and good judgment should be used when preparing pro forma financial information.

This section also requires disclosure of off-balance-sheet transactions, arrangements, and obligations (including contingent liabilities) and changes in financial condition, revenues, expenses, results of operations, liquidity capacity, capital expenditures, or capital resources.

Section 402: Enhanced Conflict-of-Interest Provisions

This section places prohibitions on personal loans to executives, directors, or officers of a company. It makes it unlawful for any issuer, either directly or indirectly, to extend, maintain, or arrange for the extension of credit in the form of a personal loan to these officers. However, this Act does not preclude any home improvement and manufactured home loans, any extension of credit under an open-end credit plan, a charge card loan, or any extension of credit by a registered broker or dealer. In addition, this Act does not apply to any loan made or maintained by an insured depository institution unless the loan is subjected to the insider lending restrictions.

Section 404: Management Assessment of Internal Controls

This section consists of two parts. First, in each annual report filed with the SEC, company management must state its responsibility for establishing and maintaining an internal control structure and procedures for financial reporting; it must also assess the effectiveness of its internal control structure, including controls over financial reporting and the results of management's assessment of the effectiveness of internal control over financial reporting.

Second, it also requires the firms that serve as external auditors for public companies to attest to the assessment made by the companies' management and report on the results of their attestation and whether they agree with management's assessment of the company's internal control over financial reporting.

This section requires the SEC to issue rules that require all annual reports filed under the SEC's Exchange Act to include certain statements and assessments related to the issuer's internal control structures and procedures for financial reporting.

Section 406: Code of Ethics for Senior Financial Officers

This section requires the SEC to issue rules about (1) disclosing whether the issuer has adopted a code of ethics for its principal executive officer (CEO), principal financial officer (CFO), principal accounting officer, or controller and, if not, the reasons why such a code has not been adopted and (2) promptly disclosing any change to, or waiver of, the issuer's code of ethics. The board of directors must approve any waivers of the code for directors, executives, or officers of the organization.

The SEC rules define **codes of ethics** as written standards that are reasonably necessary to deter wrongdoing and to promote:

- Honest and ethical conduct, including the ethical handling of actual or apparent conflicts of interest between personal and professional relationships.
- Full, fair, accurate, timely, and understandable disclosure in reports and documents that a company files with, or submits to, the SEC and in other public communications made by the company.
- Compliance with applicable governmental laws, rules, and regulations.
- The prompt internal reporting of code violations to an appropriate person or persons identified in the code.
- Accountability for adherence to the code.

Section 407: Disclosure of Audit Committee Financial Expert

Public companies must disclose in periodic reports to the SEC whether the audit committee includes at least one member who is a financial expert and, if not, the reasons why the audit committee does not include such an expert. This financial expert must be independent of management.

The financial expert on the audit committee must possess the following major attributes:

- An understanding of:
  - Financial statements and GAAP, including their application to accounting for estimates, accruals, and reserves
  - Internal controls and procedures for financial reporting
  - Audit committee functions
  - Experience in preparing, auditing, analyzing, or evaluating financial statements

The financial expert can be a principal financial officer, principal accounting officer, controller, public accountant, or external auditor but not an internal auditor. The SEC rules will provide a safe harbor provision to make clear that an audit committee financial expert will not be deemed an "expert" for any other purpose and will not impose any duties, obligations, or liabilities that are greater than those imposed on a normal audit committee member.

Major Improvements in the SOX Act

According to the PCAOB, the following is a list of major improvements made to the SOX Act in the 10 years since its inception from 2002 and until 2012.

- It restored investor confidence.
- It established the PCAOB, ending more than 100 years of self-regulation by the accounting profession.
- It dealt with the conflicts of interest in the accounting profession by prohibiting accounting firms from performing certain auditing and consulting services for the same company the firm was auditing. For example, it prohibited an accounting firm from setting up a valuation system for valuing financial assets and then auditing that system.
- It mandated independent audit committees and required issuers to disclose whether a "financial expert" is available on the audit committee. Today, an internal audit function must report functionally to an independent audit committee.

Major Improvements in the SOX Act (continued)

- It increased corporate accountability and dealt with tone at the top by requiring CEOs and CFOs to personally certify their companies' financial statements.
- It instituted clawback provisions, requiring CEOs and CFOs to give up bonuses or other financial incentives based on financial results that later had to be restated or were fraudulent.
- It essentially ended the backdating of stock options. Backdating is a misrepresentation of the dates on which stock options were granted to executives and employees during the course of their employment with a company. Through backdating, it does not appear to the outside world that the option grants were approved with a fake retroactive date when the company's stock prices were the lowest, although the actual approved date is much later, when the stock prices are higher. Backdating is a management fraud, resulting in an artificially low exercise price for stock options that could lead to financial restatements.

About the Author

S. RAO VALLABHANENI is an educator, author, publisher, consultant, and practitioner in business with more than 30 years of management and teaching experience in auditing, accounting, manufacturing, and IT consulting in both public and private sectors. He is the author of more than 60 trade books, study guides, review books, monographs, audit guides, and articles in auditing and IT, mostly to prepare for professional certification exams in business. He holds 24 professional certifications in business management in the fields of General Management, Accounting, Auditing, Finance, Information Technology, Manufacturing, Quality, and Human Resource. He taught several undergraduate and graduate courses in business administration and management programs at the university level for many years. He has earned four master's degrees in Management, Accounting, Industrial Engineering, and Chemical Engineering.

Index

B

C

E

I

P

Q

R

S